Reconfiguring the Natures of Childhood

In this fascinating new book, Affrica Taylor encourages an exciting paradigmatic shift in the ways in which childhood and nature are conceived and pedagogically deployed, and invites readers to critically reassess the naturalist childhood discourses that are rife within popular culture and early years education.

Through adopting a common worlds framework, *Reconfiguring the Natures of Childhood* generates a number of complex and inclusive ways of seeing and representing the early years. It recasts childhood as:

- messy and implicated rather than pure and innocent;
- situated and differentiated rather than decontextualized and universal;
- entangled within real world relations rather than protected in a separate space.

Throughout the book, the author follows an intelligent and innovative line of thought which challenges many pre-existing ideas about childhood. Drawing upon cross-disciplinary perspectives, and with international relevance, this book makes an important contribution to the field of childhood studies and early childhood education, and will be a valuable resource for scholars, postgraduate students and higher education teachers.

Affrica Taylor is Associate Professor of Education at the University of Canberra, Australia.

Series Title: *Contesting Early Childhood*
Series Editors: Gunilla Dahlberg and Peter Moss

This groundbreaking series questions the current dominant discourses surrounding early childhood, and offers instead alternative narratives of an area that is now made up of a multitude of perspectives and debates.

The series examines the possibilities and risks arising from the accelerated development of early childhood services and policies, and illustrates how it has become increasingly steeped in regulation and control. Insightfully, this collection of books shows how early childhood services can in fact contribute to ethical and democratic practices. The authors explore new ideas taken from alternative working practices in both the western and developing world, and from other academic disciplines such as developmental psychology. Current theories and best practice are placed in relation to the major processes of political, social, economic, cultural and technological change occurring in the world today.

Titles in the *Contesting Early Childhood* series include:

Reconfiguring the Natures of Childhood

Affrica Taylor

Routledge
Taylor & Francis Group

LONDON AND NEW YORK

First published 2013
by Routledge
2 Park Square, Milton Park, Abingdon, Oxon OX14 4RN

Simultaneously published in the USA and Canada
by Routledge
711 Third Avenue, New York, NY 10017

Routledge is an imprint of the Taylor & Francis Group, an informa business

British Library Cataloguing in Publication Data
A catalogue record for this book is available from the British Library

Library of Congress Cataloging in Publication Data
Taylor, Affrica, author.
Reconfiguring the natures of childhood / authored by Affrica Taylor.
pages cm. -- (Contesting early childhood)
Includes index. 1. Early childhood education--Philosophy. 2 Philosophy of nature. I. Title.
LB1139.23.T38 2013
372.21--dc23
2012036991

ISBN: 978-0-415-68771-3 (hbk)
ISBN: 978-0-415-68772-0 (pbk)
ISBN: 978-0-203-58204-6 (ebk)

Typeset in Galliard by Fakenham Prepress Solutions, Fakenham, Norfolk NR21 8NN

MIX
Paper from
responsible sources
FSC
www.fsc.org   FSC® C004839

Printed and bound in Great Britain by
TJ International Ltd, Padstow, Cornwall

Contents

Acknowledgements

This book would not have come to fruition without an array of contributions and contributors. I would like to acknowledge some of the key ones.

Miriam Giugni, Lesley Instone, Mindy Blaise and Carmel Richardson have been my closest fellow travellers. Over the years, each of them has contributed countless hours of nourishing conversation that have somehow found their way into this book. Miriam's commitment to pursuing 'worldly' early childhood activism, her advocacy for the praxis of theory and inclusive early childhood practice, and the sheer force of her enthusiasm were integral to dreaming up the common worlds project. Lesley's creative approach to environmental and cultural geography has inspired me enormously. I am particularly grateful to her for keeping me in touch with everything I love about geography while I have been working in education. She has helped me make the difficult shift of allegiance from nature to naturecultures that underpins this book. Mindy has been a great collaborator in bringing a queer eye to early childhood education, and in thinking through the nexus of children and dogs. Carmel has been a stalwart early childhood research collaborator and opened my eyes to the various ways in which queer theory can be put to use in early childhood education.

It is always important to have mentors, and Pam Christie and Katherine Gibson have certainly fulfilled this role for me. Thanks to you both for your considered advice and sustained encouragement. Kathie supported my earliest efforts to apply a geographical lens to the natures of childhood and to bring the more-than-human into the collective. Pam and I have had many productive grapplings over the composition of the commons and the notion of agency. I am particularly grateful to her intellectual provocations and challenges. Margaret Somerville's work on post-colonial place pedagogies and her commitment to indigenous/non-indigenous collaboration have also inspired me and I thank her for her generous interest in and support for my project.

I am also grateful to a number of colleagues at the University of Canberra for their various forms of support. Thanks to Geoff Riordan for freeing me up to complete the manuscript and to Katja Mikhailovich, Sandra Heaney-Mustafa, Ting Wang and Barbara Pamphilon for being such solid workmates. Thanks to early childhood educators Adam Duncan, Kate Ellison and Peter Kirkup, in the Wiraduri Centre, for bravely trialling ways of putting common worlds principles into practice. Thanks, as always, to Kerry McIntyre for her customary willingness, warmth and ongoing positive support.

The Childhood Research Collective provided a stimulating home base throughout the gestation of this book. Lots of people are involved, but my special thanks go to affiliated doctoral students Kath Whitty, Jane Hargreaves, Robyn Faulkner, Lara Drew, Brendan Briggs and Lily Petkovska for offering their open and lively minds to the collective process of intellectual inquiry. It is great fun working with you.

Lyn Fasoli at Batchelor Institute for Indigenous Tertiary Education in the Northern Territory has been a wonderful associate of the Childhood Research Collective and a close colleague in the Three Sisters project. Thanks also to Barbara Pederick from Atitjere Aboriginal Community in Central Australia for being such a great early childhood educator 'sister' to the Wiradjuri mob.

Also in Central Australia, I would like to thank past and present members of the Yipirinya School community. Special thanks go to Rhonda Inkamala, former cultural principal, for supporting my efforts to tell the Yeperenye story. In particular, I would like to acknowledge the late Kwementyaye Raggett for her patient tutelage many years ago. The window you offered me into your world has changed mine forever. Carrying on the family tradition in Alice Springs, Alice Taylor from the Central Australian Aboriginal Media Association was an invaluable help in accessing material for the book. Thank you for this, Alice, and for sharing valuable inter-generational perspectives on life in Alice Springs.

In the small community of Micalong Creek, in the Wee Jasper valley where I wrote this book, Maureen Murphy also told me many cross-generational childhood tales, Rodney Murphy kept my firewood supply stocked during the cold winter months and Kate Howarth from Wee Jasper Reserves filled me in on the local wombat scene. One of the many wombats of Micalong Creek was an underground companion. First Hen and later Reg were constantly by my side as I wrote. Both of them kept me healthy by insisting on taking me out for regular walks and making sure I did not spend too many continuous hours glued to the computer. While ever patient, Reg also became quite good at nudging my hands from the keyboard and bringing me my walking shoes.

Series editors Peter Moss and Gunilla Dahlberg were fantastic. Thanks to you both for your support and valuable feedback on final drafts.

Finally I would like to acknowledge and thank the publishers, authors and artists who granted me permission to use their works: Jeannie Baker and Walker Books; Jackie French and HarperCollins Australia; Beck Cole and CAAMA Productions; Shaun Tan and Hachette Australia; Ruby Elliott; Miriam Giugni; and Patricia Piccinini and Drome Studios for permission to use Graham Baring's photos of the 'Undivided' installation.

Portions of the common worlds framework outlined in Chapter 4 appeared in Taylor, A. and Guigni, M. (2012), 'Common worlds: Reconceptualising inclusion in early childhood communities', *Contemporary Issues in Early Childhood*

Education, 13 (2): 108–20. Portions of the wombat/settler story appeared in Taylor, A., Blaise, M. and Giugni, M. (2012), 'Haraway's "bag lady storytelling": Relocating childhood and learning within a "post-human landscape"', *Discourse: Studies in the Cultural Politics of Education*, 34 (1), DOI:10.1080/0 1596306.2012.698863

In the spirit of living well together in inherited past-presents and futures, I dedicate this book to Hen – and to Ruby Jean, Ollie, Mo-Mo, Liv, Miri and Lou-la.

Affrica Taylor
November 2012

Introduction by the series editors

Gunilla Dahlberg and Peter Moss

This series – *Contesting Early Childhood* – has two main goals. On the one hand, it 'questions dominant discourses surrounding early childhood', those ways of thinking, talking and practicing that make universal truth claims, implying or asserting they are inevitable, essential, self-evident, seeking to enforce a dictatorship of no alternative and to stifle new thought and action. But at the same time as being critical, the series aims to offer 'alternative narratives of an area that is now made up of a multitude of perspectives and debates'. The good news is that diversity has not been stifled despite the best efforts of dominant discourses, and this series provides one of the forums where that diversity of perspectives and debates can find expression, as well as vivid examples of how they can be put into action and made to work. To borrow the sub-title of one of the books in the series, we hope to contribute to 'movement and experimentation in early childhood education.'

The nine preceding books in the series have lived up to our intentions, combining the deconstructive and the reconstructive. This tenth and latest book maintains that track record. The dominant discourse, which is the target of author Affrica Taylor's critique, is the relationship between nature and childhood in the western tradition, a 'romantic coupling of childhood with Nature', leading to an idea of both being in a state of innocence, authenticity and purity, to be protected from the contamination of adults and society; and to the construct of 'Nature's child', whose development follows 'sequentially unfolding sets of natural dispositions.' Taylor tracks this conflation of childhood and nature, and its consequences, from Rousseau through European Romantics such as Wordsworth and Coleridge and North American transcendentalists such as Thoreau, to contemporary manifestations, including modern media for children, 'developmentally appropriate practice' and nature kindergartens – acknowledging en route the important role played in the reproduction and effecting of this relationship by early childhood pioneers such as Fröebel and Montessori.

There are many other examples. To cite just one, in *Förskola och skola – om två skilda traditioner och om visionen om en mötesplats* [Preschool and school – two different traditions and the vision of a meeting place], a paper written in 1994 for a Swedish government commission, one of us (GD) together with a colleague

Hillevi Lenz Taguchi analysed how early childhood education in Sweden has been built on the concept of the child as nature. This construction has been highly productive, contributing to a tradition of early childhood education that values: a holistic view of the child; free play and creativity, giving rise to free and self-confident people; free expression of ideas and feelings; fun; and the present. Put simply, the authors state, 'one could say that the construction of the child as nature is naturally in the child – everything is in the child, and must be given the freedom to be expressed, reworked and developed'; and that 'today's pre-school is permeated with this type of thinking' (for a fuller discussion of this paper, see an earlier book in this series, *Early Childhood and Compulsory Education: Reconceptualising the Relationship*).

But Taylor's critical gaze is not restricted to the deeply embedded relationship between childhood and nature. Her thinking leads her to challenge a number of prominent dualisms that follow from this relationship, such as that between nature and nurture (expressed in that well-worn question, what percentage of the child is due to nature and what to nurture?) and between nature and culture; and a number of much used concepts, such as 'child-centredness' and the 'social construction' of childhood. If the former emerges, in Taylor's exploration of the complex relationships between people and matter, as hopelessly simplistic and reductionist, the latter similarly fails to acknowledge the embeddedness of culture within a material world. As Taylor warns 'if childhood is reduced to nothing more than a human concept, this also implies that the only real action is human meaning making. The world itself, beyond the meaning that humans attribute to it, is more or less abandoned, rendered inert and/or easily malleable, and left to the nature realists to interpret, as before. This is a highly unsatisfactory situation – and a stand off that I aim to tackle in this book.'

Thus if Taylor is critical of a certain way of thinking about the relationship between childhood and nature, it is not because she wants to discard nature. Quite the contrary: she takes it very seriously. And it is here that the book displays its reconstructive qualities. It certainly contests conventional wisdoms, but it also offers some unconventional ones, that place the highest value on natures and their relationships with children and childhood. If her critical gaze on the Romantic relationship leads her to ask 'what does nature do when coupled with childhood in this way?', her reconstructive gaze leads to a second strategic question: 'how might we do nature otherwise in early childhood studies?'

In addressing this question, Taylor introduces important new concepts – 'naturecultures' and 'common worlds' – that help to reconceptualise the relationships, setting out to 'mess up the categorical divisions between nature and culture in order to queer the natures of childhood and to reconfigure them as enmeshed natureculture common worlds.' She goes beyond introducing these concepts to enacting them, exploring the 'pedagogical possibilities of reconfigured early childhood common worlds – envisioning these natureculture worlds as an opportunity for learning *with* others and as a way to practise an expanded and worldly form of inclusion.' She argues that common worlds pedagogies are 'relevant to the real-world challenges facing twenty-first century children':

> As an alternative to child-centredness and an exclusive focus upon the needs of the individual child, [the book] urges early childhood educators to attend to children's relations with others when designing inclusive, ethical and useful common worlds pedagogies.

A recurring theme is enmeshing, of children and natures. It is a theme that foregrounds relationships, connectedness and assemblages, together with hybridization, complexity and messiness. It is a theme, too, that contests the dualistic and disconnected thinking that pervades so much of the dominant discourse in today's early childhood education, with its need to categorise, to reduce and to normalise and its will to know and govern the child.

In developing her argument, Taylor draws on a wide range of scholarship, well established in other fields but much less so in early childhood education. She gains inspiration from scholars such as Karen Barad (who also figures prominently in an earlier book in the series – *Going beyond the Theory/Practice Divide in Early Childhood Education* – by Hillevi Lenz Taguchi), Bruno Latour, and (a particular favourite of Taylor) Donna Haraway. They introduce new theoretical perspectives, including queer theory (though perhaps we should say, as Taylor does of Haraway, a 'queer sensibility'), with its purpose of denaturalising what is taken to be natural and normal, for example to depart from 'the 'natural' and 'normal' associations of childhood with nature.

This readiness to border cross also takes the author, and early childhood education, into new and exciting disciplinary territory, in particular human geography and science studies. This creates a 'fertile dialogue' with early childhood education: 'one of the key strategies I adopt in this book, and perhaps my most original contribution, is to bring reconceptualizations of nature from science studies and human geography into conversation with reconceptualizations of childhood.' We are again reminded that some of the most original and creative work to be found in early childhood education today draws inspiration from trans-disciplinarity, escaping the dominant discourse's insular pre-occupation with developmental psychology to open up a myriad of new and provocative perspectives that introduce movement and experimentation into the field.

In enacting her new perspectives, Affrica offers a variety of richly documented examples, drawn from her own country of Australia and her own experiences with contemporary Australian children. She pays particular attention to Australia's indigenous peoples, the Aborigines, and does not gloss over the terrible abuse they have suffered from colonial rule and settlement. But she also shows them to be far more than victims. They are supremely successful constructors of sustainable naturecultures and common worlds, with child–animal relations serving as 'a testament to the adaptive capacity of Arrernte culture, and hence to its survival', and contributing to 'the creation of continually re-imagined pastpresent modern "hunter gatherer" subjectivities, lifestyles and practices' – a striking alternative to the western relationship.

In a book that is beautifully written, lucidly argued and richly documented, Affrica Taylor has made a welcome addition to our series. She has focused attention on a relationship that has been prominent in early childhood education for over two centuries, yet today is more important than ever. For as we face the fearful prospect of global warming (the Arctic sea ice, it is just announced, has receded more in summer 2012 than ever before; the United States has just endured its hottest summer on record, the United Kingdom its wettest summer for a century), the loss of bio-diversity (with talk of a sixth great extinction in the offing), chronic shortages of water and other basic resources, and the spread of toxicity – all consequence of human activity – the question of the relationship between nature and people has become a matter not just of scholarly research, but of our very survival as a species.

As Taylor points out 'human induced global warming is perhaps the ultimate hybrid nature/culture phenomenon'. What it and the other gathering perils confronting the human species, indeed all species, make clear is that we cannot have a future that is more of the same. We need new relationships, and urgently. This book, therefore, is more than usually timely, a contribution not only to early childhood education, indeed all education, but to thinking about future relationships between human beings and their environment.

Introduction

... [C]hildren have a special affinity for the natural environment – an affinity that is connected to the child's development and his or her ways of knowing.

(Wilson, 2008)

If we really want our children to thrive we need to let their connection to nature nurture them.

(Warden, 2007, cited in Mindstretchers, 2012)

Childhood and nature seem like a perfect match. Young children are often declared to have a natural affinity or connection with nature, and in turn, Mother Nature is often deferred to as the exemplary guide and nurturer during the early childhood years. The very concepts of childhood and nature are imbricated in a myriad of ways. Sharing an entangled epistemological trajectory, their close relationship has been firmly cemented within the western popular imaginary as a reassuring fact of life. In fact, childhood and nature seem bound together as the essential and original raw materials of life itself – or at least the human chapter of it. What life-giving partnership could possess a more self-evidently 'good', 'natural' and 'normal' character and quality than childhood and nature? The compelling romance of this coupling is underpinned by the premise that childhood and nature constitute a predestined, wholesome and enduring match. Supported by the certitude and moral authority of its affiliation with nature, the naturalness of childhood is confidently reaffirmed on an everyday basis. It is a most seductive and reassuring partnership.

Against this tide of conventional wisdom, I set out to queer the relationship between childhood and nature – to deromanticize it, to render it less assuredly natural and normal and to reconfigure it as infinitely more dynamic and complex. Bruno Latour's provocative comment, 'We have no idea what things would look like if they had not always been engaged in the battle of naturalization' (Latour, 2004: 42), spurs me on to ponder how we might conceive of childhood differently, if its naturalization was not already signed, sealed and delivered by its romantic coupling with a singular, or personified Nature (Williams, 1983: 221). How else might we think about childhood, if this relationship was not already demarcated and foreclosed – a done-deal between idealized perfect partners?

My purpose is not just to ridicule and discard the relationship between nature and childhood, but to hijack it from the Romantics, to politicize, reorient and reconfigure it as a lively and unforeclosed set of relations with a different set of political and ethical affordances. Despite the fact that I am setting out to denaturalize the conventional way of understanding the relationship between nature and childhood, I want to be clear from the outset that it is not my intention to jettison nature altogether, and redraw the boundaries around childhood as a purely social construct. In other words, I am not advocating a complete abandonment of nature in favour of an exclusively cultural under-standing of childhood. For me, the point of denaturalizing the more familiar, 'normal' and predictable couplings of childhood and nature is not simply to dismantle a fiction, but to clear a space for some queerer envisionings. These queer (as opposed to 'natural' and 'normal') envisionings of what counts as nature and childhood not only promise to be unexpected and lively, but, most significantly, have the potential to reveal a different kind of inclusive ethics for coexisting in more 'liveable worlds' (Haraway, 1994: 60).

What makes these envisionings queer is the very peculiarity of the assembled partners and the unpredictability of the circumstances in which they come together. If only we could think beyond the exclusive, monogamous and romantic union of childhood and singular Nature, all manner of interestingly variegated childhoods, natures and cultures could be rearticulated. This book is my attempt to turn the relationship between childhood and nature into a much more promiscuous, multifarious, generative and open-ended affair.

Strategic moves and guiding questions

To this end, I make two strategic moves. The first is a deconstructive one, to unravel some of the connective threads that have firmly sutured familiar tropes of nature and childhood from the Enlightenment to the present. These unravellings are guided by the question *What does nature do when coupled with childhood in this way?* Although I am by no means outside the discursive force field of 'natural childhood', this question helps me to better understand the seductive appeal of these naturalistic tropes by putting the spotlight on their effects and exploring their unintended consequences.

Throughout the book I am just as concerned with the task of troubling the naturalization of nature as I am in unravelling the effects of naturalized childhood. It is this double move that helps me to queer the sacrosanct union between singular Nature and childhood. Thankfully, I do not have to start from scratch. In my second strategic move, which is much more of a reconstructive one, I draw heavily upon the ground-breaking conceptual work that has already been undertaken to knock singular Nature off its capitalized pedestal – but also to reclaim nature (or natures) in other forms. This involves many trans-disciplinary forays into science studies (especially Latour, 1993 and 2004; and Haraway, 1994, 2003, 2004a, 2004b, 2004c, 2004d; 2004e, 2008a, 2011) and human geography (in particular Whatmore, 2002; Castree, 2001 and 2005; Massey, 1993, 2005; Hinchcliffe, 2005, 2007). Scholars from these disciplines specialize in interrogating nature, so there is much to be learnt from them. One of the key strategies I adopt in this book, and perhaps my most original contribution, is to bring reconceptualizations of nature from science studies and human geography into conversation with reconceptualizations of childhood. This fertile dialogue also supports the pursuit of my second question: *How might we do nature otherwise in early childhood studies?*

In addressing this challenging question I turn to the work of Donna Haraway (1985, 1989, 1991, 1994, 1997, 2004a, 2004b, 2004c, 2004d, 2004e, 2008a, 2008b, 2011), whose self-declared project of 'queering what counts as nature' (1994: 60) first inspired me to think that it might also be possible to queer the relationship between singular Nature and childhood. Through reading Haraway's extraordinary body of seriously playful, politically insightful and highly idiosyncratic work, I have come to appreciate that thinking differently about nature and what it means to be human – or to be a child in this case – is only half the game. Haraway's queer sensibility is not only evident in her ability to think outside of the box, but also in her predilection to strategically do, or perform, her scholarship in quite a different way. Consistent with her commitment to pursue alternative feminist methods, she seeks to move beyond 'the more "normal" rhetorics of systematic critical analysis', when it becomes clear that this form of analysis only serves to 'repeat and sustain our entrapment in the stories of the established disorders' (Haraway, 2004a: 47). It is the congruence between her message and her method that makes it so performatively and productively queer. For instance, her writings are replete with strategies for refusing essentialisms and messing up binary categories (such as the nature/culture binary, which is the prime concern of this book) without recourse to more conventional methods of systematic deconstruction.

One of Haraway's favourite queering strategies is to deliver feminist 'bag lady stories', assembling 'unexpected partners' and 'irreducible details' (2004b: 127) across the nature/technology/culture divide. Perhaps the most famous example is her boundary-blurring feminist cyborg figure (1985, 1991, 2004d), which is configured across the human/technological/bio-scientific/semiotic domains. Also defying her own categorization, Haraway insists that her work is neither 'realism', nor 'biological determinism', nor 'social constructionism', but a 'serious ... effort to get elsewhere' (Haraway 2004c: 330). Her serious, but also very playful, efforts guide my attempts to reconstruct, reconfigure and rearticulate some alternative natures of childhood. They help me to take the possibilities of childhood and nature 'elsewhere', not only in terms of the ways we think about them but also through the ways that we 'do' them in our research and writing.

Working to denaturalize childhood: An overview

Challenges to the naturalist assumptions about childhood and the universalist premises that flow from it are not new to the academy, although it seems that they have had limited uptake outside of the academic domain. Spearheaded by childhood sociologists (Buckingham, 2000; Corsaro, 2005; James, Jenks and Prout, 1998; James and Prout, 1990; Kehily, 2004; Jenks, 2005; Lee, 2001; Qvortrup, 1993; Wyness, 2008), clear delineations have been drawn between the state of human biological immaturity and the cultural interpretations of and social responses to this biology – which we call childhood. It is commonly conceded that while biology might be natural, there is nothing natural about our interpretations of and responses to this biology. The main game for sociologists is therefore to study how different understandings of childhood are produced or constructed (including within the academy), and/or to use empirical research to better understand how these constructions, in turn, shape the real-life experiences of children.

Within childhood studies – a field populated by sociologists and scholars from cognate disciplines – it is now axiomatic to refute the naturalization of childhood and to approach childhood as a social construct. In reflecting upon the changes in this field over the last couple of decades, Jenks (2005: 49) observes that it is as if childhood scholars have redoubled their efforts to 'transform the natural into the cultural'. There is no doubt that these intensified efforts to present childhood as above all a cultural or social construct (and at the same time to discount the significance of its nature or biology) are closely linked to the late twentieth-century cultural or linguistic turn. This paradigmatic shift, commonly referred to as post-structuralism, is characterized by a set of powerful new conceptual tools and methods that have given childhood scholars additional means for denaturalizing childhood. For instance, Michel Foucault's (1982, 1990) central and generative notion of 'discourse' as a linguistic practice that produces (rather than simply describes) social subjects and truth regimes has facilitated new insights about the technologies of power associated with social construction. This, in turn, has allowed scholars to redouble their efforts to debunk essentialist or truth claims about childhood (MacNaughton, 2005; Dahlberg and Moss, 2005; Dahlberg, Moss and Pence, 2007). Such truth claims are typically established and defended in the name of Nature, and nowhere is this more apparent than in relation to children's gendered behaviours. Inspired by Judith Butler's (1990 and 1993) extensions of Foucault's theories, post-structural feminist childhood scholars have been active in denaturalizing children's gendered behaviours by showing the ways in which they are performatively enacted and normalized by the heterosexual matrix (Blaise, 2005; Blaise and Taylor, 2012; Renold, 2005; Robinson, 2005; Taylor, 2008, 2010a, 2010b; Taylor, Blaise and Robinson, 2007; Taylor and Richardson, 2005a).

Also associated with the cultural turn is Jacques Derrida's (1976) deconstructive method, which aims to destabilize the binary categories that support modern western logic. Throughout modern western history, the apparent logic, or 'common sense' of these same binaries has been used to justify the subjugation of all manner of people deemed to be self-evidently or 'naturally' inferior – such as indigenous people, women, gays and lesbians. Deconstruction has assisted childhood scholars to take on the binary categories of childhood and adulthood (Buckingham, 2000; Lee, 2001) and the radical polarization of nature and culture, a foundational Enlightenment dualism that underpins so much categorical western thinking, including thinking about childhood (Lenz-Taguchi, 2010; Prout, 2005; Taylor, 2011).

The positioning of childhood within the polarized camps of nature or culture has been most popularly expressed within the long-standing 'nature/nurture' debates. Spurred on by the potential for socialization theory to explain (and by feminists' desires to redress) children's stereotypical gendered behaviour (Denzin, 1977), this debate reached its zenith in the 1970s and 1980s, but it still holds currency, both within and beyond the academy. Within this debate, disagreement pivots around the proportional influences of biology (nature) and socialization (nurture) upon the child. This is a zero-sum formula, most often expressed in terms of percentages. The actual categories of nature (biology) and culture (nurture) are not in dispute, let alone the concepts of childhood that they support. Even though the nature/nurture debate keeps us 'zig-zagging between the poles of culture and nature' (Wyness, 2008: 22), it does not reflect the conceptual polarization, or epistemological schism, that has spread within the academy post the cultural turn. For the last few decades, these deep-seated epistemological differences have been manifest in the disciplinary demarcations between the nature realists on the one hand and the social constructionists on the other. The nature realists are predominantly physical or behavioural scientists, seeking the biological/chemical/neurological determinants and 'hard facts' of childhood. The social constructionists are those social scientists who argue that we can only ever know childhood through our culturally produced discourses about it – including scientific discourses about the 'facts' of childhood.

This epistemological schism is most apparent in the field of early childhood education and care. This is because the theories of child growth and development and theories of learning that frame the field are informed by developmental psychology – a behavioural science with a nature realist orientation (for a notable exception, see Walkerdine, 1988). It is because developmental psychology, rather than sociology, is the foundational discipline of early childhood education and care, that this field is largely, but not exclusively, one that assumes a nature realist perspective. There have been significant internal challenges to this naturalistic perspective, spearheaded by those early childhood scholars who have engaged with post-structural theories. For instance, scholars such as Canella and Kincheloe (2002), Cannella and Soto (2010), Cannella and Viruru (2004), Dalhberg, Moss and Pence (1999), Dahlberg and Moss (2005), Hultqvist and Dahlberg (2001), O'Loughlin and Johnson (2010), Ryan and Grieshaber (2005) and Zornado (2001) not only insist that childhood is a discursive rather than a natural construction, but also point to the dangerous political effects of its naturalization. In contesting naturalist assumptions about childhood, they call for reconceptualized (post-structural) understandings to inform new approaches to early years education, policy and care. The following provocative assertion by Kenneth Hultqvist and Gunilla Dahlberg (2001: 9) exemplifies the post-structuralist counter-naturalist argument: 'There is no natural or evolutionary child, only the historically produced discourses and power relations that constitute the child as an object and subject of knowledge, practice, and political intervention.' As an explicit rebuff to the naturalization of childhood, this statement also implicitly evokes the paradigmatic gulf that exists within the field of early childhood education and care – a gulf between the nature realists and the social constructionists.

Reproducing or redressing the schism?

More recently, some of those who have been schooled in the social constructionist side of the divide are expressing a growing discomfort with this schism. Most notably, Alan Prout (2005), in his book *The Future of Childhood*, offers a challenge to the social constructionist position that he himself spent decades promoting (James and Prout, 1990; James, Jenks and Prout, 1998). To explain this challenge, he picks up on the argument that Bruno Latour (1993) puts forward in *We Have Never Been Modern* (see Prout, 2005: 40–3). In this groundbreaking work, Latour argues that modernity is both a paradoxical and a delusional intellectual project. This is because on the one hand, it works hard to purify and maintain an epistemological and ontological separation between nature and culture (through disciplinary schisms similar to those discussed above). On the other hand, it uses its scientific knowledge and technological inventions to meddle with the natural world, thereby facilitating the proliferation of mediated and thus hybridized 'nature-culture' entities and effects. Human-induced climate change is perhaps the ultimate example of a nature-culture effect. In other words, modernity is working at odds with itself – insisting on pure categories while creating new hybrid ones. Prout points out that by insisting that childhood is an entirely discursive production, social constructionists risk unwittingly contributing to this flawed modernist project. In other words, if they claim childhood to be semiotically autonomous, they are turning it into a purely cultural phenomenon. If this is the case, it is not only nature realists who are engaged in what Latour (1993: 10–11) calls 'the work of purification'. As Prout (2005: 56) puts it, social constructionism now 'stands in danger of becoming merely a reverse discourse, declaring "society" where previously had been written "nature"'.

The future of childhood studies, according to Prout, lies in doing something different. He is not calling for scholars to discard insights about the discursive construction of childhood and default to accepting its realist definitions, but rather to pursue ways of studying childhood that do not require mutually exclusive choices between the assumed-to-be-purely-natural or the assumed-to-be-purely-cultural. Borrowing Latour's (1993: 11) hybridized (as opposed to pure and differentiated) notion of 'nature-culture', Prout proposes that 'the future of childhood studies rests on ways of treating childhood as a "nature-culture"... [O]nly by understanding the ways in which childhood is constructed by the heterogeneous elements of culture and nature, which in any case cannot be easily separated, will it be possible to take the field forward' (1993: 44).

Prout is not the only childhood scholar to declare the perpetuation of the nature/culture divide to be futile. Inspired by the work of the material feminists (see Alaimo and Hekman, 2008), and in particular the work of Karen Barad (2003 and 2007), Hillevi Lenz-Taguchi (2010) also warns against the constructionist propensity to privilege the discursive and dismiss the significance of 'matter'. She proposes an 'intra-active pedagogy', based on Barad's insistence that matter (or nature) and meaning (or culture) are not separate but 'mutually implicated' and 'mutually articulated' through the 'dynamics of intra-action' between the 'material and the discursive' (Barad, 2007: 152, cited in Lenz-Taguchi, 2010: 5). As Lenz-Taguchi elaborates, this kind of thinking represents a clear departure from the existing 'either-or' and 'both-and' responses to the discursive/material divide (2010: 28–9). Unlike these existing approaches, her intra-active pedagogy does not entail choosing between nature and culture or privileging one over the other. It does not attempt to reduce nature to culture or culture to nature – as both hyper-constructionist accounts and biological essentialist accounts tend to do. Nor does it formulate the proportional influence of nature and culture – as in the nature/nurture debate. Following Barad, Lenz-Taguchi (2010: 29) keeps her focus on the 'in-between of intra-activities' – on what goes on between the discursive and the material. This is where the generative action is – and where, she surmises, real learning takes place.

Concerns, motivations and aspirations

My overview of the reinvigorated efforts by scholars to denaturalize childhood by engaging with the discursive analytics of the cultural turn highlights some of the unintended consequences of this move. Most significantly, it highlights the paradoxical correlation between the increasing sophistication of this denaturalization project and the intensification of the nature/culture divide. This is most clearly played out within the field of early childhood education. One of the unfortunate side effects of reproducing this division, which concerns Prout and Lenz-Taguchi as well as me, is that if childhood is reduced to nothing more than a human concept, this also implies that the only real action is human meaning making. The world itself, beyond the meaning that humans attribute to it, is more or less abandoned, rendered inert and/or easily malleable, and left to the nature realists to interpret, as before. This is a highly unsatisfactory situation – and a stand-off that I aim to tackle in this book.

Having made this brave assertion, I am the first to admit my trepidation. A potential web of tangled contradictions faces anyone who attempts to deconstruct the nature/culture divide and at the same time refuses to abandon this world that we so problematically refer to as 'nature'. Not the least of these challenges is the fact that no western subject can entirely step outside of the categorical divides that structure western thought. However, as Derrida (2005 (1978): 358–9) notes, we can resist the truth-value of these structuring dualisms, and we can reappropriate categories, such as 'nature', as useful tools. I hope the reader can forgive any clumsiness as I undertake the ambitious and fraught process of refuting the familiar idealized and singularized Nature that issues from the nature/culture divide, while reclaiming and embracing a motley collection of less familiar and non-innocent on-the-ground natures. Despite some apprehension, I am spurred on by Haraway and Harvey's (1995) encouragement not to shy away from this daunting task, and I am very grateful for their acknowledgement that it is both 'terribly important to overcome these divides' and at the same time 'terribly hard to find a language to do so' (1995: 515).

It is my schooling in human geography that motivates and supports me to take on the nature/culture divide in early childhood studies, to queer the romantic coupling of nature and childhood, and to retain an active sense of the world that we tend to reduce to singular Nature within childhood studies. As I mentioned earlier, human geography has long addressed the fraught question of nature and human relationships to it, and the various articulations of nature within the nature/culture divide. It seems to me that the project of denaturalizing childhood can only gain by taking on these insights about nature.

For although much critical attention has been paid to denaturalizing and reconceptualizing childhood within childhood studies, little or no attention has been paid to denaturalizing and reconceptualizing nature. Despite its long-standing cameo role in early childhood education, nature, to date, has remained a relatively taken-for-granted concept in the project of denaturalizing childhood. I argue that this omission, in turn, is accentuating the nature/culture schism in early childhood education. As a 'go-between' between the human geographies of nature and childhood studies, I take on the precarious double role of (singular) Nature critic and advocate for queerly reconfigured natures within the bigger project of denaturalizing and reconceptualizing childhood.

These dual roles need further explanation. My nature critic role is driven by my abiding distrust of unitary and valorized discourses of nature. By this I am referring to those discourses that sanctimoniously uphold an unspecified singular notion of Nature as an indisputable cover-all explanation or rationalization. I am well aware of how this nature has been and still is deployed to 'naturalize' and 'normalize' associated terms, such as race, gender and sexuality, in order to justify the unequal valuing of human lives, political exclusions and to claim the moral high-ground. This effect is intensified when the additional associative term of childhood is added to the mix, and nature is evoked as the moral authority to regulate children's gender and sexuality (Taylor, 2007, 2008,

2010a, 2010b). I readily agree with Latour's (2004) claim that for too long now, a singular and generic notion of Nature, or what he also refers to as 'mononaturalism', has performed a similar function to the old unmarked category of Man. The main difference is that while Man has now been thoroughly critiqued and differentiated (in terms of gender, human diversity, multiculturalism, etc.) Nature has not (2004: 48–9). The continuing uncritiqued deployment of capital N nature acts as a political foil. In this form, Nature functions as the final word – it reduces politically contentious 'matters of concern', to use Latour's words, to indisputable 'matters of fact' (2004: 51).

Despite the best efforts of some childhood scholars to denaturalize childhood, a sentimental attachment to a singularly virtuous and thus valorized nature is still widespread in the field of early childhood education. Although it might appear that this is a benign attachment, I think it needs challenging. I realize that I risk offending by being a critic of valorized nature, but it is not my intention to be a cynical spoiler or to ridicule those who seem to be 'sucked in'. Rather, I intend to look closely at what this romantic coupling or conflation of childhood and nature actually does and to unravel some of its tightly-knotted imbrications and unintended consequences. Typically the work of deconstruction ends when the structuring relationship between key concepts and their epistemological and ontological effects have been exposed. However, this is the moment when I shift into my second role, as an advocate for queerer understandings of nature and of childhood.

In this role, I set out to reclaim nature from the Romantics and to reconfigure its relationship with childhood through a series of enacted naturecultures (Law, 2004). I am aware that the ways in which we know nature determines what it *does* (Hinchcliffe, 2007), including what it does to childhood. For this reason, I argue that the field of early childhood education can only benefit from knowing this relationship differently. In place of the sentimental attachment to the romantic coupling of childhood with capital N Nature, I offer a grounded, ethically and politically attuned and queer reconfiguration of the relationships between diverse children and their diverse or 'multinatural' worlds (Latour, 2004). Following Haraway's lead, I offer these reconstructed or reconfigured otherwise childhoods and natures in the hope of cohabiting in more inclusive and 'liveable worlds' (Haraway, 1994: 60).

Structure of the book

This book is divided into two parts that reflect these deconstructive and reconstructive moves. Each part has three chapters.

The first part – 'The Seduction of Nature' – offers a genealogy of the western Romantic couplings of capital N Nature and childhood from the Enlightenment to the present. Taking a geo-historical perspective, the chapters in this section pay attention to the circumstances and conditions in which the singular notion of Nature was initially produced and attached to the notion of childhood, and subsequently reproduced in different times and places. They consider how and why this conflation of Nature and childhood has had such an enduring and seductive appeal and address the question of what Nature does when coupled with childhood.

Chapter 1 – 'Rousseau's Legacy: Figuring Nature's Child' – focuses upon the earliest dissemination of idealized notions of Nature and childhood in the western world. It starts by providing a detailed examination of Rousseau's seminal eighteenth-century ideas about nature, childhood and education. It deconstructs Rousseau's rhetorical strategies and the structuring logic he used to conflate Nature and childhood and to produce the prototypical figure of Nature's Child. The chapter concludes by looking at the ways in which Rousseau's Nature's Child figure has been reproduced by nineteenth-century European Romantic writers and artists and by the Transcendentalists in North America.

Chapter 2 – 'Representing Nature's Child' – picks up on Rousseau's legacy and traces it through twentieth-century popular culture representations. Focusing upon the ways in which Rousseau's generic Nature's Child figure has been adapted in different geo-historical contexts, it deconstructs four very different Romantic children's texts: two Disney nature animation feature films featuring US nature; and two well-known Australian children's nature books which have been made into feature films. The deconstruction foregrounds the ways in which the structuring logic of the nature/culture divide has secured the continuity of the Nature's Child figure in each of these texts. It also highlights the specific ways in which the Nature's Child figure has been transmitted in modified form in different historical and geographical circumstances and contexts, thus ensuring its continuing relevance to widespread adult and child audiences.

Chapter 3 – 'Educating Nature's Child' – traces the various ways in which European early childhood educators have drawn upon Rousseau's Nature's Child figure to inform curriculum and pedagogical design from Fröebel's original German kindergarten through to the establishment of contemporary Nature Kindergartens. It deconstructs the ways in which Rousseau's idea of Nature as Teacher has been variously interpreted and permeated these early childhood education initiatives. It also considers the impact of recent calls to prevent the demise of children's first-hand experiences of nature, and how these have been taken up in a revival of natural outdoor education within early childhood.

The second part – 'Reconfiguring the Natures of Childhood' – takes a reconstructive turn. The chapters in this part draw upon contemporary trans-disciplinary reconfigurations of natures to guide reconceptualizations of the relationship between situated childhoods and natures. Following the lead of these trans-disciplinary interventions, chapters in this section deliberately set out to mess up the categorical divisions between nature and culture in order to queer the natures of childhood and to reconfigure them as enmeshed natureculture common worlds. They enact, or perform, some queerly reconfigured childhood natureculture common worlds, which bear no resemblance to Rousseau's purist and singular Nature's Child figure that was the subject of the first section of this book.

Chapter 4 – 'Assembling Common Worlds' – constructs a new conceptual framework for simultaneously reconfiguring the natures and cultures of childhood. It surveys trans-disciplinary nature retheorizations that have been produced through conversations between human geographers, science and technology studies scholars, feminist eco-philosophers and indigenous peoples. It draws upon these retheorizations to suggest that reconfigured natures of childhood can be productively engaged as inclusive common worlds, composed of all manner of assembled entities: material and discursive; living and inert; human and more-than-human.

Chapter 5 – 'Enacting Common Worlds' – uses the common worlds conceptual framework assembled in the previous chapter to enact some reconfigured natures of childhood. Drawing upon Haraway's queer methods, it performatively addresses the question 'How might we do natures otherwise in early childhood?' It enacts some child–animal relations that are specific to two distinctively Australian common worlds. The first of these offers a window into the contemporary indigenous Mparntwe world of desert child–animal relations. The second relates to predominantly east-coast post-colonial white settler, immigrant child–animal relations. Both of these enactments attend to the ways in which contemporary Australian children and animals inherit and coinhabit messy and mixed-up post-colonial worlds. The ethical and political dilemmas and challenges that are thrown up within these messy and non-innocent common worlds are featured in these enactments.

The Conclusion – 'Towards Common Worlds Pedagogies' – reflects upon the difficulties and rewards of making the shift from idealized Nature's Child to messy common worlds childhoods. It surveys the pedagogical possibilities of reconfigured early childhood common worlds – envisioning these natureculture worlds as an opportunity for learning *with* others and as a way to practise an expanded and worldly form of inclusion. It explains how and why common worlds pedagogies are relevant to the real-world challenges facing twenty-first-century children. As an alternative to child-centredness and an exclusive focus upon the needs of the individual child, it urges early childhood educators to attend to children's relations with others when designing inclusive, ethical and relevant common worlds pedagogies.

Part 1

The seduction of Nature

Chapter 1

Rousseau's legacy: Figuring Nature's Child

> Everything is good as it comes from the hands of the Author of Nature; but everything degenerates in the hands of man.
>
> (Rousseau, 2003 (1762): 1).

> Here is this vast, savage, howling mother of ours, Nature, lying all around, with such beauty, and such affection for her children, as the leopard: and yet we are so early weaned from her breast to society, to that culture which is exclusively an interaction of man on man.
>
> (Thoreau, 2009 (1862))

Introduction

In 1762, the Enlightenment philosopher Jean-Jacques Rousseau wrote an impassioned educational treatise, called *Emile*, in which he pontificated that 'Nature' is the child's best teacher. Two hundred and fifty years later, Rousseau's treatise is still widely regarded as the foundational modern western educational canon, and his ideas can still be traced within contemporary discourses promoting natural childhood. Although his extended treatise is replete with the kinds of contradictions and paradoxes that beset anyone who appropriates Nature as their muse, his crude argument is encapsulated in the opening line: 'Everything is good as it comes from the hands of the Author of Nature; but everything degenerates in the hands of man' (Rousseau, 2003 (1762): 1). Rousseau staunchly believed that children are born into an originary natural state of essential goodness, but both their affiliation with Nature and the natural goodness and innocence associated with it are threatened by the corrupting influences of society, or what he scathingly referred to as the degenerative 'hands of man'. Rousseau was not the only Enlightenment philosopher to elicit a singular and essentially good Nature and to distinguish this Nature by counterposing it against essentially corrupt society (Daston and Vidal, 2004; Williams, 1983). However, it was Rousseau who famously used this distinction to align essentially good childhood with essentially good nature and to argue that children's natural goodness and innocence could only be ensured by returning them to Nature.

Rousseau's romantic coupling of childhood with Nature has found enduring expression in the figure of Nature's Child. The seductive appeal of this Nature's Child figure and the various nature figurations that support it are the main concerns of this chapter. In approaching these concerns, I ponder two broad questions – why the romantic coupling of childhood with Nature makes Nature's Child so compelling, and how the nature/culture divide consolidates and validates this relationship. I begin by charting the historical emergence of the key nature figurations that constellate within Rousseau's composite Nature's Child figure. I then trace the ways in which Rousseau's original Nature's Child prototype was taken up by English and North American nineteenth-century Romantic writers in slightly different ways. I conclude by reflecting upon how the differences between European and North American natures have afforded geo-historical variations to these Romantic Nature's Child figures.

Figuring Nature

It stands to reason that if we can better understand why nature is such an 'intoxicating idea' (Latour, 2004: 43), it will help us to comprehend the enduring seductive appeal of the Nature's Child figure. So my first move is to explore the etymology of nature itself, and to focus, in particular, upon the modes of its *singular* deployment as a clue to understanding its affects. In other words, what is it about Nature with a capital N, or 'mononature' as Latour (2004) also calls it, that we find so compelling? My fascination about the hold that singular Nature has upon us is fuelled by the paradox, noted by many scholars of nature (Castree, 2005; Daston and Vidal, 2004; Hinchcliffe, 2007; Latour, 2004; Soper, 1995), that despite, or perhaps because of, nature's unitary façade, this concept has countless referents and applications. Nature is simultaneously 'very familiar and extremely elusive' (Soper, 1995: 1), a 'portmanteau word' and a 'chaotic concept' (Castree, 2005: 36). It appears to be a monolithic self-evident idea with a high degree of integrity, and yet we use it so promiscuously. In *Keywords*, a cultural history of critical words in the English vocabulary, Raymond Williams (1983: 219) surmises that nature is 'perhaps the most complex word in the language'. He notes that it is an established convention to use a singular notion of Nature, but that this convention has a 'precise history' (1983: 220). It is this history that I intend to pause and consider. By so doing, I hope to throw some light on why singular Nature is paradoxically such a cacophonous notion and at the same time, as Haraway points out, a notion 'which we cannot *not* desire' (2004b: 125; my italics).

Like so many other corresponding English and French words, nature comes from Latin. It is an adaptation of 'natura', the past participle of 'nasci', the verb 'to be born' (Williams 1983: 219). Williams traces nature's earliest appearance in the English language back to the thirteenth century, when it was first used as a descriptor of 'the essential character and quality *of* something' (1983: 219).

A century later, nature was used as an abstract noun to refer to 'the inherent force which directs either the world or human beings or both' (Williams, 1983: 129). It was not until the seventeenth century that the third and concrete sense of nature began to emerge in reference to 'the material world itself, taken as including or not including human-beings' (Williams, 1983: 219).

All three of these original meanings of nature – nature as characteristic or essence, nature as force, and nature as the material world – are still in use. Williams notes that while it is easy for us to distinguish between these three meanings, we also commonly elide them through habitual use (1983: 219–20). This elision is also possible because the meanings have historically built upon each other, moving from the original and notably singular notion of characteristic or essence, to a more abstracted but still singular notion of force, and finally to the 'reduction of multiplicity into a singularity' when the one word nature is used to refer to all the things that make up the material world (Williams, 1983: 220–1). Rather than being contradictory, or posing a disjuncture of meaning, these three natures appear to be mutually reinforcing.

For Williams, and also for me, the most interesting aspect of these unfolding yet overlapping meanings of nature is the way in which they were accompanied by a corresponding set of personifications, or figures of nature. Most significantly, these personified figures secured the singularity of nature. They simultaneously made it universal and intelligible. Personifications of nature gave form to the more abstract meanings, and functioned as projections of their historical moments. For instance, Williams describes how even from the time of their earliest usage, the first two senses of nature as essence and nature as force were personified in the mythical figure of Mother as Goddess, or Mother Nature (Williams, 1983: 221). From medieval times, a benevolent and pure Mother Nature was seen as God's deputy or minister. As God had to remain the primary personified figure with absolute power, it was Mother Nature's role to carry out God's providential will. At other times, and especially when a more malevolent nature's omnipotent force was seen to have 'destructive effects on men', nature was personified as a despotic absolute monarch (Williams, 1983: 221).

Along with the eighteenth- and nineteenth-century European social and political transformations, the personification of nature as an absolute monarch morphed into one of nature as a constitutional monarch and a lawyer (Williams, 1983: 222), lending authority and legitimacy to the new social order. The personification of nature as lawyer also coincided with the consolidation and extension of the third meaning of nature as the material world – a world now believed to be constituted by hidden, yet discoverable natural laws (Williams, 1983: 223). Williams (1983: 223) quotes the eighteenth-century poet, Alexander Pope, to illustrate this convergence of modern science, nature as the material world, nature as God's minister and nature as lawyer:

Nature and Nature's laws lay hid in night;
God said, Let Newton be! and all was light!

This new personification of nature as law was pivotal. For not only did nature now appear to embody everything in the world, but its laws gave it the capacity to reveal everything. Williams notes that from the time of the Enlightenment, and on into the Romantic movement that followed it, this 'emphasis on law gave a philosophical basis for conceiving an ideal society' (Williams, 1983: 223). If natural laws were to be found in the forces and materialities of nature, this in turn positioned nature as the dispenser of indisputable facts, as a neutral judge, and ultimately, as Lorraine Daston and Fernando Vidal (2004) argue, as a transcendent 'moral authority'. Further fortified by the authority of its new legal dimension, the emerging notion of a 'state of nature' became an idealized external benchmark against which 'obsolete or corrupt society' was judged (Williams, 1983: 223). Williams claims that by the end of the eighteenth century, and in contrast to the perceived imperfections of the state of society at that time, this idealized 'state of nature' had come to personify a unitary repository of everything essentially good. This singularly perfect 'state of nature' encompassed all the natural beauties of the material world, it was irrefutably constituted by natural laws, it included a regenerated version of nature as an inherently good force, and its purity was ensured by the absence of 'man's' artificial creations (Williams, 1983: 223).

At this point in history, nature's ultimate authority, and its seductive appeal, was secured by two key attributes: its radical alterity from society and its inherent truth and goodness. It was now incumbent upon philosophers, such as Rousseau, to interpret the significance of nature's 'moral authority' (Daston and Vidal, 2004) for the human condition.

Rousseau's contributions to figuring Nature

As an Enlightenment philosopher, Rousseau's project was to envisage an ideal society and he turned to nature to help him do this. The perfect 'state of nature' was the template for Rousseau's ideal society and he evoked nature's 'moral authority' (Daston and Vidal, 2004) to justify his vision. All of the same patterns and idealized personifications that Williams (1983) saw emerging in eighteenth-century English writings about nature are clearly evident in Rousseau's French writings. In many ways, Rousseau's thinking and writing can be seen as a product of his European lifetime. For instance, his embracing of Nature as the antithesis of society's shortcomings was entirely congruent with the increasing uptake of the nature/culture (or nature/society) dualism during the Enlightenment period in which he lived. In addition to the historical shaping of his thinking, there were a couple of distinctive features to Rousseau's arguments that set him apart from his contemporaries. These quickly earned him the reputation as a 'revolutionary' thinker (Harris, 2003 (1892)) and consequently ensured the perpetuation of his legacy. The first of these arguments was the twist he added to the proposition of Nature as the antithesis of society. In Rousseau's utopian vision, Nature was not only an antidote to society but paradoxically promised to be society's ultimate salvation. The second distinguishing feature of Rousseau's work was his conflation of childhood with Nature and his subsequent insistence upon the resolutely natural education of (male) children as the precondition for any successful, morally intact, future civil society.

These two propositions are obviously entwined and they have a circular logic. Rousseau (2003 (1762)) argued that because 'man' had been ruined by corrupt society, he must be returned to the 'state of nature', from infancy, to relearn how to become self-governing, to develop 'his' moral fibre and to become a new kind of model citizen. Likening growing up in 'civilized' European society to living in 'a state of slavery' (2003 (1762): 10), he advocated that children should be rescued from such bondage by being brought up to be free in Nature. As he put it, 'leave to infancy the exercise of that natural liberty ... let them once learn the method of Nature' (2003 (1762): 51). His reasoning was that only a 'free man' educated from infancy by 'the method of Nature' could rebuild a new social world modelled on the perfect state of Nature. This line of argument runs through a number of Rousseau's works, but is particularly apparent in the *Discourse of the Origin of Inequality* (Rousseau, 2007 (1755, 1762)) and *The Social Contract* (Rousseau, 2007 (1755, 1762)), and it is fully articulated in *Emile: Or Treatise on Education* (2003 (1762)). It is important to recognize that Rousseau's natural educational treatise, that culminated in the story of *Emile*, was not so much driven by his interest in childhood and education per se, but by his commitment to denouncing the evils of eighteenth-century French politics, religion and society and his ultimate goal of providing a road map for revolutionary social change[1].

In fact, Rousseau appeared to have very few credentials for writing *Emile: Or Treatise on Education*. He was neither a practising educator nor a successful parent, surrendering his own children, as infants, into 'foundling homes' (Doyle and Smith, 2007). Despite his lack of first-hand experience, Rousseau's famous fictionalized philosophical treatise about the ideal natural education of a boy in the countryside gained sufficient credibility and traction to become a canon on childhood and education. For the last 250 years, Rousseau's ideas about natural education have shaped the course of early childhood education (as charted in the next chapter), and his ideas about natural child development (personified in the fictional character Emile) have indelibly marked the ways in which we conceive of and value childhood. While Rousseau's extraordinary impact upon the ways we approach childhood and education cannot be justified on the basis of his experience and expertise, it can certainly be explained by his passionate advocacy for returning childhood to Nature and by his ingenious invention and deployment of two powerful new figures of nature: Nature as Teacher and Nature's Child. With Nature as his ally, his muse and his moral arbitrator, Rousseau managed to become an enduring authority on two subjects that he knew very little about: child rearing and education. Rousseau's curious legacy appears to be a testimony to nature's powerful seductive appeal and to the dictum that if you have nature on your side, you must be right.

Figuring Nature's Child and Nature as teacher

So exactly how did Rousseau carry this off? How did he bring Nature's Child and Nature as Teacher to life so convincingly? What role did Nature play in giving *Emile: An Educational Treatise* such enduring appeal? An initial and partial answer to the first two questions can be found in Rousseau's passionate rhetorical style, which according his late nineteenth-century translator, William Payne (2003 (1892)), was very much more emotional than intellectual. With his own rhetorical flourish, Payne goes on to describe Rousseau as 'a genius in literary art', whose 'winged words ... are still making the circuit of the world, and wherever they go they touch the human heart and so produce an effect that is perennial' (2003 (1892): xxii). It may well be true that Rousseau's emotive rhetoric touched the hearts of those who read his original works, but it was also the winning combination of the subject matter and his rhetorical positioning of this subject matter that ensured its enduring legacy. For in conflating childhood and Nature, Rousseau melded two subjects of high sentimental value and emotional investment. Personified in a singular figure, Nature's Child achieved intensified quixotic appeal. Rousseau further heightened the seductive appeal of his Nature's Child figuration by ambiguously positioning it as radically distant from, and yet perpetually threatened by, the corrupting influence of adult society. Through this ambiguous positioning, Rousseau's philosophy continues to romance us with the intoxicating possibilities of a radical alterity that represents all things pure and good that our own lives are not, while simultaneously reminding us of the precariousness and vulnerability of this pure 'other' life.

Within Rousseau's broader political project, *Emile* functioned as a treatise that posited Nature's Child as radically other to corrupt 'civilized' adult lives, and Nature as Teacher as radically other to European socialization. Throughout the book, Rousseau deployed Nature's Child and Nature as Teacher as idealized counterpoints. He argued that a child's salvation could only be achieved through 'his' complete removal from society, returning 'him' to a 'state of nature' in which 'he' would undergo only the 'education of Nature' and 'the education of things' encountered in the natural environment, from infancy until 12 years of age. Rousseau argued that in this 'state of nature', Nature's Child would be free to follow his innate 'nature' or what he also called his 'primitive dispositions' (2003 (1762): 5) and to learn by his sensory and physical experiences of the external natural world to be practical, moral and self-sufficient. Rousseau did not offer any educational techniques or formal lessons, but delegated the job entirely to his personified figure of Nature as Teacher. His advice to educators was simply to '[o]bserve Nature and follow the route which she traces for you' (2003 (1762): 13). In fact, Rousseau argued that by following the 'Education of Nature' and the 'Education of things' (within Nature), educators could altogether avoid formal education, or 'the education of Man' (2003 (1762): 3). 'As soon as education becomes an art,' he warned, 'it is well-nigh impossible for it to succeed' (2003 (1762): 3). He actively promoted avoidance of the artful 'education of Man' until puberty, and called this avoidance 'negative education'. In his words, 'The first education ... ought to be purely negative. It consists not at all in teaching virtue or truth, but in shielding the heart from vice, and the mind from error' (2003 (1762): 59). Rousseau's 'negative education' was devoted to keeping the corrupting socialization effects of formal education at bay. It was to be exclusively delivered by Nature as Teacher.

It is apparent that Rousseau did far more than offer a straightforward utopian vision of natural education. Throughout *Emile*, he consistently counterposed this utopian 'state of nature' against the dystopian 'civilized' world. In fact, his rhetorical strategy of radical alterity relied upon constant negative comparisons. Interdispersed through the detailed descriptions of Emile learning by following the 'order of nature' (2003 (1762): xliii), Rousseau scattered regular reminders of the evils of society from which Emile is being protected or saved. 'Civilized man is born, lives and dies in a state of slavery' (2003 (1762): 10) is one of his most famous declarations. Some of these warnings, as Payne (2003 (1892)) pointed out, were far more emotional than rational. In the following tirade against city life, for instance, Rousseau revealed his visceral repugnance of living at close quarters with other 'men' and his profound lack of faith in human sociality:

> Men were not made to be massed together in herds, but to be scattered over the earth which they are to cultivate. The more they herd together the more they corrupt one another ... The breath of man is fatal to his fellows; this is no less true literally than figuratively ... Cities are the graves of the human species.
>
> (Rousseau, 2003 (1762): 24)

Emile was not only a treatise *for* Nature's Child and Nature as Teacher, but overwhelmingly a treatise *against* the evils of western 'civilized society'. Rousseau valorized nature, and by association childhood, by denigrating European society and distancing childhood from it. His passionate aversions to European society appear to be powerful psychological drivers of his thinking, adding to the emotional force of his rhetoric. In additional to his emotional predilections, his thinking clearly traded on the increasingly popular division between nature and culture, or nature and society, which had been gaining momentum throughout the Enlightenment. Rousseau's contempt for European 'civilized man' and society seems to have driven his infatuation with pure nature as a form of radical alterity. The emotionality of his rhetoric was escalated by this polarity – his passionate idealization of nature was matched only by his obsessive demonization of society. In other words, Rousseau's figurations of Nature as a perfect child and a perfect teacher were not only shored up by the nature/culture divide, but were the products of his emotional investment in reproducing the binary logic of *good* nature as opposed to *evil* culture.

Binary logic and collateral terms

The binary logic of the nature/culture divide was clearly not Rousseau's invention, but he made a major contribution to reversing the value ordering of its binary terms. Within the logic of this 'Great Divide' (Latour, 1993: 12), nature was (and in many instances still is) paradoxically positioned. It was simultaneously regarded as an inferior state, waiting to be improved upon by 'Man's' superior intellectual and cultural capacities, and a transcendent innate law and impartial judge that could endow a sense of truth and 'moral authority' (Daston and Vidal, 2004) to this same 'Great Divide'. Nature's key 'collateral terms' (Castree, 2005) were also subject to the same paradoxical logic. For instance, even though most of the terms associated with human culture (or society) were widely assumed to be superior to those associated with nature – such as relations between men and women, between 'civilized' and 'uncivilized' human races, between aristocracy and peasantry – the inequities of these binary relations were nonetheless regarded as the natural order of things. In this era of rapidly expanding European empire, one of the clearest examples of this paradoxical naturalization of inferiorized nature can be seen in prevailing European attitudes towards colonized indigenous people. Within the nature/culture divide, prevailing colonialist notions of native primitivism and savagery were pitted against the assumed-to-be-superior European markers of culture, domestication and civilization (Anderson, 2001 and 2007; Gregory, 2001). In fact, the belief in the 'natural' inferiority of native people, as evidenced by their living in a state closer to nature than to human society, was used to justify their colonization.

Childhood was another nature-associated category that was differentiated from adulthood through its implication within the nature/culture divide. Childhood was lined up and commonly characterized, alongside some of nature's other key collateral terms such as women and native peoples, as lacking rationality, full capacity and sophistication. Rousseau played a significant role in co-locating childhood and native people within the 'state of nature', however he deviated from conventional wisdom of the day by resignifying this 'state of nature' as superior, rather than inferior, to society. By approximating childhood and native people with valorized nature, he also resignified them as superior states of being. In *The Social Contract* he repopularizes Dryden's (1672) notion of native people as 'noble savages' because of their 'natural man' status (in Cranston, 1991), and in *Emile* he likened the qualities of Nature's Child – such as 'his' 'primitive dispositions', strength of body and moral character and innate wisdom – to those of 'natural man'. Most importantly, Rousseau's thinking marks the pivotal moment at which concepts of 'natural childhood' and 'natural man' emerged from the shadows of 'civilization', 'culture' and 'rational man' to become the locus of all things essentially good, pure and innocent and worthy of protection.

Purifying Nature's Child

Rousseau's revisioning of childhood as one of nature's key collateral terms has provided us with new composite nature figurations that continue to perform what Bruno Latour (1993: 10–11) calls the 'work of purification'. As I flagged in the Introduction, Latour argues that the 'work of purification' is a key feature of modernity. It consists of those discursive practices that aim to ensure the epistemological separation of nature and culture and to keep them 'in two entirely distinct ontological zones' (1993: 10). This purification work takes place in the paradoxical context of a world of increasingly blurred boundaries, which emerged during the scientific era and produced 'mixtures between entirely new types of beings, hybrids of nature and culture' (1993: 10). Latour describes the proliferation of nature and culture hybrids, or 'nature-cultures', as 'the work of translation' (1993: 11). He points out that despite the fact that 'purification' and ' translation' appear to be diametrically opposed projects, the former would be 'fruitless or pointless' without the hybridized forms produced by the latter (1993: 11). For the 'work of purification' is an anxious reaction to the blurring of boundaries between nature and culture brought about by 'advanced' society's interventions in 'natural' processes.

This anxiety over the blurring of boundaries between the 'state of nature' and the 'state of society' can be clearly discerned in the opening paragraph of *Emile,* when Rousseau elaborates upon his assertion that 'everything degenerates in the hands of man':

> Everything is good as it comes from the hands of the Author of Nature; but everything degenerates in the hands of man. He forces one country to nourish the productions of another; one tree to bear the fruits of another. He mingles and confounds the climates, the elements, the seasons; he mutilates his dog, his horse, and his slave; he overturns everything, disfigures everything; he loves deformity, monsters; he will have nothing as Nature made it, not even man ...
>
> (Rousseau, 2003 (1762): 1)

In the face of society's perceived disfiguring and mutilating effects, Rousseau envisaged and deployed the figures of Nature's Child and Nature as Teacher to carry out the 'work of purification'. These figures allowed him to rescue childhood from the degenerative 'hands of man' and return it to Nature. Through enacting 'negative education', his personification of Nature as Teacher offered a means of purifying Nature's Child and ultimately promised the salvation of Natural Man. These rescue, purification and salvation tropes, enabled by Rousseau's Nature's Child and Nature as Teacher figurations, can be traced into the present, as I do in chapters 2 and 3 respectively. For the remainder of this chapter, however, I look at the ways in which Rousseau's Nature's Child prototype figure was embraced and perpetuated by nineteenth-century Romantic writers and artists in England and in North America, albeit in slightly variant ways.

Romancing Nature's Child in the pastoral idyll

With the onset of industrialization, Rousseau's idealizations of nature as an antidote to the corrupting influences of an increasingly urbanized society gained momentum in the nineteenth-century western world. Nostalgic representations of perfect nature became the central motif of the cultural productions associated with the Romantic movement of that time. By its association with nature, childhood also figured prominently in the work of the Romantics (Jones, 2000). Even the most renowned Romantic writers in different geographical locations and from different literary genres, such as William Wordsworth and Henry David Thoreau, who were not primarily concerned with the subject of childhood, conflated childhood with nature in many of their sentimental musings on nature as a mother, muse and teacher. However, the kinds of ways that they depicted nature and Nature's Children did vary somewhat, and this variation related to the specificities of their own geo-historical contexts.

From the turn of the nineteenth century, the European Romantic literary tradition was closely associated with the highly emotive, nature-worshiping poetry of William Wordsworth and his friend and colleague Samuel Taylor Coleridge. Wordsworth famously claimed, in his 1802 essay 'Preface to Lyrical Ballads' (Wordsworth, 2001 (1802)), that the authenticity and authority of this new Romantic form of poetry was based upon the poet's spontaneous expression of powerful emotions springing from the 'tranquility' of nature. In his view, the Romantic poet was nature's alchemist. Wordsworth spent the majority of his life communing with 'tranquil' nature in the scenic Cumbrian Lakes District of northern England, and his lyrical odes to this countryside (or channellings of it) are full of impassioned homages to its 'daffodils', 'brooks', 'clouds', 'lakes', 'dales' and 'rainbows'. Following in Rousseau's steps, Wordsworth also projected his ecstatic deference to nature onto childhood (Coveney, 1982). This is encapsulated in his oft-cited line 'the child is father of the man' from his poem 'My Heart Leaps Up When I Behold' (Wordsworth, 1888 (1802)). In writing this line, Wordsworth was referring to his belief that only in childhood are we able to see the essential truth and beauty of nature. Reflecting on his own life experiences, he observed that as we grow up we come to take nature for granted and lose the ability to be fully attuned to it. Wordsworth fretted over the loss of a direct line to nature with the passing of childhood (Day, 1996), and like Rousseau before him, he also evoked nature as teacher within the figure of Nature's Child.

To reconnect with what he saw as childhood's innate affinity with nature, Wordsworth encouraged his readers to tap back into their early childhood experiences. His longer poem, 'Ode on Intimations of Immortality from Recollections of Early Childhood' (1888 (1803–6)), further elaborates upon this idea. Written in a very melancholic tone, he wistfully reflects not only upon the loss childhood, but on the concomitant loss of connection with nature.

> There was a time when meadow, grove, and stream,
> The earth, and every common sight,
> To me did seem
> Apparelled in celestial light,
> The glory and the freshness of a dream.

It is not now as it hath been of yore; –
Turn wheresoe'er I may
By night and day,
The things which I have seen I now can see no more.

(Wordsworth, 1888 (1803–6))

Wordsworth's Romantic representations of nature are closely associated with a revival of the European literary and artistic tradition of the pastoral idyll (Cuddon and Preston, 1998). Pastoral exponents, typically well-educated members of the urban establishment, idealized rural life for its charming lack of sophistication, its simplicity, peacefulness, beauty and innocence. It was common for them to associate childhood with all of these same characteristics (Jones, 2000). Children were typically centrally positioned within bucolic landscapes, harmoniously communing with grazing or farm animals. These kinds of images of cultivated rural nature are exemplified in the paintings of the nineteenth-century British artists Reynolds and Gainsborough. The absence of adults, infrequent markers of human settlement, and the presence of domesticated farm animals with whom the children appear to have a close and 'natural' empathy, are all recurring and noteworthy features of these pastoral idyll landscapes. Again within the Romantic pastoral traditions, such images draw heavily upon the nature/culture dualism to reaffirm the desirable separation of children's worlds from adults' worlds, and to represent children as located within a state of pre-social or asocial nature (Prout, 2005: 11). The work of purification in these pastoral representations is achieved by semiotically opposing childhood to adulthood (Higonnet, 1998) and rural life to urban, industrial society. The result is a utopian pure world of peace and harmony, where children and animals coexist in nature and are 'blessed through their proximity to and interaction with nature' (Holloway and Valentine, 2000: 17).

Romancing Nature's Child in wild Nature

The romanticization of both nature and childhood found a modified form of expression in the 'New World' colonies of North America. From his nineteenth-century European settler perspective, Henry David Thoreau, like his contemporaries John Muir and Ralph Waldo Emerson, was writing about a distinctive kind of nature. Thoreau's nature writing is still regarded as an expression of Romanticism, but the nature he wrote about was much less tame and 'tranquil' than Wordsworth's pastoral idyll. Thoreau was inspired by the wildness of the North American landscape, not the bucolic tranquillity of the cultivated European landscape. He particularly idealized the western frontier as the pinnacle of wild nature. His urgings for the protection of this wild, uncultivated nature gained him the reputation as 'father' of North American environmentalism, and his declaration – 'In Wildness is the preservation of the world' (Thoreau, 2009 (1862)) – was to become a guiding mantra for the wilderness movement a century later.

Thoreau belonged to the North American Transcendentalist movement, an intellectual and literary movement concentrated in the New England region where he lived. Following Kant's essentialist philosophies and Rousseau's valorization of nature, the Transcendentalists promoted the essential goodness of nature and protested the threats that industrial urban society posed to it. Rejecting the rationalism of the Enlightenment and organized religion, they sought truth in nature, which they regarded as the embodiment of 'heaven on earth' (Gura, 2007: 150). Thoreau not only wrote his Transcendentalist philosophy on nature, but also practised it. He famously retreated to a hut on the banks of Walden Ponds, Massachusetts, to 'live deliberately' and 'simply' with nature and to 'learn what it had to teach' (Thoreau, 2009 (1854)). Reviving Rousseau's figure of Nature as Teacher, he recounted what he had learnt from nature in his book *Walden* (2009 (1854)). In returning to nature, one of Thoreau's driving quests was to find the source of 'man's' connection to this wild nature. He sought to find the essential truths about 'man' in nature that he found lacking in conventional social forms and cultural practices, including formal religions. Like the other Romantics, he closely associated childhood with nature, and like Rousseau and Wordsworth before him, he bemoaned the lack of time that children spend in nature and advocated a return to nature as the remedy for this untimely 'weaning'. This can be seen in this excerpt from his lecture 'Walking', which he delivered several times between 1851 and 1860 and was published posthumously in 1862 (Stabb, 2009):

> Here is this vast, savage, howling mother of ours, Nature, lying all around, with such beauty, and such affection for her children, as the leopard: and yet we are so early weaned from her breast to society, to that culture which is exclusively an interaction of man on man.
>
> (Thoreau, 2009 (1862))

In this passage, Thoreau offers a powerful and animalistic personification of wild Mother Nature and her children. Thoreau was very interested in what he referred to as the 'animal in us' as our primal connection to wild nature, and he located this 'animal within' in childhood (Aitken, 2001: 33). Thoreau's North American version of Nature's Child, influenced by his perception of the nature around him, was a feral or wild Nature's Child. He was not the first to associate childhood with wild animals. Two centuries before him, Puritan religious perceptions of children as inherently wild and evil 'little devils' (Jenks, 2005; Valentine, 1996) justified the exercise of harsh discipline to exorcize and tame them. In fact it was negative and punitive views such as these, in the Puritan dominated New England context, which he and his fellow Transcendentalists challenged. Unlike this Puritan version of the essentially evil wild child in need of civilizing, Thoreau's wild child was essentially good and worthy of emulation because of being driven purely by natural instincts. Both Rousseau and Thoreau transferred their reverence for external nature, or the natural physical world around them, onto a reverence for internal human nature, or natural instincts ('primitive dispo-sitions' in Rousseau's terms). And they both located these natural instincts within the equally revered child. In this way, Thoreau reiterated the essentialist logic of Rousseau's perfect Nature's Child – although for Thoreau this essentialism was primarily defined by the power of natural instinct rather than the vulnerability of innocence. Thoreau did not fully elaborate upon childhood in his writings, as Rousseau had done. However, I mention his work here because his philosophies about wild nature have had such a formative influence upon nature conservation and nature education movements in the United States and beyond. I trace these threads of connection in the following chapters in this section.

Conclusion

Although the philosophical musings of Rousseau, and the Romantics that he inspired, might seem quaintly other-worldly – both temporally and geographi-cally – I have detailed some of their ideas in this chapter to provide a firm basis for understanding and further exploring how the conflation of essentially good and pure nature and childhood has come to have such a powerful grip on the western imaginary. Despite successive attempts by intellectual critics to expose the dangerous politics of naturalization and to thereby challenge naturalist assumptions, idealized notions of nature and its associated key collateral terms, like childhood, still exert a seductive hold upon us. Singularly deployed nature still sets the standards for what we think about as 'the good, the beautiful, the just, and the valuable' (Daston and Vidal, 2004: 1), and naturalization still 'imparts universality, firmness, even necessity – in short, authority – to the social' (Daston and Vidal, 2004: 3).

I agree with Daston and Vidal's (2004: 12) assessment that 'no amount of well-intentioned intellectual and political hygiene is likely to get rid of nature'. Indeed, as I have already declared in the Introduction, it is not my mission to try to dispose of nature by reducing it to nothing more than a series of discourses, or false ideologies. Rather, I am working towards reclaiming the multiple materialities of nature and reconfiguring them along with childhood. So my deconstruction of the figures of Nature's Child and Nature as Teacher, in this section, is not driven by the conceit that I will be able to dismantle these sentimentally naturalized figures, once and for all, by simply exposing their false structuring binaries. Rather, I am motivated by the desire to better understand the geo-historical specificities and effects of these particular figurations – to understand how the variant meanings of nature itself, in different times and places, affects the sway of its authority on childhood.

The historicity of the Nature's Child and Nature as Teacher figures is quite apparent. When we trace them into the present, as I will continue to do in the following chapters, it is not hard to see their historical continuities and contin-gencies, and the strategic moments of their reappropriation. However, in tracing the historical trajectories of these figures, I am also keen to attest to the ways in which geography disperses history (Foucault, 1972, 1980), to draw attention to the simple fact that things turn out differently in different places (Philo, 1992). By doing this, I am opening up a space for reconsidering the ways in which the physical geographies of places, or material natures, also come to 'matter' (Massey, 2005) in our comprehensions of childhood and our relationships with children.

In this chapter, I have begun to make these geographical distinctions by noting the variations between the Romantic European and North American uptakes of the Nature's Child figure within the nineteenth century. I suggest that the European pastoral uptake of Nature's Child was one that drew on a relatively domesticated notion of nature as a rural idyll and projected it onto childhood by affirming the harmonious and natural affinity between children, domesticated farm animals and features of the peaceful rural landscape. In variation to this, I point to the white settler North American uptake of Nature's Child as one that was far more attuned to the inherent wildness of nature. From the colonial settler perspective, or what Homi Bhabha (1990) called the 'gaze of the colonizer', the kind of nature surrounding the Romantics in the vast frontier landscapes of the revealingly-named 'New World', appeared to be gloriously untamed and uncultivated. Inspired by their perceptions of this vast, wild nature, they produced, by association, a much wilder and more instinctual idealized figure of Nature's Child.

In the next chapter I take note of these geo-historical variations, as I trace elements of the pastoral and the wild trajectories of Nature's Child and Nature as Teacher across the landscapes of children's literature and popular culture.

Notes

1   The 1789–91 French Revolution was partly inspired by Rousseau's philosophies about the innate natural goodness of 'man' and his vision for a free and natural utopian society.

Chapter 2

Representing Nature's Child

> Two hundred years after the publication of *Emile*, young people are still thought to be naturally closer to nature with little thought to how childhood is constructed closer to nature.
>
> (Aitken, 2001: 36)

Introduction

Much of western children's literature and popular culture is imbued with 'mythical representations of nature' that 'glorify nature and animals' (Aitken, 2001: 26). These same texts are often replete with Nature's Child figures that attest to Rousseau's legacy and to the Romantic and Transcendentalist nature traditions that he inspired. Figures of Nature's Child come in various forms, all of which are shaped and modified by their geo-historical contexts and overlaid by accompanying racialized, classed and gendered discourses. There are a number of ways in which these Nature's Child figures are represented in children's fictional texts. They can revolve around children's intimate relationships with animals (*Winnie-the-Pooh*, *Lassie Come Home*, *My Friend Flicka*, *Flipper*, *Skippy the Bush Kangaroo*, *Owls in the Family*, *Storm Boy*), children's adventures in natural environments (*The Secret Garden*, *Huckleberry Finn*, *Heidi*, *Pippi Longstocking*, *Storm Boy*), or in natural fantasylands (*Peter Pan*, *Snow White and the Seven Dwarfs*). They can rehearse the Romulus and Remus story of the archetypal wild Nature's Child raised by wild animals (*Jungle Book*), or be evoked, by proxy, through children's identification with animal characters in anthropomorphized stories (*The Tale of Peter Rabbit*, *The Muddle Headed Wombat*, *Bambi*, *The Lion King*, *Finding Nemo*, *Charlotte's Web*, *Babe*). The representations of Nature's Child that I examine in this chapter take a number of these forms.

When we reflect upon the Romantic writings that I charted in the previous chapter, and which gave rise to subsequent generations of Nature's Child representations, it is clear that these Romantic musings had everything to do with wistful and nostalgic adult imaginaries of some kind of 'Golden Age' of childhood (Buckingham, 2000: 9) and almost nothing to do with the real-life experiences of actual children. This is because the very qualities that make the Golden Age of childhood golden are also those that temporally and spatially distance it from the less-than-ideal real world in which we live. However, even though the Golden Age may be an atemporal and displaced adult fantasy, and even though it may be far removed from actual children's lives, it is not only adults that buy into it. In discussing the cultural transmission of adult imaginaries of childhood to children through representational practices, David Buckingham (2000: 9) observes that: '[c]hildren are often extremely interested in certain forms of discourse *about* childhood'. Why would they *not* be drawn to utopian narratives of the Nature's Child variety? These offer them a highly aestheticized imaginary world in which children are independent, competent and free, often in communion with animals, and who can act without adult interference, control and surveillance. The fact that these narratives of childhood are so 'unrealistic' – so different to their own lives – no doubt enhances their appeal. While adults might be nostalgically captivated by the romantic ideal of a lost natural childhood that probably never existed, children seem to enjoy the escapism and the empowerment of the same fantasy. So as Buckingham (2000: 9) notes, it is not only adults but also children who have 'fantasy investments in the idea of childhood'.

It is the *idea* of childhood, or to be more precise, the cultural transmission of the idea of idealized natural childhood, that is the subject of this chapter. The underlying question I am pursuing is: how do variant understandings of idealized nature affect the cultural transmission of idealized childhoods? Personifying the idea of idealized nature, the Nature's Child figures that I examine testify to the ways in which Rousseau's legacy has been disseminated in children's texts through Romantic and Transcendentalist appeals to glorified nature. But as well as allowing us to trace the continuities of Rousseau's legacy, these figures also reveal the ways in which idealized understandings of nature (and thus childhood) are modified and reshaped by the specificities of the times and places in which they are produced. Although these Nature's Child figures can trace a direct lineage back to Rousseau, they are nevertheless clearly representative of quite specifically situated natures (Instone, 2004). They move with the times, but also with the geographies of their production. To retain their currency, relevance and seductive appeal, these Nature's Child representations must offer creative adaptations of the recurring Rousseau motifs, tropes, rhetorical strategies and narrative devices that I outlined in Chapter 1.

To illustrate this dynamic combination of representational continuity and adaptation, I offer a selection of early and late twentieth-century children's cultural texts from the United States and Australia. These ex-British colony settler nation texts transmit specifically *wild* (i.e. non-European) nature imaginaries to their child audiences. By tracing their continuities and divergences, I show how each of these texts has contributed in quite distinctive ways to perpetuating 'adults' and children's fantasy investments' (Buckingham, 2000: 9) in Rousseau's original idealizations of nature, through appropriating and adapting the figure of Nature's Child to suit a variety of geographical and historical contexts and concerns.

Disney Nature's children

There is arguably no other body of Nature's Child representations that have had the same worldwide reach and exposure, and emotional impact on successive generations of child audiences, than Disney' fantasyland popular culture animations. Nor have many others rivalled the seductive appeal of Disney's formulaic and hyper-sentimentalized fantasy nature representations. Despite their geo-historical specificities, the ones I focus upon here, *Bambi* and *Pocahontas*, both run to this stock-in-trade Disney formula. They both conflate wild nature and childhood within a figurative motif of wild Nature's Child and explicitly structure the narrative dramas around the threats posed to innocent, wild and free nature by morally corrupt and destructive human culture. They emotionally engage their young audiences in 'wild sentiment', as Disney scholar David Whitley (2008: 1) calls it, by filling the highly aestheticized, brightly coloured and reverentially pristine natural scenery with a plentitude of heart-warming, cute and comic anthropomorphized wild North American animals. Both narratives include the obligatory romance between the main characters (human and animal), but much more powerfully, they foster an audience romance with the wild nature they portray. Their moral appeal is intensified by the ways in which they overtly exploit the trope of wild nature as originary, pure and sanctified.

Bambi (Hand, 1942) was Disney's first full-length wild nature fantasy animation. Based upon an early twentieth-century German children's novel (Salten, 1998 (1928)), elements of *Bambi*'s sentimental formula have been rehashed many times, but it remains Disney's signature perfect wild nature fantasy film. At face value, *Bambi* is the straightforward story of a deer's life, beginning with his birth, focusing upon his survival in the forest without his mother and ending with the birth of his own fawns. With his famed enormous eyes, extended eyelashes and disproportionately large head, not to mention his ability to speak English, Bambi is an overtly anthropomorphized character. Even as he grows up, Bambi's exaggerated and infantilized humanesque features convey a sense of his perpetual youth, allowing him to function as an easy point of identification for his young human viewing audiences. Bambi is a doe-eyed, frolicking, cloven-footed version of the pure and innocent Nature's Child. Not only does Bambi the fawn personify perfect childlike innocence, but the forest world in which he lives visually resembles the Garden of Eden, that Judaeo-Christian archetype of perfect (prelapsarian) nature with which childhood innocence is so closely associated. *Bambi*'s film-makers have exploited the rich visual repertoire of animation techniques to simulate a paradise on earth and to enhance the child audiences' sense of intimacy with this natural paradise. But as Whitley (2008) notes, *Bambi* does not just offer us a generic version of Eden. The animated landscapes bear a strong resemblance to North America's most iconic grand wilderness area – the spectacular glacial Yosemite valley and mountains of north-east California, made famous by the wilderness photography of Ansell Adams (see Adams, 2010). By interspersing the intimate close-up Garden of Eden images with simulated wide-shots of the majestic North American wilderness, *Bambi*'s film-makers evoke the Romantic sublime of the North American wilderness tradition. This combination of biblical and wilderness referents produces, as Whitley endorses, '[t]he purest evocation yet of Disney's vision of a perfect world' (Elliot, cited in Whitley, 2008: 62).

It is also important to note that the absence of humans within *Bambi*'s pristine wild nature is entirely consistent with the highly externalized notion of wilderness as pristine *unpeopled* nature that grew out of the nineteenth-century North American romantic Transcendentalist traditions and frontier ideologies (Cronon, 1996, 1998) and gathered momentum during the twentieth century. A number of nature scholars have additionally noted the symbolic erasure of indigenous people from twentieth-century wilderness discourses (Braun, 2002; Instone, 2000, 2001; Plumwood, 1993 and 2002; Spence, 1999; Taylor, 2011; Willems-Braun, 1997), and in the Australian colonial context, likened it to the legal fiction of 'terra nullius' (or land without people) that justified British occupation and indigenous dispossession (Langton, 1996).

Images that reproduce the discourse of wilderness as unpeopled nature, such as those offered in *Bambi* (and in Ansell Adam's original photographs), invite us to internalize a sense of the powerful integrity of wilderness and to endow it with a spiritual status (Taylor, 2011). The culturally transmitted *idea* of unpeopled wilderness is often sanctified and revered as an undefiled, virginal space, and in this way has become 'the ultimate landscape of authenticity' and moral authority (Cronon, 1998: 484). As the most radically pure and separate form of exter-nalized wild nature, consecrated wilderness has become the moral compass against which human actions can be judged (Taylor, 2011). The unpeopled wilderness discourse that *Bambi* evokes, clearly fortifies the moral authority of its narrative. At the same time, *Bambi* symbolically transfers the sacred significations of unpeopled nature (or wilderness) onto childhood.

Consistent with the dualistic underpinnings of purist discourses of unpeopled wilderness, the narrative tension in *Bambi*'s otherwise perfect natural world pivots around the absented and yet always potentially threatening presence of evil humans. Although we never see them, it is clear from the (off-screen) shooting of Bambi's mother early in the film that the baddies in this story are the human hunters. As Whitley (2008: 67) also notes, there is no other bad or threatening living presence within *Bambi*'s perfect world. The forest animals never prey on each other. They live in perfect harmony, exuding love for one another, thereby evoking the pastoral trope of nature as the locus of simplicity, tranquillity, balance and goodness. Only the lurking human hunters threaten life within this natural paradise. They kill Bambi's mother, threaten his love-interest and at the film's climax, it is the hunters campfire that gets out of control and quickly engulfs the forest. Of course, ultimately nature survives the onslaught and it all ends happily. Purged of its human intruders, the forest and its animals spring back to life. The work of purification is done. Bambi lives on to father his own progeny and to become the majestic patriarchal 'prince of the forest'. The natural order of things is restored in paradise.

It is hard to image a work that visually embodies and emotionally bleeds the trope of nature as inherently pure and good more than Disney's *Bambi*. Both the virginal wilderness environment and the infantilized wild animals frolicking in forests and meadows are the epitome of sacred vulnerability and innocence. The film blatantly exploits the nature/culture binary, by positioning wild nature and its animals as radically apart from, and yet intermittently threatened by, the lurking evil influence of 'man'. While *Bambi* summons many of the essential ingredients of the European pastoral idyll – such as the harmonious relations between the animals, the lingering intimacy with natural elements (magnificent blossom and floral displays, crystal raindrops and dancing falling leaves), and a general sense of sacred tranquillity – it also repositions these familiar traditions within an unpeopled North American wild nature setting. This is significant, for it not only serves to reiterate familiar (European) Romantic pastoral idyll tropes, but with the additional signification of (North American) Transcendental unpeopled wild nature, it secures the complete separation of 'man' and 'nature'. In this way, *Bambi* shows us that cultural representations, including those of Nature's Child, contain historical continuities as well as points of divergence that are produced by geo-historical specificities. In other words, as well as drawing upon and reproducing traditions (such as Rousseau's Romantic traditions that I am tracing here), representations are also contingent upon and reflective of the characteristics and concerns of the time and place in which they are produced.

By the end of the twentieth century, and nearly 60 years after the release of *Bambi*, *Pocahontas* (Gabriel and Golberg, 1995) revisited and reworked the Transcendentalist North American wild nature imaginary from yet another very distinctive geo-historical perspective. This time around, the reformed Walt Disney Feature Animation production company was much more critically attuned to the politics of nature representations. The film's producers were keen to respond to broader environmental concerns that had by now become part of the global political agenda (Whitley, 2008: 80–1) and they were much more cognizant of the political implications of gender and race representations. In particular, they were aware of the strategic value of affirming indigenous peoples' (by now widely revered) spiritual relationship with nature in an age of commodified New Ageism. Motivated to respond to these late twentieth-century sensitivities, predilections and concerns, Disney's *Pocahontas* offers up a very differently configured idyllic imaginary of wild North American nature to that of *Bambi*'s unpeopled wilderness. Set in the eastern 'New World' territories, at the violent human interface of Native American and British colonial encounter, it draws heavily upon Rousseau's romantic conflation of pure nature with noble savagery (Anderson, 2001, 2007) and his inversion of the nature/culture binary to reaffirm the original fusion of Native Americans and North American nature and to cast the white colonists as the ignorant 'savages'. By conflating nature with the twin collateral concepts of child and native, Disney's *Pocahontas* adds an additional element to the configuration of the Nature's Child imaginary. In this film, the essential moral goodness of wild North American nature is value-added by its association with Native American spirituality and given voice by Pocahontas, the original Native Nature's Child. So uncompromising is the film's pro-native naturalist agenda that it would be hard for audiences, presumably consisting of primarily non-indigenous children, not to be interpellated by its moral dictums, which appear to come directly from nature through Pocahontas.

Disney's *Pocahontas* is just one of many romantic fictionalizations of the British colonization of the 'New World' which features the legendary Native American figure Pocahontas, virgin daughter of Powhatan, the chief of the Algonquian nation. On one level, the Pocahontas story is human romance promoting white settler/Native American reconciliation in the face of colonial conflict, but the Disney version overlays the human narrative with an additional environmental message. It suggests that white settlers not only need to learn how to respect and coexist peacefully with the original people of the so-called 'New World', but also how to recognize and respect its special (spiritually powerful) nature. Despite its susceptibility to historical revisionism, this story is still widely regarded as one of the 'key founding narratives of the American nation' (Whitley, 2008: 82). It combines the vital ingredients of romance and learning how to become authentically American. The Disney version revolves around a fictional love story between Pocahontas and the British sailor and colonist John Smith, but this romance is also a narrative device for exploring the colonists' and Native Americans' very different perspectives on the nature of this land. One of the films most overt messages is that the 'New World' is not only a colonial frontier of physical conflict, but also a conceptually or symbolically contested space. With more than a tinge of romantic New Ageism, and its accompanying valorization of indigenous naturalist spirituality, it hammers home that the conflict between Native Americans and white settlers is based upon their very different under-standings of and relationships to the nature of this place. It makes it crystal clear that the native understanding and relationship is the correct and righteous one and that the white settlers' attitudes are ignorant and exploitative.

As in *Bambi*, there is no human child in this story, but because of her noble savage status, Pocahontas is a symbolic child of nature. The film's successful deployment of a lead female character who simultaneously represents nature, noble savagery and childhood was contingent upon its historical moment. It was released at a time in which many within the western New Age movement turned to Native American spirituality and all things associated with 'Mother Nature' to find alternatives to the hyper-materialism of the late industrial age. However, despite the film's distinctively North American New Ageist romantic reformulation of Native Nature's Child, the film still draws upon the standard set of formulas that Rousseau set in place in Europe two centuries beforehand. By conflating Pocahontas, as the noble savage child, with wild American nature, and setting her superior value system against that of the invading so-called 'civilized' but actually fatally flawed white colonists, the film's narrative is still entirely dependent upon the nature/culture divide. The resolution to the culminating binary dilemma – in which Pocahontas chooses not to sail away with John Smith but to remain with her people and her land – both represents a strategic win for nature and reconfirms the authenticity of her status as a forever-native child of nature.

Consistent with popular New Ageist romanticized notions of noble savagery, much of the film's rhetoric is designed to emphasize Pocahontas's essential oneness with the natural world, her spiritual kinship with the animals and her custodianship of the land. Not only does this consistently reconfirm Pocahontas's authoritative status as Native Nature's Child, but it also allows her to channel nature. This provides an additional and interesting adaptation of Rousseau's Nature as Teacher figure. When Pocahontas speaks as (native) nature, it is to re-educate her smitten lover, John Smith, and in turn, her adoring audience. As a Native Nature's Child, Pocahontas is the conduit of nature's higher-order moral truths. As Nature's Teacher and Nature's Judge, she opens his eyes (and those of her audience) to the morally bereft and exploitative relationships that white 'men' have to nature. She condemns the 'white man's' systems of land ownership and the material greed associated with it as an ignorant and corrupt ideology and counterposes it to the holistic Native American world-view of human-nature relations as dynamic and mutually constitutive. These messages are epitomized in the lyrics of the film's theme song, 'Colours of the Wind', which Pocahontas sings to John Smith in an impassioned moment.

> You think you own whatever land you land on,
> the earth is just a dead thing you can claim,
> but I know every rock and tree and creature
> has a life, has a spirit, has a name.
> …
> Have you ever heard the wolf cry to the blue corn moon,
> or ask the grinning bob cat why he grins?
> Can you sing with all the voices of the mountain,
> can you paint with all the colors of the wind?
> Can you paint with all the colors of the wind?
>
> (Gabriel and Golberg, 1995)

The visuals, including sweeping wide-angle shots of sublime natural scenery, moments of raw passion (kissing), soaring eagles and transforming shamanistic native-animal forms, are designed to support the lyrics. And yet, as Whitley also observes, 'Everywhere in *Pocahontas* there is a gap between words and the images which are designed to embody them' (2008: 87). Despite the rhetoric, the kinds of images we see of Pocahontas interacting with the natural world around her, particularly with the animals, belie any real intimacy or spiritual connection. She pays scant attention to the racoon and the hummingbird, her constant faithful companions, and the otters claimed as friends in the theme song, for instance, appear to be nothing more than Pocahontas's sleek and graceful 'fashion accessories' (Whitley, 2008: 87). In true Disney form, all of the 'wild' animals in *Pocahontas* are fetishized as cute playthings, aesthetic appendages or comic extras. As Whitley (2008: 88–9) also notes, Pocahontas herself is a visual anathema. Her arresting good looks and hour-glass body was allegedly inspired by a famous supermodel and the film certainly goes to a lot of effort to draw the audiences' attention to it. It is full of lingering close-ups and elevated long shots of the stunning Pocahontas, often standing on the top of the cliff, hair flowing in the wind, which mimic cliched fashion magazine advertisements. Such visuals signify the status of a glamorous celebrity rather than that of Native Child of Nature. Disney seems to be having it both ways here – overlaying the moral authority of this legendary Native American chieftain's daughter, famed for her anti-materialistic ethics and native ecological and spiritual wisdom, with the superficial appeal of a fashionista celebrity princess.

Both of these twentieth-century Disney animations offer a particular variant of the wild Nature's Child figure, and each of them contains internal contradictions. My point here is not just to mock these wild Nature's Child figures, but to draw attention to the vicissitudes of their cultural construction, and to highlight the specific historical, geographical, social and political conditions of their reproduction. Because of the exaggerated naivety of Disney fantasy texts, which often border on the kitsch, it is not hard to identify the ways in which they strategically exploit 'pure' and 'good' nature's semiotic potency and associate it with childhood. Once recognized, it is easy to appreciate that it is these same naturalization strategies that transmit adults' and children's fantasies about the fundamental idea of natural childhood and at the same time reformulate and repopularize Nature's Child figures. Despite the transparency of their techniques and their contradictions, it is these kinds of children's popular culture nature texts that have done much of the adaptive 'work of purification' that Latour (1993) talks about, and have also kept Rousseau's romantic Nature's Child figure in creative flux and currency.

Australian Nature's children

The Australian wild Nature's Child variants that I move on to now are ones that have shaped my own idealizations of natural childhood. Even though I consumed my share of transatlantic Nature's Child narratives in my early years, courtesy of Beatrix Potter (2002 (1902)), A. A. Milne (1994 (1928)), Enid Blyton (2010 (1942)), and, of course, Disney productions, it was the reincarnation of wild Nature's Child around the very distinctive Australian native animals and indigenous people that captured my mid-twentieth-century childhood imagination and helped to construct my sense of belonging to this young modern western nation but ancient cultural land. It was no coincidence that in the early days of nationhood, Australian children's authors such as Ethel Pedley (1977 (1906)), May Gibbs (1916; 1918) and Mary Grant Bruce (1910) began to rework Romantic European and North American traditions to produce a distinctively Australian version of Nature's Child, based upon a very different kind of antipodean nature.

Inspired by the bush legendary of nineteenth-century colonial art and literature, these children's authors were intent upon generating new national imaginaries of quintessentially Australian childhoods, based upon children's relationships with Australian nature, or, as it had come to be known, with the Australian 'bush'. Instead of associating childhood with the Romantic natural norms of northern hemisphere flora and fauna (Instone, 1998) – the rabbits, bears, deer, squirrels, otters, acorns, fir trees and daffodils – these Australian authors constructed their children's narratives around kangaroos, koalas, wombats, kookaburras, and eucalyptus and banskia trees. Perhaps more than any other Australian Nature's Child characters, it was May Gibb's (1916; 1918) hybrid 'gumnut babies' or 'bush babies' – half eucalyptus seed case and half child – that came to personify the naturalization of Australian settler childhoods (Walsh, 2007: 2). As well as perpetuating Romantic western traditions, the Australian variant of Nature's Child had a specific function in this very young modern nation. This was to encourage the identification of white settler Australian children with Australian nature and thereby to secure their naturalization as Australians.

Dot and the Kangaroo (Pedley, 1977 (1906)) is one of the earliest distinctively settler Australian Nature's Child narratives. It exemplifies the ways in which white Australian childhood was 'naturalized' in the early days of nationhood through its close association with native flora and fauna, and also with Indigenous Australian people. It is noteworthy that nineteenth-century colonial natural histories commonly represented the original human inhabitants as a part of this country's curious, exotic and 'primitive' vegetation and marsupial animals (Anderson, 2007). Without full recognition of their humanity, Aboriginal people were subsequently excluded from the 1901 Australian Constitution. Dispossessed of their country and without the rights of Australian citizenship for nearly seven decades, they remained as paradoxically non-Commonwealth Australians and yet as highly regulated and ambiguous state subjects, often under the jurisdiction of state flora and fauna acts.

For its time, *Dot and the Kangaroo* was a very unusual children's story – offering a frank, critical and alternative viewpoint on colonial race relations and relations to Australian nature. Like Disney's *Pocahontas*, it promotes a 'native' perspective on Australian nature, but this time through the authority and wisdom of Australian animals. These native animals transform Dot from a hapless and naive white child into a re-educated wise settler Australian Nature's Child. Also specific to its geo-historical Australian context, the book draws upon the recurrent theme of the lost child in the bush. The motif of the lost child in the bush was prevalent in late nineteenth-century colonial art and literature and is widely regarded as a projection of colonial anxieties about 'settling in' to this inhospitable and unfamiliar antipodean land – with its non-cultivating Aboriginal inhabitants, its harsh climate, infertile soils and very peculiar animals and plants (Pierce, 1999;

Tilley, 2007, 2009). The lost child is usually interpreted as a metaphor for the colonial subject, feeling uneasily out of place and unsafe in this strange new bush nature, which offered few of the reassuring referents of the European pastoral idyll that were so much more apparent in the North American landscape. Within the 'Great Divide' (Latour, 1993:12) of nineteenth-century lost children motifs and narratives, Australian natures (and Indigenous Australians) were inevitably cast as an enigmatic threat to new settler Australian cultures. However, in *Dot and the Kangaroo*, Ethel Pedley inverts the binary. She reframes the Australian bush as the haven and the settlers' culture as threatening it.

Right from the start, Pedley makes it crystal clear where her sympathies lie. She prefaces her story, which marks the 'birth' of the modern Australian nation, with a dedication and an appeal to Australian children. In a rhetorical flourish, which evokes Rousseau's sentiments and immediately establishes the reversal of her sympathies within the Great Divide of lost child narratives, she writes:

> To the children of Australia, in the hope of enlisting their sympathies for the many beautiful, amiable, and frolicsome creatures of their land, whose extinction, through ruthless destruction, is being surely accomplished.
>
> (1997 (1906): 3)

Moving on to the story's opening line, we are altered to the fact that this is a lost child narrative: 'LITTLE DOT had lost her way in the bush ... and she was very frightened' (1997 (1906): 1). However, almost immediately, little Dot seems to lose her fear and quickly realize that Australian nature does not endanger her. To the contrary, the child is nurtured and rescued by the real heroes of the story – the Australian native animals she meets. In the process, the animals teach her about the cruelty of humans, overtly demarcating and reiterating the good nature/bad culture divide. Befriended by an empathic kangaroo, who has herself lost a joey while being hunted by white settlers, Dot learns that the Australian bush animals have much more cause to be afraid of 'Humans' than Dot has to be afraid of them.

Kangaroo gives Dot some magic bush berries to eat, and these allow her to understand what the animals are saying and to become an audience for their concerns. The mind-altering berries help Dot to cross the 'Great Divide'. After ingesting them, she moves from the bad world of 'Humans' into the good world of native animals. As an honorary Australian native animal, now ensconced in Kangaroo's pouch, Dot has the scales lifted from her eyes. In the tradition of that archetypal Nature's Child figure – the figure of the feral child raised by wild animals – Dot learns from these Australian native animals, what it means to be human. Nature's central moral lesson about human behaviour is delivered by Kangaroo, when she points out: '"how easily one can live in the bush without hurting anyone; and yet Humans live by murdering creatures and devouring them ... Humans become so cruel that they kill, and kill not even for food, but for the love of murdering"' (1997 (1906): 18).

As well as teaching Dot some harsh truths about what it means to be human, the native Australian animals also help her to find her way back to her parent's home. Curiously the imperative to get Dot home seems to be entirely Kangaroo's, as Dot herself never appears to be homesick. To the contrary, she seems to be enchanted by the many animals that she meets – including the platypus, nightjar owl, koala, wombat, possum and cockatoo – and fascinated by their eccentricities, their perspectives on life and the wisdom that they share with her. Throughout the journey home, Dot establishes a series of empathic relationship with the animals, and it is these relationships that transform her into a child of Australian nature. However, it is not entirely an easy journey – the lessons that Dot has to learn are quite challenging.

There are two noteworthy difficult transformational moments. The first occurs midway through the journey, when Dot and Kangaroo come across a 'tribe of Black fellows' performing a 'corroboree'. In this encounter, Dot is confronted by Kangaroo's responses to her racialized comments, and by the realization that Kangaroo does not share her belief in the subhuman status of Aboriginal people and the natural superiority of the 'white Australian race' (as it was then described). As they near the clearing where the 'corroboree' is taking place,

> 'Dot nearly screamed with fright at the sight. She had thought she would see a few Black folk, not a crowd of such terrible people as she beheld. They did not look like human beings at all, but like dreadful demons. They were so wicked and ugly in appearance.'

> 'Oh, Kangaroo!" she whispered, 'they are dreadful, horrid creatures.'
> 'They're just Humans,' replied the Kangaroo, indulgently.
> 'But white Humans are not like that,' said Dot.
> 'All Humans are the same underneath, they all kill kangaroos,' said the Kangaroo.
>
> (1997 (1906): 39)

Chastened by this response, and even more dismayed by Kangaroo's further elaborations that 'Black folk', unlike 'white Humans', only kill to eat, not for pleasure, Dot seeks redemption from her mentor:

> 'I wish I were not a white little girl,' she whispered to the kangaroo. The gentle animal patted her kindly with her delicate black hands.
> 'You are as nice now as my baby kangaroo,' she said sadly, 'but you will have to grow into a real white Human … you may become an improved Human.'
> 'How could I do that?' asked Dot, eagerly.
> 'Never wear kangaroo leather boots – never use kangaroo skin rugs, and … never, never eat kangaroo tail soup!' said the Kangaroo, solemnly.
> 'I never will,' said Dot, earnestly, 'I will become an improved Human.'
>
> (1997 (1906): 41)

Dot's second challenging transformational moment occurs near the end of the story, when she is unexpectedly called before a court of native animals. The personification of nature as law, judge and jury is quite overt. Cockatoo is the presiding magistrate and Magpie is Dot's defence lawyer. Pelican explains the situation: '"We are here to place you on trial for the wrongs we Bush creatures have suffered from the cruelty of White Humans"' (1997 (1906): 63). Luckily for Dot, when Kangaroo is called as a key witness, she tells the judge and jury that the little white girl is suitably remorseful and has committed to becoming an 'improved Human'. She tells the others that she has already forgiven Dot for all the sins of the white Humans, including the 'hunting', 'the rugs', 'the boots' and 'the kangaroo-tail soup' (1997 (1906): 70), and the trial is abandoned.

Dot's education by the native Australian animals to become an 'improved Human', and her subsequent trial to establish her status as a redeemed white child, is an explicit inversion of the nature/culture divide and an interesting settler Australian adaptation of Rousseau's treatise on the 'Education of Nature'. In having Dot declare her desires to be an 'improved Human', Pedley was clearly defying the prevailing discourses that portrayed nature as being improved by human intervention. This is very much an echo of Rousseau's inverted valuation of the nature/culture divide, and is similarly driven by a passionate contempt for 'degenerative' (cruel) adult human behaviours. The stated purpose of Dot's education by the native animals (just like Emile's 'Education of Nature') was to make her into a better human being. Once re-educated by nature and certified by the court of the native animal republic as an 'improved Human', she was returned back to human society – redeemed, enlightened and with new moral fortitude and vision. Pedley's version of the child's redemption through nature is clearly overlaid with a strong early Australian nationalist agenda. It seems that Improved Little Dot is destined to become a 'naturalized' white settler Australian child, and a symbol of hope for the future reconciliation of settler Australians with Australian nature.

Seven decades later, YoramGross Films Studios released an animated film version of *Dot and the Kangaroo* (Gross, 1977). Not surprisingly, the Australian political climate had changed considerably since the early days of federation, when the book was written. The national government had just legislated for its first official multicultural policy, and no longer was it acceptable for Australians to defer to the 1901 White Australia Policy, and its declared purpose to 'ensure the purity of the white race'. In the decade preceding the release of this film, Indigenous Australians had been finally recognized as Australian citizens, and the first Aboriginal Land Rights Act had been enacted. The 'second wave' of the environmental movement had gathered considerable momentum after the Second World War and spurred a number of environmental protection campaigns in the 1970s (Hutton and Connors, 1999). The newly established Australian Film Commission was keen to promote children's films and television that reflected these changes. It had a charter to promote a national identity for young Australians that incorporated the distinctiveness of the Australian natural environment and was politically attuned to the originary status of Indigenous Australians within the national story. As an Australian children's classic, the story of *Dot and the Kangaroo* contained all these elements; however, the animated film version deviated far from the original hard-hitting text.

Despite the imprinting of the animated animals upon realist background footage of the Australian bush, the film version does not convey any of the book's political realism. It delivers a highly sentimental and soft romantic image of Australian wild nature, strikingly resembling the stylistics of Disney wild nature animation. This is so much so, that few of the Australian animals are easily recognizable. They seem to take normative forms that might be more palatable for northern hemisphere audiences. With her enormous ears and large wistful eyes, Kangaroo bears an uncanny likeness to Bambi, and the wombat, often seen standing upright, resembles Yogi Bear much more than the resolutely squat and four-footed Australian marsupial. The film's message is also very tempered. While the animals still communicate their fear of humans to Dot, there is no discussion of the distinctive cruelty of white humans. Instead of the trial to determine Dot's guilt or innocence for white human crimes against animals, there is a 'council of animals' to decide the best course of action to help Dot find her way home. The political rhetoric of the original text has been replaced by a series of whimsical animal song and dance routines, interspersed with extended interludes of Kangaroo hopping through the bush with Dot in pouch. Instead of being horrified by the sight of Aboriginal people at the corroboree scene, ever-innocent Dot begs to stay 'a bit longer', as she is enchanted by the dancing. There is none of the original commentary upon the racialized division between black and white people or the need for white humans to be 'improved' by Australian nature. Unlike the book, the film ends by symbolically reaffirming the division between wild Australian animals and white settlers. When Kangaroo finally delivers Dot back to her human family, she declines her invitation to meet the family. At the boundary of nature/culture – the post and rail fence surrounding the homestead – Kangaroo turns around and hops her way back into freedom in the wild. It seems that the film's parting message is quite different from that of the book. Whereas Pedley clearly promotes the potential for white settler Australian children to reconcile with wild Australian nature, the film reconfirms the inevitable hyper-separation (Plumwood, 1993) of humans and wild nature.

Storm Boy (Thiele, 1964) is another Australian Nature's Child narrative, originally written as a children's novel and subsequently adapted to film, but this time with a lot more care to be faithful to the original text. The film *Storm Boy* (Safran, 1976) was released at the same time as *Dot and the Kangaroo*. It was promoted by the Australian Film Commission as a high-quality and quintes-sentially Australian children's drama. Both the novel and the film, which tell the story of a relationship between a boy and pelican, explicitly promote the protection of the Australian wilderness and acknowledge the significance of Indigenous Australians' relations to the land. The film was shot in the rugged Coorong estuarine wilderness area of South Australia, which fronts onto the stormy Southern Ocean. The film-makers used this spectacular scenery to elicit a range of emotional responses. The scale of wild nature is at times delivered in broad sweeping shots, which are majestically uplifting and evoke the calm transcendental sense of the Romantic sublime. At other times of high narrative tension, the wild nature of the ocean is portrayed as an uncontrollable force. As in *Dot and the Kangaroo*, wild Australian nature is more than a backdrop to this film: it functions as a narrative focal point (Zonn and Aitken, 1994).

As the title suggests, the central human character, Storm Boy, is the child of this wild Australian nature. He is a white settler child, taken out of human society and away from his mother (who subsequently dies) by his reclusive father. Tom, the father, and Storm Boy eke out a subsistence life, sheltering behind the sand dunes on the wind-blown and 'deserted' coast. The trope of nature as a restorative or therapeutic refuge is central to this film. Storm Boy spends his days beachcombing and fishing. He lives a wild and free Robinson Crusoe-style life (minus the cannibals), sheltering in the obligatory beach shack that he and his father construct from the driftwood they find washed up on the beach. Storm Boy spends all of his days out of doors in nature. Storm Boy's father is a man of few words and apart from bringing Storm Boy to this place and ultimately making the decision to leave it, he has a relatively background role in the unfolding narrative. Much more important are the supporting Australian nature characters – Mr Percival the pelican, and Fishbone Bill, Storm Boy's Aboriginal mentor.

Mr Percival comes into the story as an orphaned pelican chick, rescued and reared by Storm Boy. Once mature, and upon Tom's insistence, he is released back into the wild. On the strength of the early bond established with the boy, Mr Percival regularly returns of his own free will, to become Storm Boy's close seasonal companion, his primary relationship and his partner in heroic coastal adventures. This makes him a wild animal that can also cross the nature/culture divide and live in 'two worlds'. At the film's dramatic climax, and as he is flying back to be with Storm Boy, Mr Percival is killed by the evil white hunters. As well as consolidating Storm Boy's emotional relationship with the nature of this wild place, Mr Percival, as the sacrificial hero, teaches Storm Boy about the importance of mateship, loyalty and a sense of community. He also teaches Storm Boy and his father Tom that it is possible to enter in and out of the world of human domestication without entirely sacrificing the freedom of wild nature. In this way, this ambiguously domesticated-wild animal teacher subtly subverts the absolutisms of the 'Great Divide' (Latour, 1993).

Fingerbone Bill is the other significant character in the story. He is a traditional Aboriginal man from this country, who is camping behind the beach uncharacteristically alone. We learn that he is by himself because he has been cast out from his 'tribe' as a punishment for engaging in an illicit romance that contravened traditional lore. Fingerbone Bill is a custodian of the indigenous stories of this place. He knows the ways of this country and becomes Storm Boy's native guide and mentor. As a lore-breaker, Fingerbone is not quite a noble savage figure, and, like Mr Percival, retains some interesting ambiguities that allow him to escape the stereotyping that goes with being cast on one or either side of the nature/culture divide. Through his mentoring of Storm Boy, Fingerbone finds a pathway back to his own spiritual restoration. As a not entirely heroic Native Nature's Teacher, he nevertheless educates the white boy by telling him the traditional creation stories of this wild place, which feature pelicans and storms. It is Fingerbone who names this settler child 'Storm Boy', symbolically initiating him as a white native child of this place. The mentoring relationship between the Aboriginal elder and the young white settler child carries some national symbolism – gesturing towards the need for the newcomers to this country to learn from the ancient traditional knowledge base of its original custodians. Like Pocahontas in the Disney film, the Fingerbone character has the indigenous authority to speak for nature, but he does not speak with Pocahontas's unflinching moral certitude and he does not rehearse a crudely racialized binary of goodies and baddies.

Despite its more nuanced treatment of the nature/culture divide and Indigenous/non-indigenous relations, Storm Boy still has its own lacunae. With its all-male cast, the *Storm Boy* story additionally reiterates the inherent masculinity of the quintessential Australian bush legend, which is so central to the national imaginary and yet bears little resemblance to the lives and identities of most Australians. *Storm Boy*'s coastal nature narrative and its settler boy/beachcomber character offers a slightly different take on the 'white native' bushman that is typified in the *Man from Snowy River* and *Crocodile Dundee* figures, but it still draws upon a similar set of gendered values and binary logics. It reiterates the blokey form of Australian masculinity that is so closely associated with the attributes of anti-authoritarianism, rugged independence, mateship and above all freedom (Zonn and Aitken, 1994). The narrative is infused with this idiosyncratically Australian gendered take on the nature/culture divide. This can be seen in the way that nature is aligned with the freedom of the central male characters while culture is aligned with the confines of town life and the female characters associated with it (such as the ex-wife and the schoolteacher who pressures Storm Boy to return to school) (Aitken, 2001: 38).

After the death of Mr Percival, Tom is finally convinced to return to town and to send Storm Boy to school. This ultimate choice is supported by the sense that Storm Boy's education in nature is now complete and wild nature has done its recuperative work. The slightly wayward adult male characters are more or less 'healed' and ready to return to society. Moreover, the wild natural world of the Coorong, along with Mr Percival, has grown the boy up, delivering him strength of character and moral judgment from both the wondrous and the bitter lessons of life and death. In Rousseau's terms, Storm Boy will return to society much stronger and wiser because of his education in Nature. But the final decision is not without its shades of ambivalence. While there is an acknowledgement of the need for more community, there is also a fair amount of wistful nostalgia about the freedom in nature that must be sacrificed in order to return Storm Boy to society.

Heterotopic purification

When returning to the question of what representations of idealized nature *do* to our understandings of childhood, I find it useful to draw upon Foucault's (1986) analytic concept of heterotopia, or 'other spaces'. Heterotopias are similar to utopias, but instead of representing perfectly imagined alternative societies, they are ambiguous in-between spaces that remain as a part of the existing 'real' world while offering possibilities beyond it. Foucault identified a number of different kinds of heterotopic spaces with different functions, but of particular relevance to these Nature's Child representations is the kind of heterotopic space that is 'consecrated to ... activities of purification' (1986: 26). *Bambi*'s pristine and unpeopled wilderness paradise, *Pocahontas*'s perfect Native American world of spiritual harmony with nature, *Dot and the Kangaroo*'s wise Australian native animal republic, and *Storm Boy*'s free, wild Australian beachcombing life can all be read as textual 'other spaces' of purification.

According to Foucault, entry into these kinds of heterotopic spaces entails submitting to the rules and rituals of purification. *Bambi, Pocahontas, Dot and the Kangaroo* and *Storm Boy* all emulate Rousseau's rules and rituals around childhood and nature. Each of these texts follows Rousseau's original directive to dissociate childhood from modern 'man's' degenerative society and each of them partakes in the redemptive rite, promoted by Rousseau, of allowing children to be re-educated by Nature. It is through being interpellated by such routine cleansing activities that child and adult audiences are drawn into Nature's Child representations as heterotopic spaces of purification.

Heterotopias function on a number of levels, and Foucault also outlined one of the additional roles of purification heterotopias as a compensatory one: 'Their role is to create a space that is other, another real space, as perfect, as meticulous, as well arranged as ours is messy, ill constructed, and jumbled' (1986: 27). With reference to these different levels of functionality, Foucault described heterotopia as a kind of 'enacted utopia, in which the real sites, all the other real sites that can be found within the culture, are simultaneously represented, contested and inverted' (1986: 24). Each text represents the 'real world' by drawing upon a unique set of natural referents (North American and Australian post-colonial landscapes, native animals and indigenous people) to act as symbolic markers of that particular nature's authenticity and moral authority. Each text contests the 'real social world' by drawing upon the logic of oppositions encapsulated in the nature/culture divide, and constructing an alternative utopian natural world. Each one inverts the 'real world' by romancing nature as an idealized form of other-worldliness.

But as Foucault stressed, the most interesting thing about heterotopias is that by simultaneously 'representing, contesting and inverting', they reveal their own paradoxes and slippages. These heterotopias of pure natural childhood, or imaginaries of nature and childhood as purified 'other spaces', inevitably become sites of contradiction and displacement (Taylor and Richardson, 2005a). The

most obvious contradiction relates to the status of Nature's Child as simultaneously a cultural desire, an aspirational idea and an idealization that paradoxically
seduces us precisely because its key referent, nature, 'appears not to be an idea
at all' (Castree, 2005: 137). The very artifice of Nature's Child, as a cultural
production, belies its own claims to natural authority, authenticity and truth. It
displaces itself and reveals the ways in which 'external nature is not a given, but
rather the result of an explicit procedure of externalization' (Latour, 2004: 242).

If we reconsider Nature's Child as a serial representational act that reconfirms
and reproduces the desire for childhood as a heterotopia, an 'other space' of
purification and natural perfection, we can start to identify the cracks that might
allow us to prise apart and 'queer' this seductively perfect (monogamous) liaison.
We can look for the slippages that reveal how these Nature's Child figures, as
well as seducing us with the lure of pure and perfect other-worldly worlds, might
also be doing something quite different and unintentional. For instance, we can
question what else child audiences might take away from these glorified nature
representations that are so 'other' to their own lives, but which interpellate them
so strongly. Do these heterotopic nature representations become their primary
referents for nature – as simulacra, do they become more authentic than 'real'
nature? Does the pure nature heterotopia inspire their love of nature or effect
disappointment in or disassociation from the less-than-pure and perfect material
natures that they encounter in their everyday lives? Do they feel reassured by
their association with an unpeopled world, or compromised by being called to
choose nature over the human world? Do they aspire to follow nature in order to
become better humans or do they disavow their humanness in order to identify
with nature? How do these nature purification rites and rituals affect their sense
of self and belonging in the world?

Conclusion

In this chapter I have examined some popular children's cultural texts to see
how the seductive work of nature is expressed through the fictional representations of the Nature's Child figure. I have traced the continuities as well as
some of the geo-historical points of divergence in the cultural transmission of
Rousseau's original notion of Nature's Child. These have flowed and dispersed
from Rousseau's romantic conflation of nature, childhood and noble savagery,
through the romantic filters of the pastoral idyll, Transcendentalism and New
Ageism and into these four very different North American and Australian wild
nature children's texts. The main continuities can be identified within the central
organizing structure of the nature/culture divide. Time and again it is this
'Great Divide' (Latour, 1993) that shores up the representations of idealized
nature and Nature's Child against the potential threats of society and the various
humans who constitute it (adults, hunters, colonists, women, white Humans).
Also common to these children's popular narratives is the way in which the
distinctive features (animals, plants, landforms) of (non-European) wild nature,

in particular, have become key motifs in the transmission of cultural stories, the production of national imaginaries, the endorsement of noble savagery, the improvement of newcomer (settler) human children, the reconciliation of colonial conflicts and the naturalization of settler identities. The geo-historical specificities of these distinctive nature referents are marker points of difference and dispersal. But instead of diffusing the cultural transmission of Rousseau's Nature's Child figuration by modifying it, they do the important work of simultaneously customizing and spreading the seductive appeal of pure natural childhoods to geographically, culturally and historically diverse child audiences.

Whatever intentional or non-intentional messages children take away from these texts, there is no denying that representations of Nature's Child perform a pedagogical function. Within each of the texts we have looked at, the Nature's Child figure is entwined with that of Nature as Teacher. One of the universal themes is that by learning from nature we can become better people, or 'improved Humans' as Dot put it. Within the texts, children are represented as learning how to become better people through being taught by nature. If they are not directly represented, they are encouraged to identify with other natural characters, in order to learn about and aspire to nature's innate higher moral order. This entanglement of the figures of Nature's Child and Nature as Teacher, and the theme of humans learning from nature, is even more explicit in the next chapter – where we move on to look at the ways in which Rousseau's (2003 (1762)) *Emile* treatise has influenced the unfolding traditions of modern 'natural education' and been translated into a range of early childhood nature-related pedagogical practices.

Educating Nature's Child

> In the beginning was Rousseau. His pedagogical anthropology, so it seems, marked the turning point to a new 'natural pedagogy.' His vision was called 'nature's gospel of education.'
>
> (Fuchs, 2004: 155)

> ... leave to infancy the exercise of that natural liberty ... let them once learn the method of Nature.
>
> (Rousseau, 2003 (1762): 51)

Introduction

Rousseau's status and reputation as the prophet of natural education has almost biblical proportions, as the quote above from Fuchs implies. In this chapter, as in the previous one, I trace the continuities and dispersals of Rousseau's natural 'gospel of education'. But this time my focus is upon the ways in which his prophetic philosophies have filtered through to subsequent generations of natural pedagogies, and shaped the history of mainstream and alternative branches of early childhood education. I look at the ways in which, following in Rousseau's footsteps, educationalists have variously reiterated the relationship between Nature's Child and Nature as Teacher to ensure that young children learn how to become better (smarter, healthier, wiser, emotionally stronger and more spiritually developed) humans. Starting with Fröebel's evolving early nineteenth-century kindergarten design, the chapter spans three centuries of early childhood education. It considers the impact of modern science upon the delivery of Rousseau's 'method of Nature', and concludes by looking at the ways in which Rousseau's ideas still have currency within the contemporary outdoor or nature early childhood education movement.

Formal education's engagement with Rousseau's 'vision' of 'the education of Nature' has been very uneven. While his urgings to match learning against the child's innate stage of natural development have been universally embraced, his ambiguous notion of 'the method of Nature' has had a more tempered and checkered uptake within mainstream education. Not surprisingly, Rousseau's radical negative education thesis (on the need to shield young children from 'the Education of Man') has found a very small following amongst modern educators. Those that do advocate for children to be educated directly *in* and *by* nature, as opposed to *about* nature, are positioned well outside of the mainstream. While tracing the trajectory of nature-based education from Rousseau to the present, I consider how and why the different aspects of his 'gospel' of natural education have been variously adopted, appropriated, avoided and ignored.

Quite recently, a 'back to nature' movement has given a boost to those who advocate education *in* nature and by 'the method of Nature'. This has been precipitated by the release of Richard Louv's (2008) book *Last Child in the Woods: Saving Our Children from Nature-Deficit Disorder*. Louv's arguments, and the ways in which they have been taken up by nature-education proponents, offer a new twist to the relationship between Rousseau's Nature's Child and Nature as Teacher. I reflect upon the ways in which rearticulations of Romantic nature traditions alongside scientific discourse have reinvigorated a movement to return children to nature, both without and within early childhood education, and how they have also injected new life into Rousseau's thesis of negative education.

My guiding mantra in this chapter, once again, is Steve Hinchcliffe's (2007) observation that how we think about nature determines what it does. This time, my interest is focused upon how different perceptions of nature produce different applications of natural early childhood education. As a starting point, I look at the pedagogical implications of Rousseau's own ever-Romantic but also layered understandings of nature. From this baseline, I then consider how such Romantic philosophical understandings of nature have been rearticulated and/or superseded within education, along with the increasingly hegemonic status of modern science. Science has become *the* major player in interpreting and representing nature in the secular arena of modern western education. The intersection of Rousseau's Romantic nature philosophies and western science's empirical and pragmatic relationship to nature has produced a very interesting tension. This tension between Romantic and scientific iterations of nature, and their relative authority, runs throughout all the natural early childhood education approaches that I study, as well as through Louv's warnings about the endangered status of Nature's Child in *Last Child in the Woods*. In concluding this chapter, I reflect upon how this tension between Romantic and scientific iterations of natural education is deployed to secure the seduction of Nature as Teacher.

Revisiting Rousseau's 'gospel' of natural education

Before tracing Rousseau's legacy within European traditions of natural early childhood education, I revisit his *Treatise on Education* in order to recall the ways in which Rousseau himself conceptualized nature – or Nature, as he reverentially called it. Needless to say, Rousseau drew upon idealized notions of nature in order to impart authority to his educational treatise. He used multiple meanings, which were sometimes contradictory, and he often elided them. In his editorial preface to *Emile*, W. T. Harris (2003 (1892)) remarks that Rousseau's 'appeal to Nature is always a piece of jugglery'. He notes that Rousseau opportunistically used this 'high-sounding word' in many different senses and for many different purposes. I can distinguish three main senses in which Rousseau used nature to purposefully promote what he often referred to as the 'education of Nature' (2003 (1762): 20). Each of these deployments of nature has impacted upon modern theories of 'natural education', but in varying ways and degrees.

The first sense of nature adopted by Rousseau was of nature as an internal force. This is aligned to the more common sense of innate human nature, but Rousseau offered a specific variation of it. He deliberately described the innate nature of the child as different (and superior) to that of the adult. He articulated this in terms of the child's pure natural 'primitive dispositions' (2003 (1762): 13). According to Rousseau, these 'primitive dispositions' are the child's hard-wired urges, instincts and curiosities to explore and inquire. They are uncomplicated sensory urges, unfolding in sequential stages, and exist independent of adult intervention (instruction, explanation or reasoning). Rousseau's core idea of the child as being essentially different in nature from the adult (much purer and more authentic), and driven by sequentially unfolding sets of natural dispositions, was radical for its day, but it is now an axiom of modern educational theory. It is not hard to trace the modern-day premise of the unique and special child and the emphasis upon careful child-centred approaches that respect the natural stages of her of his growth and development (as exemplified in the idea of 'developmentally appropriate practice' or DAP (Bredekamp, 1986)), directly back to Rousseau's original conceptions of the child's unique inner nature or 'primitive dispositions'. This is by far his most universally adopted and greatest legacy to modern western educational theory.

Rousseau's belief that perfect nature resides within the child as an essential life-driving force led him to postulate that the young child should be left alone to freely explore the external natural world and learn by 'his' sensory and physical experiences of it (not adult explanations of it). This ties in with his second and yet rather contradictory notion of nature as other-to and better-than 'man' – although not other-to or better-than the child. The idea of nature as 'not-man' was most clearly expressed within Rousseau's theory of 'negative education' (2003 (1762): 59). This is the idea that children need to be protected from 'the education of Man' for as long as possible, at least until they are 12 years old. Rousseau believed that adult intervention derailed the child's innate natural learning processes, and in a sense also robbed children of their unique and special (superior) natures. He explained that the purpose of negative education was 'not to gain time' by prematurely rushing the child into the adult reasoning world, 'but to lose it' by allowing the child to learn in 'his' own time within nature (2003 (1762): 58).

Rousseau justified his advocacy of 'negative education' by explaining that the child that 'receives his lessons from Nature ... learns the more rapidly ... his body and his mind are called into exercise at the same time. Acting always in accordance with his own thought, and not according to that of another, he is continually uniting two processes; the stronger and the more robust he makes himself, the more sensible and judicious he becomes' (2003 (1762): 86). His argument is that 'negative education', as a 100 per cent natural education without any interference from 'rational man', is a better education and ultimately makes the child a better thinker and a better human. Rousseau's underlying premise that 'experience precedes lessons' (2003 (1762): 25) can also be seen within this passage on 'negative education'.

In this sense of embodied experience leading learning, Rousseau's idea of 'negative education' can be traced through to the constructivist school of modern educational thought, championed by John Dewey (1859–1952). This is the theory that promotes experiential learning, based as closely as possible upon real-life experiences, as far more effective than purely abstracted and decontextualized teaching and learning. In Dewey's words we can see the resonances of Rousseau's ideas about natural education: 'if knowledge comes from the impressions made upon us by natural objects, it is impossible to procure knowledge without the use of objects which impress the mind' (Dewey, 2009 (1916): 217–18). The point at which Dewey's thinking departs from Rousseau's is around the latter's insistence that the child's embodied experiences should only 'act in accordance with his own thought, and not according to that of another' (Rousseau, 2003 (1762): 86). For Dewey, it is the two-way interaction of the child's experiences and the teacher's input that create the optimal learning conditions. It is not surprising that Rousseau's advocacy for the radical autonomy of the child's learning process in nature, and his explicit insistence upon the elimination of all adult interference in this process, has not been widely espoused in mainstream educational theory. It is really only within the free play philosophies of early childhood education, and within the field of outdoor education, that we find the remaining traces of Rousseau's more radical non-human interference aspects of 'negative education'.

The third sense of nature that Rousseau evoked was that of nature as the external and material world in which we live – more specifically, the material world that is *not* made by 'man'. Obviously this external nature is an elision of his second idea of nature as radically other-to and better-than 'man', and better than anything 'man' can make. Rousseau evoked this third understanding of nature alongside his 'education of Nature' when he advocated the 'education of things' (2003 (1762): 2). As already noted, Rousseau's belief in the pedagogical significance of material experiences has travelled directly into constructivist educational theory, via Dewey. It has also, and perhaps most notably of all, been formalized within theories of natural child development. This is particularly apparent in Piaget's (1928, 1952) canonic cognitive development theory, in which the development of 'figurative' and 'operative' cognitive skills are founded upon the child's repeated physical and sensory concrete experiences of the material world, particularly in the 'sensory motor' (birth to two years) and 'preoperational' (two to seven years) stages of early childhood. In these extremely foundational ways, Rousseau's 'education of things' has become a fundamental guiding principle of educational theory and practice, particularly in the early years. However, the stock-in-trade modern-day educational equipment – the stuff of concrete educational materials – bears little or no resemblance to the purity and integrity of the resolutely natural things that Rousseau described as affording the child a natural education. In fact the ubiquitous modern school classroom, with its desks, boards, books, computers, and the ever-present knowledge-disseminating teacher, is the antithesis of Rousseau's vision of 'negative education'.

Nature's method in Fröebel's kindergarten

Just as the Romantics represented childhood in a special relationship with nature, the field of early childhood education is cast in a unique relationship to Rousseau's 'method of Nature'. It is obvious that this is at least partially due to the premise that the younger the child, the closer s/he is to her/his natural instincts and nature and the further away s/he is from reason and logic. But the perception of a special relationship between early childhood education and the 'method of Nature' has another dimension. It is also attributable to the fact that Freidrich Fröebel, the 'father' of the kindergarten movement, bore direct lineage to Rousseau. His own teacher in educational theory was the Swizz educationalist Johan Pestalozzi, a second-generation follower of Rousseau's ideas. As a committed Romantic, Pestalozzi espoused Rousseau's beliefs in the essential goodness of human nature and the infallibility of nature. He insisted that education must be respectful of the child's inherent nature and subordinated to the external laws of nature (Fuchs, 2004: 161). His student, Fröebel, took these Rousseau-inspired guiding principles quite literally and this is exactly what he set out to do when he reverentially designed the kindergarten, or children's gardens, as a literal manifestation of 'the method of Nature', to educate pre-primary aged children.

Fröebel's interest in education, and in particular the education of young children, emerged later in his life. Before setting up his kindergartens he had had previous careers in surveying, forestry and mineral classification, and had studied architecture and crystallography. So he already had a well-developed multidisciplinary understanding of and investment in nature. Unlike Rousseau's rather vague Romantic notion of the laws of nature, and nature's method, Fröebel's understanding about nature's laws was based upon his substantial knowledge about and experience in spatial geometry and the natural sciences of plants and crystals. Fröebel's kindergarten design was the manifestation of a complex set of understandings about nature. On the one hand it drew closely upon his scientific understandings of and devotions to studying nature's law and order, and on the other, it was also an expression of his deeply held Romantic beliefs in nature as truth and perfection (Brosterman, 1997, 2002–3).

Indeed, Fröebel was motivated by a conviction that the infallible natural laws that govern the growth of plants and the formation of crystals also parallel the child's natural growth and development processes. As he reflected in his autobi-ography, 'my rocks and crystals served me as a mirror wherein I might descry mankind, and man's development and history ... Nature and Man now seemed to me mutually to explain each other, through all their numberless various stages of development' (Fröebel, cited in Brosterman, 2002–3). Fröebel's kindergarten design was a systematic attempt to formalize these correspondences, by applying nature's perfect laws of plant growth and crystal formation to support the young child's optimal growth and development.

Fröebel's reverential study of nature's laws was also driven by his strong religious faith. As the son of a Lutheran pastor and a Romantic naturalist, he developed a personal spiritual philosophy of 'Unity', within which nature's laws were divinely ordained. His Unity philosophy was one that demonstrated the interconnectedness of God, external nature, human nature and an ideal society (1912a (1826)). As Norman Brosterman (2002–3) surmises, Fröebel's philosophy was simultaneously 'embracing the spiritual potential within a person, relations between people in a free society, the place of the individual in relation to the nature that surrounds and includes him, and the [divine and natural] life force that controls growth in all things' (Brosterman, 2002–3). For Fröebel, education that was faithful to 'the method of Nature' and revealed 'the divine essence of things' was a way of manifesting his Unity philosophy and would lead 'man' towards 'a clear knowledge of himself, to peace with nature, to unity with God' (1912a (1826): 32).

Because of his adherence to the Romantic belief that it is young children who maintain the closest relationship to nature, Fröebel eventually focused his interests upon four- and five-years-olds, who were not at that time included within formal education. It was within his detailed road maps for kinder-garten education, written during the period 1838–40 and quite late in his life, that Fröebel eventually constellated and materialized all of his passions. His kindergarten design drew upon the resolutely Romantic beliefs about nature and young children that he inherited from Rousseau; his religious faith in and personal philosophy of spiritual interconnectedness; and his scientific obsession with applying nature's laws. He effectively channelled the emotional force of Rousseau's Romantic treatise on the natural education of the child into his simultaneously spiritual, scientific and natural design for kindergarten education and produced the first comprehensive template of 'Nature's method' for early childhood education.

For Fröebel, the kindergarten was both a metaphorical marker of and a physical space for the cultivation of nature in the child. He spoke of the kinder-garten as both a '*garden of children*', an environment in which children's true natures are cultivated, and as a place with real gardens 'for the children who attend' (1912b (1838–40): 238). To this end he provided detailed instructions for the layout of the physical gardens within the kindergarten. In these instruc-tions, he paid forensic attention to creating an order that reflected nature's own forms and rhythms, but would also lead children to cultivate habits that would prepare them for living in a perfectly ordered civil society. Each child in the kindergarten was to have their own individual plot, but these plots were to be enclosed and protected by a 'common garden' – symbolizing the ways in which 'the particular rests within the general' and is 'part to the whole' (1912b (1838–40): 238). Fröebel provided specifications for the construction of the gardens, including the dimensions and directions for main paths and branch paths, which again 'at once divide and connect the whole' (1912b (1838–40): 239). In addition to the spatial layout, which was modelled upon his civic ideals about the relations between individuals and society, he provided rules for the children's cultivation of plants. These rules were modelled upon natural rhythms and the growth processes of plants. Again, his detailed guide to systems of cultivation aimed to provide the child with 'a general knowledge of the whole and an insight into the parts, so that his memory is impressed simultaneously with relations of place, object, name, qualities, and time and combines them' (1912b (1838–40): 240). His garden design was founded upon his belief that just as children will learn how best to become good cultivators (and good citizens) by observing these natural patterns, rhythms and processes, so will their own cultivation within the kindergarten environment be ensured by pedagogical forms, patterns and processes that are modelled upon nature.

Just as the children's gardens were modelled upon Fröebel's botanical knowledge and experiences, his children's 'gifts', or inanimate geometric play objects, were modelled upon his knowledge about the structure and formation of rocks and crystals. The 'gifts' can thus be seen as Fröebel's scientific extrapolations upon Rousseau's 'education of [natural] things'. As Fröebel's expressed it, 'play becomes to the child the key to the world of things' (1912b (1838–40): 198). As much as possible, Fröebel wanted the 'gifts' to resemble simple openended natural play objects – like sticks and stones – to which children are naturally attracted. But he also wanted them to mimic the internal structure of natural objects, and for this reason he designed them to replicate the basic geometric shapes and forms of crystals. Most commonly, the 'gifts' took the form of simple and unadorned wooden cubes, spheres, bricks and tetrahedrons that children played with inside the kindergarten. Used within short guidedplay sessions, they were the 'tools' for fostering children's appreciation for what Fröebel identified as the three basic forms of life: 'the forms of Nature (or Life), forms of Knowledge (or Science), and forms of Beauty (or Art)' (Brosterman, 2002–3).

In line with his philosophy of the spiritual Unity of nature, Fröebel believed that by manipulating these simple 'gift' objects, children would develop the creative capacity to 'seek and find the particular in the general' (1912b (1838–40): 198) – to relate the more complex 'man'-made objects around 'him' back to these basic geometric building blocks of life. Through repeated handling of these gifts, 'The child attains clear knowledge of nature and of himself, though he cannot yet express it in word' (1912b (1838–40): 198). At an even loftier level, he believed that the child would develop an unarticulated but nevertheless abstracted awareness of 'the distinction of part and whole' and gain 'the ennobling sense of the unity of all life' (1912b (1838–40): 194–5). Using a similar form of nature-replicating reasoning as he did with his very deliberate garden design, 'Fröebel postulated that since the shapes of crystals ... are the outcome of the same natural laws that also result in the growth of children, people, and entire societies, handling these forms correctly would reveal and illuminate the mind of the creator itself' (Brosterman, 2002–3). In other words, the 'gifts', like the garden, were the key design elements of the kindergarten intended to formalize the 'method of Nature' and to foster children's ultimate sense of God's/nature's grand design.

Fröebel's operationalization of Rousseau's ideas in the kindergarten context has had its own great legacy – literally giving birth to and continuing to closely determine the trajectory of western early childhood education for well over a century. The influence of Fröebel's thinking can easily be traced within European education approaches, such as Montessori's meticulous methods of natural observation and inquiry (Montessori, 1912); the Steiner emphasis on environmental design, children's handling of natural materials and the connections between natural education and the child's spiritual development (Steiner, 1996 (1906–11)); and the design of the Nature Kindergartens in Scotland (Warden, 2010). Through 'inventing the kindergarten' (Brosterman, 1997), Fröebel aligned early childhood education, more than any other form of education, with a Romantic sense of the educational (and spiritual) affordances of the laws of nature, with the pedagogical significance of natural play and natural play objects, and with a desire to embed natural form and process within educational design. Through maintaining his Romantic inheritance from the author of 'nature's gospel of education' (Fuchs, 2004: 163), and substantiating it with his own grounding in natural science, Fröebel launched the field of early childhood education with a distinctively Romantic scientific template for natural education. It combined the moral authority of nature and the axiomatic Romantic belief in young children's special relationship with nature with the scientific veracity of 'nature's laws'.

This is akin to what Lorraine Daston (2004: 107) calls the 'displacement of sentiment'. In her study of the scientific writings of Enlightenment natural historians, she uses this phrase to describe the shift from a reverential adherence to a singular, 'all-encompassing' and personified notion of Nature (such as that held by Rousseau and Wordsworth) to the equally Romantically inflected scientific practice of systematically discovering and classifying the attributes and forms of 'highly specific natural objects'. This habituated practice, which Daston also describes as a 'cult of attention' (2004: 109), lent a new form of authority to nature – an authority that was not only intrinsic to nature's predetermined grand design for the world, but also linked to discovering the 'design *of* nature itself' (2004: 126). The 'displacement of sentiment' from singularly valorized Nature to the scientific detailing of nature's complex 'truths' is very much evident in Fröebel's educational theories and kindergarten design.

In his wake, other early childhood educationalists have enacted this same shift by translating the Romantic philosophical and literary idealizations of nature and its conflations with idealized childhood (via the likes of Rousseau, Wordsworth, Thoreau) into the scientific practice of observing and validating nature's truths about children and learning. It is this 'displacement of sentiment' that I am particularly interested in, as I continue to trace Rousseau's legacy, past Fröebel's kindergarten design, into the early twentieth-century scientific natural methods of Maria Montessori.

Diverging strands of natural education

As the twentieth century unfolded, the discipline of education was firmly positioned within the behavioural sciences, closely aligned with psychology, and threw its lot in with development theory. Universal education in the western world was delivered by a new class of professional teachers, who were increasingly formally inducted into the scientific study of cognitive development (Piaget, 1928). This resolutely scientific perception of the nature of children's cognition gave a new spin to the nature of education. The disciplinary alliance between education and the behavioural sciences inevitably realigned understanding about what is 'natural' about natural education. Within mainstream education, idealized nature no longer bestowed 'her' pedagogical wisdom directly upon the child. Nature's authority was now interpreted and mediated by scientists and dispensed through the pedagogical expertise of (scientifically inducted) teachers. Rousseau's command to 'follow Nature' through attending to the child's inherent 'primitive dispositions' had been replaced by calls for educators to follow the science of the child's natural development. The scientific rationalists dispensed with Rousseau's sentimental attachment to the valorized child *of* nature learning *in* nature and dismissed his regime of 'negative education'. The 'Education of (rational) Man' prevailed and children were inducted into rationality by being taught *about* nature.

Even as scientific rationalism was taking hold in western secular schooling (or what Eckhardt Fuchs (2004) calls 'rational pedagogical naturalism' in the European context), the Romantic traditions of natural education held fast in some alternative school sectors, particularly in their early years' philosophies and pedagogies. This was perhaps most evident in the Waldorf (Uhrmacher, 1995) and Montessori Schools (Whitescarver and Cossentino, 2008) that were established in Europe during the early part of the twentieth century, and quickly spread to other parts of the western world. Fuchs (2004: 168–72) describes how twentieth-century European 'romantic pedagogical naturalists', including Steiner and Montessori, brought together an array of religious, Romantic, philosophical and scientific beliefs about nature and childhood, just as Fröebel had done in the previous century. Fuchs identifies two recurring assumptions about children's special relationship to nature in the writings of the European 'romantic pedagogical naturalists'. The first is that the child is the embodiment of the 'the natural and the innocent Edenic human who lives in harmony with the divine order'. This is consistent with the transmission of Rousseau's Nature's Child figure that I have traced within children's popular culture (see Chapter 2). Connected to this, Fuchs identifies a belief that the birth of the child, as the reincarnation of the divine order of perfect nature, 'enables the adult to go back to his origin' (2004: 168). This assumption strongly evokes Wordsworth's notion of the 'child as father of the man', and his associated belief that the young child's exclusively pure and innocent disposition to divine nature is the adult's only conduit to it (see Chapter 1). It is not so surprising, then, that Romantic beliefs about idealized childhood and nature, reinforced by their ubiquitous transmission within and across literary, artistic, religious and educational discourses, were most closely adhered to in the early years pedagogies of these alternative schools. Nor is it surprising that many aspects of these alternative Romantic natural pedagogies have flowed through to mainstream early childhood education, which, after all, received its original Romantic scientific template for natural education from the 'father of the kindergarten' himself.

Italian-born Maria Montessori was arguably the most influential of the early twentieth-century European Romantic natural pedagogical theorists. Although she did not theorize exclusively about early childhood education, her methods of early years learning have had an enduring impact upon the early childhood education sector. Montessori was a woman of many strong beliefs and talents. As well as an educationalist, she was a devout Christian, a medical doctor schooled in experimental and empirical scientific methods, and a great follower of Darwin's theory of evolution. In her famous book, *Montessori Method* (1912), she promoted a 'new education' based upon the fusion of scientific child-centred pedagogical theory and the idea of children being taught how to be scientific observers of natural phenomena. Even though this sounds like a formula for 'rational pedagogical naturalism', Montessori's commitment to scientific observation was located in what she described as the 'spirit' of scientists. By this, she was referring to the reverence of many scientists (herself included) for their inquiry into natural phenomena, which she saw as more spiritual than clinical (Fuchs, 2004: 169). She melded a Romantic commitment to the practice of scientific observation with a faith in the evidential natural truths revealed by this scientific method.

Like Fröebel, Montessori passionately deployed science as a higher-order natural practice. Her reverential approach to scientific observation and the 'nature' that it studies can be read as another example of the 'displacement of sentiment' (Daston, 2004: 107). Both Montessori and Fröebel were Romantic scientists, reinvented as innovative educators, and both injected their passion for science into their natural educational methodologies and theories. In this way, they retained the legacy of Rousseau's Romantic attachment to nature and childhood, but displaced his singular ideal of Nature with their idiosyncratic scientific methods. These methods authorized and valorized the role of nature in the learning processes of young children. For Fröebel, this involved producing natural designs that replicated scientific laws, and for Montessori it pivoted around applying the methods of scientific observations. Located outside of the mainstream of education, both Fröebel and Montessori effectively conflated their scientific pedagogical methods with what Rousseau referred to as 'the method of Nature'.

Montessori clearly revealed the religious Romantic disposition of her method when she insisted that it is only through the pedagogical cultivation of children's careful observations of the world around them that they can become competent 'worshippers and interpreters of the spirit of nature' (Montessori, 1912, cited in Fuchs, 2004: 169). For Montessori, scientific observations were quasi-religious acts, bringing observers closer to the divine truths of nature. Her method involved both teachers and their students becoming such observers. The teacher's role was to prepare activities that would foster the children's observations, and to then stand back and observe the learning. Montessori regularly warned against what she called the 'obtrusive interference' (1946: 2) of the teacher in the child's learning process. As she also succinctly put it, 'with my methods, the teacher teaches little and observes much' (Montessori, 1912: 174).

This hands-off approach brought Montessori's thinking much more in line with Rousseau's notion of 'negative education', at a time in which mass education systems had teachers delivering more and more facts to students. As one of the earliest advocates of constructivist learning (see also Dewey, 1997 (1938)), Montessori used scientific observation to justify why teachers should leave children to learn by doing rather than always instructing them. 'Scientific observation has established that education is not what the teacher gives' she wrote; 'education is a natural process spontaneously carried out by the human individual, and is acquired not by listening to words but by experiences upon the environment' (Montessori, 1946: 2). Although she was a dedicated scientist, Montessori was clearly not an advocate for the rationalist approach to natural education. In her estimation, the rationalist approach to imparting scientific facts about nature was both pedagogically ineffective and failed to induct children into the practice of empirical inquiry. It was Montessori's passionate investment in scientific inquiry methods, together with her adherence to the Romantic coupling of nature and childhood, that led her to reject the rationalist approach to education. To her, the rational pedagogical approach was neither 'natural' enough nor, ironically, was it a truly scientific approach (Fuchs, 2004: 169).

It is now a hundred years since *The Montessori Method* was first published. Although play is still central to the pedagogies of early childhood, few educators maintain the pedantic scientific devotion to Nature's methods within this play that both Montessori and Fröebel promoted. The 'cult of attention' (Daston, 2004: 109), which characterized their painstaking efforts to design pedagogical methods reflecting nature's perfect forms and processes, is now largely a thing of the past. Rousseau's appeal to allow young children the freedom to follow 'the methods of Nature' does live on within early childhood education, but it is most commonly expressed in the generic notions of child-centred, experiential and play-based learning, which may or may not be nature-based.

As early childhood education itself is increasingly co-opted into mainstream education, much of the Romantic faith in children's special relationship to nature that originally shaped these core principles of child-centredness, play-based learning and even developmentally appropriate practice (Bredekamp, 1986), has been overwritten by appeals to scientific validity. However, early childhood education is neither monolithic nor even in its interpretation and application of natural education. There is still a strong Romantic impulse within early childhood education and also a significant alternative strand that takes Rousseau's dictum of education *in* nature and his vision of Nature as Teacher quite literally. This is most evident in the increasingly popular outdoor all-weather nature kindergartens that I will soon discuss. But before I do so, I take a look at some nature-based educational initiatives outside early childhood that have influenced the recent upsurge of interest in returning children back into nature, in order to learn directly from it.

Learning 'about', 'in' or 'from' Nature?

Unlike early childhood education, modern mainstream schooling has never had a template for Romantic scientific natural pedagogy. It has always taken the rationalist approach to natural education. As formal education has become more and more the vehicle of science, technology and reason, nature has been reduced to the object of study and technology has become the medium for studying it. Rather than being led *by* nature, technologically assisted school education has become the ultimate source of information *about* nature. Those that do still advocate for children to be educated directly *in* and *from* nature, as opposed to *about* nature, position themselves as counter voices to mainstream schooling. In fact their arguments for returning children to nature, like Rousseau's treatise three centuries earlier, are defined by their opposition to the status quo and their appeal to a Romantically-inverted valuing of the nature/culture divide.

Their arguments flow from a twenty-first-century perspective on the relationship between children, nature, science and technology, and are cast against the backdrop of two sets of somewhat contradictory contemporary concerns. The first is the global concern about human-induced climate change and the depletion of the earth's finite natural resources, which has spurred international policies promoting education for sustainability (UNESCO, 2012). The second is a set of concerns about the productivity of future generations of technologically-savvy 'new knowledge workers' (Jemielniak, 2012), which has led to a rush of early intervention and smart child national education policies throughout the western world. While it might seem that these concerns are not closely related, a number of pro-nature education proponents believe that the potential for education for sustainability is being sabotaged by the emphasis upon standardized, evidence-based and digital technology-assisted learning that is being pushing by the neo-liberalist productivity agendas (Kahn and Kellert, 2002; Orr, 2004; Sobel, 2008).

David Sobel (2004 and 2008) is one of the leading US pro-nature education proponents who contends that even though children are more educated than ever before about the environmental problems we face, they are not necessarily better equipped to respond to them. In fact, for some time he has been warning that children can feel so overwhelmed with age-inappropriate information about environmental crises, and at the same time so disconnected from the actual natural world around them, that they develop a fear of nature, or what he calls 'ecophobia' (1996). Whether or not they concur with Sobel's 'ecophobia' argument, all of the major pro-nature education advocates note the link between children's expanding abstracted (scientific) knowledge about the environment, often delivered by new digital technologies, and their increasingly limited direct personal experiences of it (Kahn, 2002; Kahn and Kellert, 2002; Kellert, 2002; Moore and Cooper Marcus, 2008; Nabhan and Trimble, 1994; Pyle, 2002). Their concerns about the increasing objectification of nature, and the diminishment of children's subjective experience of it, both echo and reactivate Rousseau's idea of 'negative education' and the Romantic belief in the special relationship between children and nature. As Stephen Kellert puts it, 'Nature is intrinsically and qualitatively different from anything the child confronts in the human built world, no matter how well simulated, technologically sophisticated, or "virtual" these manufactured representations may be' (2002: 140).

In the face of increasingly digitally-mediated education *about* nature, the pro-nature proponents argue that children need to be returned to nature in order to learn directly from it. Robert Pyle is a US natural scientist. He is also well known for his lyrical writings about nature, which are often based upon recollections of his own direct childhood experiences of it. This passage follows his descriptions of a childhood spent exploring the ditches behind his suburban estate and typifies the argument for children's need for embodied experiences of nature.

> It is through close and intimate contact with a particular patch of ground that we learn to respond to the earth ... a ditch somewhere – or a creek, meadow, woodlot, or marsh ... These are places of initiation, where the borders between ourselves and other creatures break down, where the earth gets under our nails and a sense of place gets under our skin ... Everybody has a ditch, or ought to. For only the ditches and the field, the woods, the ravines can teach us to care enough for all the land. (Pyle, 1993: xv, xix)

Many US writers, such as Pyle, Sobel and Kellert, who work against the tide of mainstream school education to promote the intrinsic value of children's immersion in external nature, often refer, as Pyle does here, to being taught by external nature. In so doing, they reiterate Transcendentalist philosophies (such as those enacted by Thoreau that I discuss in Chapter 1), which not only cast Nature as Teacher, but also posit that children have special relationships with nature. In other words, childhood is seen as the crucial time for children to learn these lessons directly from nature. They typically rehearse these Transcendentalist beliefs through sentimental narrative traditions, in which they nostalgically recollect their own peak childhood moments in outdoor nature.

Despite their heavy reliance upon anecdote, science is not entirely discarded in these Romantic accounts. In yet another manifestation of 'sentimental displacement' (Daston, 2004: 107), science has come to perform a validating role within the predominantly US, Transcendentalist-inspired twenty-first-century pro-nature education movement. Such anecdotes are typically supported by references to E. O. Wilson's (1984) 'biophilia hypothesis' (Louv, 1990, 2008; Nabhan and Trimble, 1994; Pyle, 1993, 2002). The biophilia hypothesis draws upon evolutionary theory to posit that humans are biologically hard-wired to seek affinity and form emotional attachments with other life forms, and that childhood is the critical moment for forming these attachments and affinities (Wilson, 1993; Kellert, 1997). In addition, most of the pro-nature school educators, as well as reiterating the Transcendentalist traditions of nostalgic nature recollections, have appropriated child psychology and learning development theory to detail and justify the emotional, cognitive and moral development aspects and stages of children's innate and special relationships with nature (Kahn, 1999; Kahn and Kellert, 2002; Sobel, 1996, 2002, 2004, 2008).

Sobel (1996, 2002, 2004 and 2008) is one of the most prolific of these Transcendentalist-inspired US pro-nature educators who enlists science to authorize children's experiences in nature. He argues that these experiences are crucial to children's cognitive, social, emotional and moral development, as well as to producing future environmental stewards (see also Kahn, 1999 and 2002; Kellert, 2002; Louv, 1990 and 2008; Myers, 1998; Nabhan and Trimble, 1994; Orr, 2004; Pyle, 1993 and 2002). Sobel also contends that in spite of the marked uprise in children's virtual engagement with the natural world, no amount of representations of nature, scientific or otherwise, can substitute for the child's direct experiences of it (2008). Evoking Pyle's (1993) earlier warnings about the 'extinction of experience' and his nostalgic writings about his childhood (cited above), Sobel wryly observes that 'The [child's] opportunity to explore the ditch gets replaced by memorizing lists of the plants you might find *if* you actually ever went to the ditch' (2008: 11). Kinaesthetic or embodied nature experiences, he suggests, are far more impactful than objectively studying the natural world and being encouraged to look after it: 'One transcendental experience in nature is worth a thousand nature facts' (2008: 13).

With his sights set on the ultimate goal of facilitating children's sense of environmental affinity, ethics and responsibility, Sobel calls upon schools to extend their role beyond simply dispensing the facts about the environment. 'If we want children to become the environmental stewards,' he says 'then one of the best things we can do is let them play in natural settings' (2008: 11). His arguments are underpinned by a declared faith in the special relationship between children and nature (2008: 7), particularly in the middle childhood years, but also by a conviction in the irreplaceability of nature's role as teacher.

By appealing to North American Transcendentist cultural traditions, Sobel and his US colleagues are calling for a reinvigorated faith in the special relationship between children and nature that can only be tapped by returning children *to* nature.

Children's special relations with Nature

Their calls constellate around a couple of core principles regarding children's special relationship to nature, that were first articulated by Rachel Carson (1998 (1956)) and Edith Cobb (1977 (1959)) in their seminal mid-twentieth-century writings. These principles are significant, as they remain as points of reference not just for the US pro-nature educators, but also for many of today's leading early childhood nature educators (Chawla, 1990, 2002; Davis and Elliott, 2003; Elliott and Davis, 2004 and 2008; Rivkin, 1995, 1998; Warden, 2010; Wilson, 1993, 1995, 2007, 2008, 2011). The first of these principles is that nature encounters fill children with a deep sense of awe and wonder about the natural world. According to Carson, these wondrous experiences offer children 'recognition of something beyond the boundaries of human existence' (1998 (1956): 54) and stimulate their sense of curiosity and discovery. Cobb argued that they motivate children to inquire and learn by acting as a 'stimulus that promises "more to come" or, better still, "more to do" – the power of perceptual participation in the known and unknown' (1977 (1959): 28). Carson further emphasized that the motivational basis of children's wondrous nature experiences are primarily emotional: 'The early years of childhood are the time to prepare the soil. Once the emotions have been aroused ... then we wish for knowledge about the object of our emotional response. Once found, it has lasting meaning' (1998 (1956): 56).

The second principle emphasized by both these writers relates to the lasting significance of these childhood encounters with nature. As Carson poetically put it, 'Those who contemplate the beauty of the earth [in childhood] find reserves of strength that will endure as long as life lasts' (1998 (1956): 100). Cobb stressed the connections between adult creativity and transcendental childhood moments of awe and wonder in nature. She identified transcendental childhood moments as the source of creativity, 'a living sense of a dynamic relationship with the outer world' that can be tapped into throughout adulthood (Cobb, 1956, cited in Chawla, 2002: 214).

Louise Chawla is one of the leading contemporary exponents of children's special relations to nature, who unashamedly reclaims Romantic traditions to explore these moments of awe and wonder that can only occur when children connect with nature. For Chawla, these moments cannot be explained by cognitive theories. She believes, like Wordsworth and the other Romantic writers, that their significance exceeds the limits of rational consciousness, and that they not only momentarily connect children to something beyond themselves, but that this sense of connection stays with them into adulthood (2002). She finds a mythical and magical dimension to these childhood experiences, which she describes as taking place in 'ecstatic places' and functioning as 'radioactive jewels buried within us, emitting energy across the years of our life' (1990: 18). Chawla completely rejects the scientific 'mechanistic and instrumentally rational view on nature' (2002: 209) and observes that 'How we ... relate to nature will influence what we see with regard to children in nature and what we neglect to see' (Chawla, 2002: 221). Her mission over the last couple of decades has been to find 'different ways of knowing nature in childhood, as well as different ways of relating childhood to adulthood' (2002: 200).

Chawla's search for meaning in children's nature encounters has largely sidestepped the standard appeal to scientific evidence or biological theory advanced by the majority of her US contemporaries. However, regardless of the kind of corroborating evidence they seek or the ways they seek to explain it, all of these nature education advocates share the same Romantic belief, passed on from Rousseau, and reiterated by Wordsworth and Thoreau amongst others, that children have an intrinsically special relationship with nature. From this basic premise, they all passionately advocate (like Rousseau) that the best kind of learning comes from children's direct, rather than mediated, nature experiences, and (yet again like Rousseau) they all bemoan the loss of these experiences

Endangered Nature's Child

The name that is now most closely associated with spreading the word about the dangers of children's lack of direct nature experiences is Richard Louv. Louv (2008) is the US author of the international best-selling book *Last Child in the Woods: Saving Our Children from Nature-Deficit Disorder* (first published in 2005 and now into its second edition), which has had an enormous impact both within and without education. Building upon research he has been carrying out since the late 1980s (see Louv, 1990), and mining the arguments of the (predominantly US) pro-nature advocates I have already mentioned, Louv passionately reiterates the Romantic premise about children's special relations with nature alongside dire warnings about its loss, in a manner that demonstrates a firm grasp on the nostalgic cultural traditions and wide appeal of North American Transcendentalism.

Louv's basic argument is that 'the American experience of nature ... has gone from romantic attachment to electronic detachment' (2008: 16) and as a consequence, childhood has been 'de-natured' (2008: 31). He blames the increasingly virtual postmodern world for alienating children from nature (2008: 3) and for denying children the kind of natural childhood experiences that he, and countless other adults that he has interviewed, recall with great affection. This is not a state of affairs that Louv can countenance as he believes that nature experiences are essential to children's well-being and healthy development. He declares today's children to be at risk of suffering 'nature-deficit disorder' and appeals to all those with an interest in children – parents, child health professionals, educators and policy makers – to save these endangered children by effecting a 'nature-child reunion' (2008: 36). Amongst other sectors, schools must play their part in ensuring this reunion. As he puts it, 'environment-based education can surely be one of the antidotes to nature-deficit disorder. The basic idea is to use the surrounding community, including nature, as the preferred classroom' (2008: 206).

By evoking the new figure of 'endangered Nature's Child', the book plays on the seductive appeal of nature and natural childhoods (courtesy of Rousseau), as well as our fears of their loss. What is noteworthy, however, is that despite the urgency of the imminent endangerment warning (which bears some of the hallmarks of a moral panic), such warnings are far from new. Rousseau was the first to famously declare the innocence of natural childhood to be threatened by 'man' and his books, and this has become a recurring historical theme, usually linked to the advent of each new communication technology (for discussions of this, see Buckingham, 2000; Jenks, 2005; Valentine, 1996). In the wake of electronic mass media (but before the advent of the internet), Neil Postman (1982) famously declared children to be an 'endangered species' in his influential book *The Disappearance of Childhood*. In this most recent incarnation, concerns about the endangerment of childhood are conflated with the endangerment of nature (for more discussion of this, see Taylor, 2011). In the face of global warming, dangerous pollution levels, rapid urbanization, the destruction of the world's largest forests, unsustainable growth and consumption on the part of the overdeveloped world, Kahn (2002: 106) has raised the possibility that children will grow up in a world in which environmental degradation is so normalized and children are so cut off from nature, that we will soon face the problem of 'environmental generational amnesia'. *Last Child in the Woods* taps into these interconnected public anxieties about the technology-precipitated 'death of childhood' and about children's ill preparedness to respond to intensifying environmental degeneration and crisis.

Nostalgic adult testimonials of 'awe and wonder' childhood nature experiences (both autobiographical and cited) are scattered liberally throughout Louv's book and substantiated by the arguments and theories of the pro-nature academic 'experts' (mentioned above). These are interspersed with statistical evidence of increasing childhood ADHD, obesity and increasing time spent indoors, and multiple good news stories of local initiatives to return children to nature and of green communities. This is a highly emotive and motivational book, which trades on the winning combination of the Romantic seduction of Nature's Child; North American Transcendentalist nature-worshipping traditions; the fear of loss of both nature and childhood; a 'can do' celebration of the transformational potential of both nature and people power; and a recourse to scientific validation. It covers all bases.

Louv's arguments have not only hit a collective nerve of concern about the endangered status of Nature's Child in the twenty-first century, but they have had a performative effect. The heavily promoted book and the national and international speaking tours that accompanied it have spearheaded, articulated and simultaneously generated widespread public concerns about the consequences of children's lack of nature experiences. In the US, it has inspired a widespread 'Leave No Child Inside' campaign (2008: 351) and led to the establishment of the umbrella organization 'Childhood and Nature Network' (2012). Founded by Louv, this not-for-profit organization has a comprehensive web-presence. It hosts a number of subsidiary networks, including the 'Natural Teachers Network' (with the slogan 'every teacher can be a Nature Teacher'), sponsors academic research, hosts a multitude of local and regional campaigns and action groups in the US, boasts a growing international membership and promotes itself as 'a world-wide movement to reconnect children with nature' (Childhood and Nature Network, 2012). In the UK, Louv's work has prompted the National Trust to commission a report to gather evidence of 'nature-deficit disorder' amongst UK children. The recently published report, called *Natural Childhood* (Moss, 2012), calls for a national campaign (similar to the US 'Leave No Child Inside' campaign) and the funding of further research.

A review of academic journals suggests that such research is indeed gathering pace, particularly within the disciplinary fields of environmental and applied psychology, outdoors education, children's health and well-being and urban planning and design. It is noteworthy, for instance, that the International Association of Applied Psychology recently ran a special theme on 'The health benefits of nature' in their journal *Applied Psychology: Health and Well-Being* (Ong and Peterson, 2011). This recent spike in publications about children's relations with nature (or lack of) are collectively delivering a body of evidence that supports Louv's endangerment claim as well as his assertion that large doses of external nature (the wilder the better) are the antidote and the remedy for children's 'nature deficit disorder'. Quantitative studies from different parts of the overdeveloped world confirm that children are spending proportionally more and more time indoors and becoming increasingly sedentary, and that these trends correspond with adverse health, cognitive and social outcomes (Brown et al., 2008; Fjørtoft, 2001; Moss, 2012; Van Den Berg and Van Den Berg, 2011; Wolch et al., 2010). Evaluative studies of programmes designed to facilitate children spending active time outdoors in natural environments consistently find evidence of physical, psychological, social and/or cognitive benefits (Blair, 2009; Faber Taylor and Kuo, 2011; Jack, 2010; Kaplan and Kaplan, 2011; Koonce, 2010; McCurdy et al., 2010; Moore and Cooper Marcus, 2008; O'Brien and Murray, 2005 and 2007; Staempfli, 2009; Van Den Berg and Van Den Berg, 2011). The spread and influence of the 'New Nature Movement' to 'reconnect childhood with nature' (Childhood and Nature Network, 2012), by taking them outdoors into natural environments, has not gone unnoticed by the child health, education and policy professionals in post-industrial countries. Now that Nature's Child seems under threat of 'extinction' (Gill, 2005), Rousseau's impassioned vision is being rekindled. All eyes are turning to the great outdoors – where Nature as Muse, Remedy (Ritalin) and Teacher resides.

Taking Nature's Child back outdoors

Early childhood education is no exception. This is hardly surprising, as early childhood, more than any other sector of education, has the greatest investment in validating the relationship between nature, childhood and learning and ensuring the 'survival' of Nature's Child. The 'Fathers'' (Rousseau's and Fröebel's) tenet that Nature is the child's best teacher is deeply imprinted within the field of early childhood, as is the Romantic coupling of innocent young children and perfect nature that pervades our adult imaginaries and children's popular culture, and features so consistently in the children's literature that is taken up within early learning environments.

There is no doubt that the 'New Nature Movement' to 'reconnect children with nature' has bolstered the efforts of existing proponents of early childhood nature-based education and raised the profile of their work within the general field of early childhood. Many of the post-2005 publications cite Louv's work to support their own arguments and findings. These include those who advocate the benefits of natural outdoor play spaces (Brown et al., 2009; Dau, 2005; Elliott, 2008; Elliott and Davies, 2008; Fjørtoft, 2001 and 2004; Little and Wyver, 2008; Waite, 2011; Young, 2008); those who argue that young children's connection with nature is a prerequisite for future environmental stewardship (Chawla, 2006 and 2009; Wilson, 2007, 2008 and 2011); and those who positively evaluate the effects and outcomes of the existing all-weather nature kindergartens and forest schools (Änggård, 2010; Maynard, 2007; Ridgers and Sayers, 2012; Robertson, 2008; Warden, 2010).

On the ground of early childhood education and care there is a corresponding rising concern that under the thumb of the industry safety regulators and risk-averse management policies, the sector has veered too far off the path of natural education. There is a growing apprehension that the safe 'indoor' environment (also perceived as the cultural hub) of early childhood has become far too dominant, and this has also spurred a concomitant surge of interest in the idea of taking children back outside to play in nature (Elliott and Davis, 2008; Passy and Waite, 2011). These shifting concerns and interests of practitioners are concurrent with the proliferation of nature and childhood endangerment discourses (Gill, 2005; Louv, 2008; Childhood and Nature Network, 2012) and responsive to the early childhood literature that reveals the diminishment of children's natural outdoor play (Davis and Elliott, 2003; Elliott and Davis, 2008; Faber Taylor and Kuo, 2011; Fjørtoft, 2001; Little and Wyver, 2008; McCurdy et al., 2010; Moss, 2012; Rivkin, 1995 and 1998; Sutton, 2008).

The revival of early childhood practitioners' interest in natural outdoor education is also sparked by the frustrating reality that for many, taking children outside to play is anything but a Romantic 'back to nature' experience. In the wake of economic rationalist policies, and their accompanying risk-averse regulatory regimes, more often than not outdoor play is simply obligatory time spent in a resolutely un-natural and uninspiring synthetic environment (Elliott and Davis, 2008: 2). In fact, the increasingly ubiquitous synthetic playground, with its characteristic low-maintenance (low-cost) artificial grass lawns, its (safe) shock-absorbing rubber surfaces and its brightly coloured plastic outdoor play equipment, has become the ultimate symbol of young children's forced disconnection from nature.

Such commonplace experiences ironically increase the Romantic allure of the exotic natural outdoors. They make the ideal of 'authentic' natural outdoor play areas that promise to function, as Sue Elliott and Julie Davis (2008: 12) enticingly suggest, as 'landscapes for children to embroider with the loose threads of nature', even more compelling. They intensify the seductive appeal of nature as something quite exotic and 'other' to the prosaic everyday realities. Just as the artificial playground has come to symbolize the denaturalization of early childhood, the natural outdoor early childhood movement has become the aspirational beacon for renaturalizing the sector. And there is growing professional support for being inducted into this renaturalization process. Early childhood practitioners' burgeoning interest in natural outdoor pedagogies is already being catered for, as well as generated by an emerging industry of nature education professional training and consultancy organizations and individuals. Some organizational examples include Mindstretchers, Creative Star Learning Company and Archimedes in the UK, Inside-Out Nature Danish Forest School Training in Denmark and the UK, and Cedarsong and Forest School Canada in North America.

Although a renewed interest in and attention to natural outdoor play is definitely on the rise in early childhood, the provision of outdoor nature education for young children is by no means new. A variety of all-weather outdoor and forest programmes for pre-school-aged children have been operating in Scandinavian countries and Germany since the second half of the twentieth century. These have their own distinctive cultural heritages and trajectories – the Scandinavian models, for instance, are closely linked to the construction of healthy outdoor Nordic national identities as well as reflecting the more generic Romantic Nature's Child traditions (see Adhémar, 2000; Änggård, 2010; Bentsen et al., 2009; Kollner and Leinert, 1998; Knight, 2009; Miklitz, 2001; Muñoz, 2008; Passey and Waite, 2011; Robertson, 2008). Although very well-established, these outdoor nature and forest kindergartens have attracted an unprecedented amount of new attention – including professional interest in learning about their practices and scientific interest in assessing and validating their effects and outcomes. This was something that Anna Adhémar (2000) foreshadowed at the turn of the millennium when she proclaimed: 'All across Scandinavia small children are running wild! … research shows that these "nature" children gain far more than rosy cheeks and bright eyes; for it is now evident that nature nursery schools are socially, physically and intellectually at an advantage over their contemporaries in conventional nursery schools' (2000: 44).

Nature and forest kindergartens and pre-schools are now mushrooming in other parts of northern Europe, the UK, North America and New Zealand (Knight, 2009). The Scottish Nature Kindergarten model, established by Claire Warden from Mindstretchers, is one of the most widely promoted and internationally connected. It also has a very active educational consultancy and training arm. Unlike many of the other outdoor and forest kindergarten ventures, the philosophies, values and practices of the Nature Kindergartens have been well documented in a number of Mindstretchers' publications written by Warden. For all of these reasons, the Mindstretchers' Nature Kindergarten model is one that clearly functions as an aspirational ideal for early childhood educators seeking to renaturalize their pedagogies. I have witnessed this first hand in Australia, when Claire Warden was given a standing ovation for her keynote presentation from a crowd of well over a thousand early childhood educators. Motivated by her conviction that 'children have always been connected to nature' (2010: 13), Warden explains that she established the first Nature Kindergarten with the vision of linking the resources to be found within a 'natural children's garden' with a 'sense of community' and with children's 'natural desire to have a choice and have one's voice heard from an early age' (2010: 13). I am particularly interested in the ways in which Warden articulates her contemporary vision, as it provides a clear example of how 'sentimental displacement' (Daston, 2004: 107) is still operating within early childhood nature education, and how it is accommodating the contemporary environmental concerns and issues of the early childhood sector.

Warden's vision is historically anchored, but it also casts a wide net to incorporate some very different kinds of contemporary thinking. To begin with, she draws upon the full range of Romantic childhood nature education exponents that I have previously discussed to authorize the foundational principles and values of her Nature Kindergarten philosophy – from Fröebel's and Montessori's early Rousseau-inspired methods, to the Scandinavian *friluftsliv* approach, to Transcendentalist-inspired US writers such as Sobel, Chawla, Cobb, Wilson and Louv (Warden, 2010: 13–14). The philosophy gains credibility from these wide-ranging historical and cultural Romantic traditions. The Romantic underpinnings are encapsulated within affirmations such as 'Nature offers "magic moments" to deepen learning in a way that is closely connected to the child' (2010: 26); 'Children are connected to nature, we need to allow them to learn through real, meaningful experiences of it' (2010: 104); and 'The emotional connection to the planet at a young age may well be the foundation for the love and protection of the earth at a later stage in life' (2010: 130).

Warden is also very keen to corroborate her Romantic commitment to the natural fit of nature and childhood with the scientific evidence – again drawing upon a number of the studies that I have previously mentioned to validate her approach. For instance, citing the findings of Fjørtoft (2001) she claims: 'Children who play regularly in natural environments show more advanced motor fitness ... and are sick less often' (2010: 13). She cites the work of Faber

Taylor's team to assert that calm 'natural playscapes' reduce Attention Deficit Disorder (2010: 13). Drawing upon Pyle's (2002) arguments, she declares: 'Exposure to natural environments improves children's cognitive development, by improving their awareness, reasoning and observational skills' (2010: 13). And in reference to Chawla's (1998), Sobel's (1996, 2002, 2004) and Wilson's (1997) work (amongst others), she mentions the links between 'regular contact with and play in the natural world during early childhood' and the development of a 'positive environmental ethic' (2010: 13).

The significance of children's future roles as environmental stewards and protectors holds high emotional and scientific currency today, and it is an additional element that is easily incorporated within the authoritative alliance of Romantic sentiment and objective science that characterize the Nature Kindergarten philosophy. Warden also uses the notions of 'community of nations' (2010: 37), 'community of culture' (2010: 38) and 'community of "local" people' (2010: 39) to create a space for the exchange of ancient and present-day cultural practices of nature and indigenous knowledge within the philosophy. This gives it global scope but also taps into the Romantic New-Ageist interests in pre-modern knowledge and cultures that offer alternatives to western science's rationalist approaches to nature. The Nature Kindergarten philosophy thus offers a broad church of 'sentimental displacement' (Daston, 2004) – passionately combining the Romantic image of the perfect union of nature and child, the wisdom of indigenous people, the multi-cultures of nature, the veracity of science, the democratic rights of the child, environmental ethics and responsibilities, and above all a sense that in nature, we find the guiding 'moral authority' (Daston, 2004) to glue it all together.

Conclusion

The field of early childhood is far from universal or even-handed in its approach to interpreting and applying Rousseau's 'method of Nature'. However, because of its Romantic ancestral foundations it has been historically positioned (certainly more than any other sector of education) to retain at least some investment in the ideals of Nature's Child and Nature as Teacher. This is the case whether or not these ideals are actually attainable. Regardless, they have inspired the application of a range of different Romantic scientific natural methods bequeathed by Fröebel and likes of Montessori, and which are being reinvented today, quite literally, in many of the natural outdoor initiatives and pedagogies for pre-school-aged children. In this chapter I have traced the historical trajectory of these figures in early years education, focusing upon the continuities and the points of dispersal. The latter have been triggered by the interventions of scientific rationalism (the push to learn *about* nature exclusively through science) and economic rationalism (through the agendas of risk-averse regulatory regimes). The former have been passed on by the enduring Romantic belief in the special relationship between children and nature, which underpins the unique methodological orientations of early childhood education.

I have also noted how the recent urgent imperative to save endangered children from 'nature-deficit disorder' (Louv, 2008) by reconnecting them with nature, which is being driven by the New Nature Movement (Childhood and Nature Network, 2012), has refocused attention upon and intensified the efforts of early childhood educational professionals and researchers who advocate for children to be educated *in* nature rather than *about* it. As well as reinstating the Romantic notion of Nature as original Teacher and reaffirming Rousseau's notion of 'negative education', this New Nature Movement has also given science a new role. By declaring external nature to be the cure (or 'Ritalin') for this disorder and offering scientific evidence for the ways in which nature also enhances cognition, self-confidence, appreciation of beauty and moral certitude (Louv, 2008: 177–200), the newly formed alliance between the New Nature Movement and the scientific experts who endorse it paves the way for science to relinquish the exclusive rights to dispense facts *about* nature to children. Within this alliance, science's new role remains one of validation, but it is no longer only called upon to validate the facts of nature. Rather paradoxically, it is now science's job to validate Nature's impeccable credentials to do its own thing. Three centuries after Rousseau offered his 'negative education' thesis, we now seem to have come full circle. But these days, it is *science* that decrees that we must return these endangered children to Nature and trust that Nature alone will restore, heal, guide and teach them, within the 'mythical and magical' (Chawla, 1990) potencies of this 'very special' relationship.

Part 2

Reconfiguring the Natures of childhood

Chapter 4

Assembling common worlds

> The world is precisely what gets lost in doctrines of representation and scientific objectivity ... 'nature' and 'realism' are precisely the consequences of representational practices. Where we need to move is not 'back' to nature, but elsewhere, through and within an artifactual social nature ...
>
> (Haraway, 2004b: 90)

Introduction

In the first section of this book, I focused upon what Romantic notions of nature *do* – and in particular, what they do when conflated with childhood. Tracing the emblematic Romantic Nature's Child figure, I showed how idealized nature does the work of purifying childhood – how it renders childhood innocent and originary and associates it with other key collateral nature figurations (Castree, 2005), such as that of the noble savage. I also noted that the 'moral authority' (Daston and Vidal, 2004) carried by idealized nature is projected onto this Nature's Child figure, making it a very seductive proposition. From this point, I considered how idealized nature has been variously interpreted as the best teacher of young children – and has served as a pedagogical guide and muse for early childhood educators. I noted that idealized nature is still being cast as the prerequisite for healthy childhoods and, correspondingly, as the remedy and salvation for endangered (denaturalized) childhoods. And last, I reflected upon the rather paradoxical ways in which the science of human development (internal nature) is increasingly deployed as evidence of children's special relationship with idealized external nature.

Donna Haraway prompts us to ask the questions: 'What counts as nature, by whom, and at what cost?' (1997: 104). When I apply such questions to the idealized natures that featured in the previous section, and extend them to think about what these particular natures have done, I can identify a number of unintended consequences. For while on the surface these nature 'doings' may seem well-intentioned, life-affirming and benign, the 'good work' of idealized nature is inevitably done at the expense of what Val Plumwood (1993, 2002) refers to as the 'hyper-separation' of humans from nature. It becomes even more complicated when childhood is conflated with idealized nature, and effectively handed over from the human to the nature side of the 'either/or' equation. This idealized union of childhood and Nature is intended to protect Nature's Child from the 'corrupting' influence of adult society and technologies, but it effectively separates children off, at least semiotically, from the rest of humanity. As I have constantly reminded, the Romantic idealization of nature, and hence childhood, depends upon the binary logic of the nature/culture divide. For nature and childhood can only be idealized through being separated off, valorized as exotic others, and counterposed or set against degenerative (adult) society. Along with the transfer of cultural understandings about nature and childhood into real life experience, this has the unfortunate flow-on effect of denying real children's real world relationships and it positions them in the paradoxical situation of needing protection from the world in which they actually reside. Another unintended and paradoxical effect is the potential displacement of the actual material world and real embodied child that are being eulogized and mythologized as perfect Nature and Nature's Child respectively. To borrow Haraway's (2004b: 90) turn of phrase, 'the [real] world is precisely what gets lost' when childhood is represented as a manifestation of idealized nature and partitioned off within a heterotopic imaginary realm. This, to me, is the biggest cost of all.

In this section I follow through on the argument that the real potential of the child–nature relationship lies not in returning childhood to some valorized notion of nature that does not actually exist, but in moving the relationship 'elsewhere' (Haraway, 2004b: 90) – beyond the wistful imaginings of Romanticism and the entrapments of its constitutive nature/culture divide. Tapping into this potential involves some major gear shifts and a completely different set of articulations of real world natures and childhoods. It entails bringing childhood back to earth – grounding it within the imperfect common worlds that we share with all manner of others – living and inert, human and more-than-human. These are not sanctified, pure and innocent *separated* worlds, but worlds that are always already full of inherited messy *connections*. Common worlds are worlds full of entangled and uneven historical and geographical relations, political tensions, ethical dilemmas and unending possibilities. I now turn to the task of reclaiming nature and childhood from the Romantics and rearticulating or reconfiguring them in the 'elsewhere' of these complex but down-to-earth common worlds.

Methodological shifts

In order to reconfigure the natures of childhood within common worlds, I make a significant methodological shift. I move from the deconstructive methods I have previously used, into the much more challenging and inventive mode of reconstruction. The experimental impetus of this reconstructive methodology will become particularly evident in Chapter 5. I also reposition myself as researcher – transitioning from the more traditional, distant and detached research perspective that allowed me to trace the geo-historical trajectory of the Nature's Child figure in Part 1, into a situated, meddling and personally invested researcher-as-bricoleur in this part. This is a researcher identity that I borrow from Claude Levi-Strauss (1966). He used the metaphor of the bricoleur to describe the work of the ethnographer who gathers or collects all manner of ideas, things or elements that 'might … come in handy', and who then selectively pieces these assorted collected entities together to create an inventive assemblage or bricolage (1966: 18). That is exactly what I am doing as I reconfigure the natures of childhood.

The collection of interdisciplinary interventions that I assemble into a common worlds conceptual framework in the second half of this chapter can also be seen as a kind of theoretical bricolage. I use it to rearticulate the theoretical grounds of nature, and thereby to reconsider childhood. Common worlds is a term borrowed from Latour, who speaks about 'composing the common world' (2004: 91). It stands for bringing nature and culture back together, and gives name to the conceptual framework that I have been piecing together for some time now with my Australian colleague Miriam Giugni (see Taylor and Giugni, 2012). Although the component parts (along with the name) of this common worlds framework are selectively borrowed, their assemblage is an original bricolage. It is also a strategic one, which allows me to advocate a particular set of political and ethical interests and concerns in which I am clearly invested. In the following chapter (Chapter 5), I put this conceptual framework to work to reconfigure some of the natures of childhood that are familiar to me. It is in this following chapter that the creative possibilities of the bricolage method of reconstruction are most apparent.

While the standard deconstructive approach of the first section was useful for exposing how and why the Romantic Nature's Child figure, supported by the nature/culture divide, has been such an enduring and seductive *idea*, it could not offer any alternative conceptualizations. This reconstructive turn affords a very different kind of inquiry that responds to the many challenging questions that have arisen from the deconstructive method of the previous section, but which could not be answered by it. For instance, the following questions arise. How might we approach the relationship between childhood and nature without rehearsing nostalgic adult idealizations, sentimentalized attachments, or heroic rescue and salvation appeals? How might we approach the pedagogical opportunities of natures and childhoods without reverting to Romantic notions of nature and/or reifying science as a form of sentimental displacement? How might we articulate the relationship between childhood and nature beyond the nature/culture divide? What might then happen to the purity and innocence discourses that adhere to this 'perfect natural' relationship? How might we proceed to reconceptualize childhood in ways that neither jettison nature nor valorize it, but 'queer' it, as Haraway (1994: 60) entreats? The reconstructive turn enables me to address these questions by selectively piecing together or reconfiguring some of the common (shared and ordinary) yet worldly (big picture and earthy) natures of childhood.

Queer reconfigurations

In the Introduction, I flagged my intention to queer the sacrosanct Romantic conflation of childhood and nature that is encapsulated within Rousseau's Nature's Child figure. I associated queering with a reconstructive impulse and indicated that it would be my way of doing nature and childhood differently. It would constitute a point of departure from the 'natural' and 'normal' associations of childhood with nature. So how will my queer reconfiguration of the natures of childhood in this section differ from Rousseau's original figuring of Nature's Child? What is the significance of this word figuration and what points of departure are signalled by the promise of queering it? The explanation requires a brief recapping. When I first introduced the term figure in Chapter 1, I was picking up on Raymond Williams' (1983) identification of a number of historical personifications or figures of nature in his cultural history of English texts. Although Williams focused exclusively upon English writings, I suggested that Rousseau (2003 (1762)) made a significant contribution to the Romantic European repository of nature figures when he invented Nature's Child and Nature as Teacher in his eighteenth-century *Emile* treatise. In my tracings of Rousseau's figures across cultural representations and educational discourses and practices, I set out to emphasize their reiteration of the nature/culture binary and their generative and adaptive qualities. I argued that over time and in different places they have not only enabled particular ways of *thinking* about nature, childhood and education (as the antithesis of 'The education of man'/society), but also ways of *doing* it. This kind of reiterative doing is what Judith Butler (1990, 1993) refers to as performativity – not just the naming of something that is self-evident and pre-exists its naming, but the bringing into being or the making of that which is named through repetitive discursive acts.

In a similar way, but emphasizing the material effects of figurations, Claudia Castaneda (2002: 3) talks about how the child is figured or 'bodied forth' through multiple figurations, the most significant of which is the developmental child (2002: 4). Although she does not mention Nature's Child, we might think of it as one of these many figures. She declares that in the processes of being figured, these figurations 'speak to the making of worlds' (2002: 3). In other words, the figuring that produces particular ways of knowing childhood, including Nature's Child, has a constitutive effect. It generates particular children's bodies and brings into being 'a particular version of the world' (Castaneda, 2002: 4). The Nature's Child figure that I have traced has constituted a whole gamut of 'natural' children's bodies – pure and innocent bodies; rosy-cheeked and healthy bodies; wild and instinctual bodies; peaceful and tranquil bodies; bodies learning through natural play; indigenized and hence naturalized national bodies;

connected (to nature) bodies; or conversely denaturalized children's bodies suffering from 'nature-deficit disorder'. Equally important, this same figure can also be seen to have constituted a particularly compelling, seductively simple and highly Romantic idea of a perfect natural world – that is, everything good and true that the corrupting social, technological and 'man-made' world is not.

My queer reconfigurations of the natures of childhood are premised upon the productive figurative processes of world making. In Chapter 5, I consciously enact common worlds, specifically to show how childhoods are figured within the world-making process. The big difference is that my common world reconfiguration is a queering strategy to undo the 'normal' category of nature (Haraway, 2008b: xxiv). In fact I am deliberately targeting the kind of nature that hails from the nature/culture divide for a makeover, which, in turn, remakes childhood. My common world reconfigurations set out to trouble, confound, breach and denaturalize the binary logic that structures purist figurations of childhood (Prout, 2005). They also use a different timbre. Taking inspiration from the queer sensibilities of Haraway's seriously playful writings (1991: 149), the tone I adopt is simultaneously irreverent and political. It is irreverent because it tackles the quasi-religious 'moral authority' (Daston and Vidal, 2004) of idealized nature and its projection onto the sacrosanct mythologies of 'pure and innocent' childhood. In fact it tackles the pious moralisms that hover around questions of nature and childhood full stop. It is political because it troubles the protectionist benchmark norms of natural childhood innocence, exposing childhood as already well and truly implicated in the production of an imperfect, impure and power-ridden world (see Taylor 2008, 2010a, 2010b; Taylor and Richardson, 2005a). By attending to queer ironies and paradoxes, I hope that my aspirations to be seriously playful also temper the tendency of political commentary to be overly earnest and heroic – especially when nature and children are concerned.

The most crucial difference afforded by specifically *queer* reconfigurations of nature, however, is the potential to de-centre the human in the world-making process. Let me explain. In reconsidering the possibilities of 'nature's queer performativity', Karen Barad (2011) speaks about the radical queerness of nature when unleashed from the nature/culture divide that attributes all the agency to the human (culture) side and renders nature passive and inert. She also points to the anthropocentric limits of Butler's (1990, 1993) early seminal writings about performativity, which offer a wonderful account of the ways in which the reiteration of discourses shape human (gendered/sexed) subjectivities, identities, lives and bodies, but do not consider the co-determinant productive effects of the bodies themselves, let alone other non-human bodies or activities (Barad, 2008: 151). By paying particular attention to the ways that human lives are mutually enmeshed with (rather than separated from) living and inert non-human others, queer reconfigurations reveal the ways in which common worlds are made, not only by human discursive practices and their material effects, but also by non-human forces, and, most importantly, by the mutually enmeshed relations between humans and non-human others. These queer reconfigurations extend the field of performativity beyond the discursive and beyond a set of exclusively human enactments. When nature is reconfigured, 'nature's queer performativity' (Barad, 2011) becomes a human/more-than-human double act.

Transdisciplinary conversations

To make my methodological shift and enact these queer reconfigurations, I trawl through a body of academic theory about nature that has been generated outside of the fields of childhood studies and early childhood education and which relish traversing disciplinary boundaries. As I noted in the Introduction, I see my major contribution to childhood studies and early childhood education as bringing new theorizations or reconceptualizations of nature into conversation with reconceptualizations of childhood. The trans-disciplinary conversations that I relay take place within and between human geographers; science and technology studies (STS) scholars; post-human, feminist and ecological philosophers; and post-structural feminist theorists involved in the 'material turn' (see, for instance, Anderson, 2001; Barad, 2003, 2011; Braidotti, 2006; Braun, 2002; Castree, 2005; Castree and Braun, 1998, 2001; Foltz and Frodeman, 2004; Haraway, 1991, 2004d, 2008a; Hinchcliffe, 2005, 2007; Instone, 2004; Latour, 1993, 2004; Law, 2004; Plumwood, 1993, 2002; Rose, 2011; Soper, 1995; Whatmore, 2002).

For the last couple of decades, such conversations have constellated around the challenge of thinking differently about nature, as well as what it means to be human. Those involved have undertaken to reconceptualize what counts as nature outside the bounds of the nature/culture divide, to build connections rather than rehearse separations and, as Haraway (2004b: 90) puts it, to locate nature 'elsewhere'. These 'elsewhere' conversations have necessitated the invention of a new lexicon – with an explicitly counter-binary and connective vocabulary. It includes the liberal use of blended concepts such as Latour's 'nature-cultures' (1993) and 'human/nonhuman collective' (2004, 2005, 2009); Haraway's 'artifactual social nature' (2004b), 'technocultures' (1985, 2011) and 'naturecultures' (2008a); Braidotti's 'bios/zoe' (2006); Hinchcliffe's 'nature/culture' (2005), and Castree's 'socionature' (2001).

The use of a hybridized nomenclature such as this typifies the trans-disciplinary conversation I am tapping into. Hybridization is one of the key strategies used to carve out a non-separatist and non-purist way of thinking and conversing about nature. It is also a way of navigating a pathway that does not inevitably lead to 'setting up camp' with either the nature realists or the nature constructionists. As others (and I) have noted (in the Introduction and elsewhere), these polarized nature realist and nature constructionist camps themselves mimic and reiterate the foundational nature/culture divide (Haraway, 2004d: 66; Prout, 2005: 84; Castree, 2001: 17; Taylor, 2011: 425). They also underpin the positivist/post-positivist methodological divisions that are apparent in many fields of research, including the field of early childhood education. To identify the main point of departure for these 'elsewhere' and hybridizing trans-disciplinary conversations, I take a moment to recap on what already counts as nature on both sides of the divided academic terrain.

The divided camps: Nature realists and Nature constructionists

Associated with positivist traditions, nature realists proceed from the premise that nature exists 'out there' as an observable, independent, external and scientifically verifiable reality. Within the nature realist approach, the inherent properties and universal laws of nature become the objects of scientific inquiry. Once 'validated', these objective facts of nature are disseminated, for instance through the publication of scientific theories and research findings, through the popular medium of nature documentaries, and through the school science curriculum. Nature realism is most often promulgated through what Haraway (2004b: 90) refers to as 'doctrines of representation and scientific objectivity', which promote the impartial delivery of the essential facts of nature and are rarely, if ever, cognizant of the politics or partialities of their own representational practices.

In stark contrast to the unreflexive 'faith' of the nature realists, nature constructionists critically determine that nature is not only socially constructed but contingent upon the cultural, historical and political circumstances of its construction. This camp is now closely associated with post-positivist approaches to research, which foreground the relationship between discourse and power in the production of knowledge. It also includes some of the Marxist analytic traditions that warn about the propensity for (objective) nature to be used to validate (false) ideological positions (Harvey, 1996; Smith, 1991; Young, 1985). Much to the chagrin of many scientists, nature constructionists tend to reposition scientific realist accounts of nature as just one set of discourses amongst a plethora of other kinds – including Romantic fictional varieties that I deconstructed in Chapter 2.

One of the most famous and contentious of these repositionings was William Cronon's (1996, 1998) declaration of 'wilderness' as the ultimate nature fiction. Contrary to many realist accounts of wilderness as the most natural of all natural environments because of its untouched-by-humans status, Cronon provocatively argued that wilderness was 'quite profoundly a human creation – indeed the creation of very particular human cultures at very particular moments in history' (1998: 471). His identification of wilderness as a white colonial invention not only exposed the political grounds upon which this particular nature discourse was produced, but also underscored the potential cultural myopia of all nature realist assumptions (see also Braun, 2002; Gregory, 2001; Willems-Braun, 1997).

While the constructionist view might be savvy to the ways in which humans 'make' nature through discourse, and to the political implication of the 'cultures of nature' (Wilson, 1991), it falls well short of engaging with nature beyond these sets of human meaning-making practices and projected imaginings. In other words, constructionists rarely recognize nature as a human–nonhuman co-production (Haraway, 2004b: 66). Through ignoring the differences to the world that the more-than-human make and only ever considering nature as a concept that is reducible to culture, the nature constructionist position in effect 'implies that nature is a *tabula rasa* on which societies can write at will' (Castree, 2001: 17).

Points of departure: Human geography and science and technology studies (STS)

Positioned at the interstices of the natural and the social sciences, the fields of human geography and science and technology studies (STS) have had a particular interest and investment in elucidating the relationship between nature and society (or nature and culture) and bridging the divide between the nature realists and the nature constructionists. So it is not so surprising that many initiatives to retheorize nature outside of the nature/culture divide have come from these disciplinary locations. For those human geographers and STS scholars who are interested in departing from the nature/culture divide and taking nature 'elsewhere', there are two complimentary tasks. The first is to unsettle the physical sciences' uncritical adherence to objectivity and realism by introducing insights about the cultural contingencies and partialities of knowledge production from the humanities and social sciences. The second task is to bring the physical sciences' interest and engagement with the non-human world into play within the humanities and social sciences, in order to challenge human-centrism and the associated belief that human society operates independently from the rest of the world. Because nature already holds the attention of scientists and social scientists, it can be regarded as a key interdisciplinary 'boundary object' (Strathern, 2004: 45–7). As a boundary object, nature creates a space for trading or negotiating meaning across the paradigmatic disciplinary divides. Finding some common ground within the boundary object is always the key to making translations across boundaries and this is exactly what the human geographers and STS scholars have set out to do.

As one of STS's most influential scholars, Bruno Latour's way of establishing common ground is to enact 'the work of translation' (1993: 11). He does this by approaching nature and culture as hybridized networks of relations and at the same time exposing 'the work of purification' that seeks to separate human cultures and non-human nature (1993: 10–11). Across all his work, Latour disputes that the two separate zones that we call nature and culture (or society) actually exist (for example, 1993, 2004, 2005). They are both artefacts, he says, produced in the process of bracketing off one from the other. They are the effects of the specifically 'modern' process of separating, or purifying; they do not pre-exist this process: 'Cultures – different or universal – do not exist, any more than Nature does. There are only natures – cultures' (1993: 104). Latour (1993) identifies this particular kind of delusional 'Great Divide' thinking about nature and culture as modernity's characterizing feature and its greatest paradox. He points out that on the one hand modern science and technology has always ensured the 'proliferation of hybrids' (1993: 1). By this he means that the modern age has produced, manufactured and invented endless entities and phenomena that cross the nature/culture divide. Human-induced global warming is perhaps the ultimate hybrid natures-cultures phenomenon. On the other hand, modernity has a separate epistemological project to maintain the purity of two 'ontological zones' – one for the human cultures and another for non-human nature (1993: 10–11). The paradox is manifest in the never-ending endeavour to keep the artifice of the nature/culture divide alive in the face of proliferating natures-cultures hybrids. This is what Latour calls 'the work of purification' (1993: 11).

A further irony is that the work of purification can also be undertaken in the cultural process of mimicking idealized nature. This is the case in the discursive trajectory of the Nature's Child figure that I traced in Part 1 of this book. As cultural texts, Rousseau's *Emile* treatise, Louv's *Last Child in the Woods*, Fröebel's 'gifts' and kindergarten design, the Nature and Childhood website, the Romantic art and literature, the *Bambi, Pocahontas, Dot and the Kangaroo* and *Storm Boy* filmic texts, the nature kindergartens and professional training courses in outdoor nature education are all examples of nature–culture hybrids, which have been produced in the effort to replicate, represent or promote nature as separate from (adult) society. In other words, all of this work to symbolically purify nature (and by association childhood) is dependent upon the production of hybrid (and thus impure) nature–culture forms (books, films, websites, educational institutions, curricula, training courses).

Latour's (2004) critique of nature as modernity's duplicitous and self-serving political ploy has led him to suggest that we abandon the term altogether. In the place of nature and society, he offers us collectivized notions of assembled 'common worlds' or 'human and nonhuman collectives' (2004, 2005, 2009). Flowing on from this, he entreats us to rethink agency in distributed, shared or collective terms. Latour uses the term 'actants' to signify that nonhumans as well as humans are active agents, and the term 'actancy' to signify nonhuman as well as human agency. He urges us to recognize that every action that takes place in the human and more-than-human collective 'is the property of the whole association, not only of those actants called human' (2009: 162). This takes us well beyond thinking about the individual human exercising agency on a passive or inert nature, including the scientist studying nature, the educator teaching students about nature, and the individual child playing with natural materials. Latour's ideas about distributed agency within human–nonhuman collectives are central to the common worlds framework that I will shortly be offering as a new way of thinking about childhood (see also Prout, 2005). There is no doubt that Latour's 'elsewhere' conceptualizations have a wide carriage, but their mark upon the field of human geography is already well established.

Many human geographers are now 'rethinking the human in human geography' (Whatmore, 1999: 22) and questioning the human-centric assumption that we (humans) are the sole actors and agents in the world. In reconsidering the relationship between humans and the physical world we inhabit (variously considered by geographers as nature, space and place), many have mobilized Latour's (2005) much more collective and generative notion of natures–cultures that recognizes the interdependencies of human activity and nonhuman actancy. Sarah Whatmore (2002: 27) stresses the intermingling of the human and the nonhuman within 'the social fabric', but also the shared agency of humans and 'nonhuman actants' in the making of worlds. In recognition of the fact that we live in a human–nonhuman collective, rather than a divided world, she calls for a 'hybrid geography'. In a similar vein, Noel Castree (2001, 2005) and Bruce Braun (Castree and Braun, 1998, 2001) also refuse the ontological Great Divide of society and nature. As Castree (2001: 15) points out, it is simply not possible to 'physically disentangle the social and the natural. In reality, all there is … is "socionature"'. By adopting the hybrid concept of 'socionature', Braun and Castree (1998: 169–268) are also arguing for a new form of politics, in which nature and society are never approached as separate entities. Their call for a hybrid politics is a deliberate move to decentre exclusively human notions of agency, and to reframe it as an effect of the imbroglio of socionatural relations.

Human geographers are not the only ones calling for a more dynamic and relational view of nature. Stephan Harrison is a geomorphologist with an interest in the philosophy of physical geography who has spearheaded 'conversations across the divide' of physical and human geography (Harrison et al, 2004), including joint conversations about the affordances of complexity and emergence theory in the study of place and landscape (Harrison, Massey and Richards, 2006) and 'the entanglements of nature and culture' (Harrison, Pile and Thrift, 2004). Combined efforts to shift beyond an exclusive concern either with the discourses of nature or with realist nature have refocused upon how nature-culture is experienced, embodied and practised (Thrift, 2007); what the multiplicities of nature do (Hinchcliffe, 2007); how 'naturecultures' are 'situated' (Instone, 2004); how the lives of human and nonhuman animals are co-constituted and mutually implicated within racialized and gendered discourses (Anderson, 1995); and how dynamic human, nonhuman and geophysical worlds are constellated together in time and space (Massey, 2005). In other words these geographers, like Latour, are collectively arguing that we cannot locate human experience outside of nature and for this reason the social and the natural are best thought about together – as an imbroglio of human and nonhuman, living and inert, geographic and engineered, discursive and material relations.

Points of departure: Feminist theory and philosophy

In parallel but also often intersecting trajectories, feminist theorists and philosophers have made major contributions to the project of taking nature 'elsewhere', albeit from a number of different points of entry. For eco-feminists, the entry point is their contestation of the gender ordering of the nature/culture divide that simultaneously structures and naturalizes the dominance of man over woman (patriarchy) and the instrumentalist scientific dominance (and exploitation) of nonhuman nature (Griffin, 1978; Merchant, 1980; Mies and Shiva, 1993). Eco-feminist philosopher Val Plumwood associates the 'mastery of nature' (1993) with both anthropocentric (human-centric) and androcentric (male-centric) rationalism (2002). She maintains that this rationalism is responsible for the 'hyper-separation' of humans and nature, the doctrine of human exceptionalism and the concomitant devaluing and inferiorizing of nature and its rendering as passive and inert (2002). For Plumwood, the way out of masculinist human-centrism and the human/nature divide is through establishing a dialogical and ethical relationship with 'earth others', that recognizes their 'subjecthood, opacity and agency' and remains 'open to the play of more-than-human forces' (2002: 229).

Another space for feminist retheorizations of nature has been created by a long-standing feminist interest in the body. This was first kindled by the post-structural French feminist philosophers in the 1970s, when they called for women, rendered invisible by phallogocentrism, to write themselves back into the world through writing the female body (Cixous, 1976). This call led to a spate of feminist theorizations of the agentic (rather than the passive and inert female) body (for instance, Grosz, 1994). More recently, the emerging 'material feminisms' (Alaimo and Hekman, 2008) have pushed these agentic body theorizations beyond the human. By arguing, as feminist quantum physics philosopher Karen Barad (2011) has done, that more-than-human matter 'matters', and that agency lies in material/discursive intra-actions, they have contributed to feminist retheorizations that take us beyond the material/discursive (and hence the nature/culture) divide. Also from within what is alternately referred to as the 'posthuman' or 'material turn', and strongly influenced by the work of Deleuze and Guattari (1987), feminist philosopher Rosi Braidotti (2006) urges us to take account of the vitality of non-human bodies and life forms ('zoe') and their intersections with discursively produced and bio-politically governed human bodies ('bios'). As a way out of the various divides that separate the human from the rest, Braidotti argues for a post-anthropocentric nomadic subjectivity (2006: 103) that seeks multiple belongings (2006: 123), follows an eco-philosophy of interconnections on a planetary scale (2006: 135) and engages in a transformative life-loving ethics that she calls 'bios/zoe ethics' (2006: 232).

Feminists retheorizations of nature, from whatever disciplinary location, emphasize the relationality of human and more-than-human worlds. Along with this emphasis they seek a relational ethics for these shared worlds. This is true for the feminist geographers Kay Anderson (1995), Doreen Massey (2005) and Sarah Whatmore (2002), for the feminist eco-philosophers Val Plumwood (1993 and 2002) and Rosi Braidotti (2006), and for feminist science studies theorists Karen Barad (2007, 2008) and Donna Haraway (1985, 1991, 1994, 2004a, 2004e, 2008a, 2011). Donna Haraway, in particular, has been relentless in this regard – calling over and over again for a feminist ethics and politics that refuses essentialist divides and pure ontologies, and flagrantly transgresses the boundaries between the human and technological, between human and nonhuman animals. These transgressions, as she continually stresses, are far from gratuitous: they are for 'fruitfully informing liveable politics and ontologies in current life worlds' (2003: 4). In other words, relational ethics respond to the irrevocably messed up world in which we live – but they do not seek pious purity.

Haraway's highly idiosyncratic and multitudinous boundary transgressions, informed by her background as a biologist as well as a feminist science studies theorist, have forged unique pathways and partnerships 'elsewhere' (think biota gone viral) within the landscapes of feminism and STS. For a few decades now, she has been messing up the kinds of categories that others take for granted – including nature, animal, human, technology, culture – and deliberately '[o]pening up their tropic quality, making them swerve into unexpected neighborhoods and form unexpected liaisons, enlarging the lexicon' (Haraway, in Potts and Haraway, 2010: 333). It was in the mid-1980s that she first attained notoriety as a category confounder, for her 'Cyborg Manifesto' (1985). This was her (self-proclaimed) 'blasphemous' call for socialist feminists to re-envisage the human as an organic and technological hybrid and as both a (science) fiction and a social reality (1985: 65). From the human cyborg, she shifted her focus to the conjoined naturecultures of apes and monkeys in science (1989 and 1991) and the technocultures of laboratory animals (1997). More recently, her panache for 'swerv[ing] into unexpected neighborhoods and form[ing] unexpected liaisons' has taken her to the 'co-habitation, co-evolution and embodied cross-species sociality' of humans and dogs (2003: 4). This deviation has brought her back to her own neighbourhood and the life she shares with her Australian Shepherd dog, Ms Cayenne Pepper, and allows her to theorize from the mundane and ordinary (2008a). The result is her second manifesto, this time a 'Companion Species Manifesto' (2003) which calls for an 'ethics and politics committed to the flourishing of significant otherness' and for a recognition that interconnected human and nonhuman 'history matters in naturecultures' (2003: 3). The 'Cyborg' and 'Companion Species' manifestos, along with the rest of Haraway's formidable opus of transgressive writings, proclaim our lives to be entangled in naturecultures and shaped by reciprocal multi-species relationships (2008a: 281). In 'queering what counts as nature' (1994: 60), Haraway is also queering what it means to be human. She often reminds us of this double move by repeating the words of her colleague Anna Tsing – 'human nature is a multispecies relationship' (Tsing, cited by Haraway, in Potts and Haraway, 2010: 320).

As well as expanding the lexicon with queerly hybridized 'nature' concepts of the likes of natureculture and technoculture, Haraway also leads the way in reclaiming reconfiguration as a central queering strategy. By adopting figures such as cyborgs and companion species, she at once queers nature, evokes hybrid relations and unravels the interwoven histories of nature-technocultures. In stark contrast to Rousseau's evocation of Nature's Child as a pure and utopic figure, Haraway's figures are purposefully impure, down to earth, confabulated and confounding. She describes them as 'semiotic-material nodes or knots in which diverse bodies and meanings coshape one another' (2008a: 4). As a locus of knotted relations, the figures function as somewhat arbitrary, but nevertheless strategic, starting points for loosening up and unraveling the threads of nature-technoculture relations, sometimes between the most unlikely partners. Haraway uses her figures as a way of getting elsewhere by other means – means that resist the romance of the sublime and stay resolutely connected to the earth and the 'flesh of mortal world-making entanglements' (2008a: 4). In this way Haraway's figures function as both theoretical devises and methodological processes through which she reconstructs what counts as nature and queerly reconfigures worlds. As she puts it, the appeal of using creative reconfiguration (as opposed to deconstruction) is that it is 'a mode of theory [to use] when the more "normal" rhetorics of systematic critical analysis seem only to repeat and sustain our entrapment in the stories of the established disorders' (Haraway, 2004a: 47). Haraway's work is anything but entrapped in the normal. Although I have been working to queer what count as natural and normal for some time now (Blaise and Taylor, 2012; Taylor, 2007a, 2007b, 2008, 1010a, 2010b; Taylor et al., 2007; Taylor and Richardson, 2005a), Haraway's queer reconfigurative methods have reinvigorated my efforts to move elsewhere via other means. It is in this spirit that I set out to assemble and enact the common worlds bricolage that I have cobbled together from these trans-disciplinary conversations.

Windows into children's common worlds

The extraordinary artistries of Jeannie Baker and Shaun Tan, two of Australia's preeminent children's author-illustrators, provide visually stimulating and thought-provoking windows into the common worlds of childhood. I offer them here, not as exemplars of what children's common worlds do or should look like, but as a way of stimulating thought and opening up discussions about their possibilities. *The Hidden Forest* (Baker, 2000) and *The Rabbits* (Marsden and Tan, 1998) are both children's picture books that are on a mission to encourage their young readers to see their worlds differently. Both indicate that the entanglement of differences within these worlds poses certain ethical dilemmas that require our (children's) response. The ethics of how to respond to human and more-than-human differences is of central concern to a common worlds view of childhood. These books offer two very different takes on it.

The Hidden Forest is a strikingly beautiful children's picture book with a strong environmental message and more than a hint of the Romantic sublime. This is communicated first and foremost through Baker's exquisitely detailed naturalistic artwork, designed to inspire awe and wonder. Each page reveals yet another breathtaking scene from Tasmania's marine environment, in southern Australia. The full-page images are reproductions of Baker's original miniature collage constructions, including many real objects. It is an assembled bricolage, a materially reconstructed miniature replica of a real world. Baker uses this art medium to evoke a sense of place (Baker, 2012). The visuals animate the story of Ben's encounters with the 'hidden' and mysterious undersea world of Giant Kelp forests. The vibrant colours and textures of Baker's collage techniques evoke a hyper-realist sense of the undersea world. They viscerally communicate Ben's highly sensory and emotional experiences to the readers. Most importantly, the evocative artistry is constructed to impress how this 'dark, tangled world of the weed' could have affected Ben so powerfully and afforded him a very different way of seeing the world.

Ben often catches 'tiddlers' in his fish trap in the bay from the safety of his small dinghy, but he avoids going into the water. He is quite anxious about touching the 'slimy' seaweed that covers the surface of the bay, and fantasizes about what might be 'lurking below'. Early in the story, Ben falls into the sea while he is yanking at the rope of his tangled fish trap, and his 'dinghy flips from under him'. In the seaweedy water, Ben wrestles with his fear: 'He is afraid some unknown creature will grab his legs as he scrambles back into the dinghy.' He tries to row away, but in his panic, it seems as if 'the kelp clings to his oars and won't let him go'.

Eventually Ben manages to row out of the kelp and to calm down, but in order to retrieve the tangled trap, he calls on his friend Sophie who is a strong diver and not afraid of swimming in these waters. Sophie agrees to help on the condition that Ben will come and 'see the world under the waves with her'. Ben is anxious at first, swimming near the surface, but he gradually relaxes, ventures deeper down and begins to enjoy the sensory pleasures of this mysterious 'underwater forest'.

The story climaxes when Ben senses 'a presence behind him', turns around and finds himself staring directly into the enormous eye of a whale. This moment of face-to-face encounter with the whale is a transformative one for Ben. He is 'overwhelmed with wonder'. From now on he 'sees things differently ... He sees how wonderful these creatures are here in their mysterious, hidden world.' He no longer keeps the fish he has caught in his trap, but swims down to release them back into the hidden forest of the Giant Kelp. 'He feels this is where they belong.'

Apart from the Romantic trope of personal transformation through wondrous nature encounters and the clear environmental message that flows from this, I also read this story and its images as gesturing towards the notion of common worlds. Read as an example of common worlding, Ben not only comes to see the beauty of the undersea world and thus to respect it, but also recognizes his co-implication in a world he shares with a multitude of more-than-human others and responds to it. His eye-to-eye encounter with the whale is particularly significant as it evokes the ethics of recognition of, and hence responsibility for, the other, that Levinas (1969) wrote about, but extends this ethics beyond the exclusively human face-to-face encounter (see Edelglass et al., 2012; Kendall, 2008).

Figure 4.1 Ben encounters the whale in *The Hidden Forest*. Illustration by
         author/illustrator Jeannie Baker. © 2000 Jeannie Baker. From *The
         Hidden Forrest* by Jeannie Baker. Reproduced by permission of
         Walker Books Australia.

John Marsden's and Shaun Tan's controversial picture book, *The Rabbits*, is
much more ominous – although, as in *The Hidden Forest*, the book's message
relies heavily upon the evocations of its striking full-page illustrations. These are
reproductions of Tan's original artworks, also bricolages, but in this case strategically 'unnatural' congregations of intertextual styles – including surrealism,

Figure 4.2 'They came by water.' Image reproduced by permission from *The
         Rabbits* by John Marsden and Shaun Tan, Lothian Children's Books,
         an imprint of Hachette Australia, 1998.

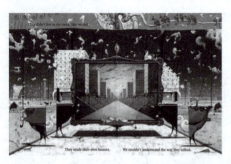

Figure 4.3 'They made their own houses.' Image reproduced by permission from *The Rabbits* by John Marsden and Shaun Tan, Lothian Children's Books, an imprint of Hachette Australia, 1998.

Australian colonial and contemporary landscape art, political cartoons and European mythical figurations (Tan, 1999). The book is narrated by rather timid numbat-like creatures, who survey the unfolding scenario (from the treetops in the images above) and recount the tragic story of the rabbits' invasion and destruction of their country. Marsden's text, although minimal, is an uncompromising political analogy of the devastating effects of British colonization upon Aboriginal people, native plants and animals and the physical environment itself.

Tan's artworks dominate the book and add layers of complexity to the narrative. Unlike the written text, the images are deliberately ambiguous and open to interpretation. In a conversation with Nick Strathopoulos called 'Rabbiting On', Tan (1999) declares that, 'The subject of colonisation has also fascinated me for some time, not simply as a political issue, but as an event of utter aesthetic strangeness where two very different worlds collide.' Tan gives visual form to this collision of different worlds through his hybrid technoculture-nature creatures. The rabbit protagonists are hybrid machinic-colonist-animal figures. Stiff, footless and faceless, their rabbit-ness is only recognizable because of their long stick ears and fluffy white tails. In 'Rabbiting on', Tan further explains that he is 'very interested in the way in which normal things can be seen as abnormal'. He achieves this subversion of normal through his hybrid figures, through the juxtaposition of worlds and through the use of mimetic forms. For instance, in the image above he responds to the normalcy of the written text, 'they made their own houses', and of the referent 'house' itself, by queerly 'furnishing' the landscape with 'rabbit-made' structures. Pretentious bedroom furniture – chests of drawers – morph into high-rise development and a formally framed painting, heralded (or guarded?) by the hybrid rabbit figures, mimics (or is it mocks?) the vision of urban progress. Throughout the book, the natural landscape is presented as a palimpsest – overwritten and progressively overwhelmed by the artefacts of colonialism and modernity in all their strange hybrid manifestations – revealing not only the wanton destructive effects of indigenous displacement but also the altered environmental legacy of weird, misplaced formations.

This provocative book has attracted a lot of controversy and criticism. As well as being accused by the nationalist right as being 'politically correct' anti-white indoctrination (discussed in Tan, 1999), it has also attracted critique from an Indigenous Australian perspective. For instance, Brooke Collins-Gearing and Dianne Osland (2010) point out that despite its intention to contest the fallacious heroic white settlement narrative and to champion the cause of the colonized, it ultimately remains an inherently white-centric story of conquest, in which the indigenes, as innocent bystanders, are stripped of any agency and the evil colonists maintain their omnipotent status. These authors also protest the crude analogy of substituting invaded native animals for invaded Aboriginal people. They judge the numbat stand-in creatures as particularly insensitive – especially given that until the 1960s, so many Aboriginal people were governed under state native flora and fauna acts, effectively denying their human status and thus their citizenship. The end line – 'who will save us from the rabbits?' – also incites their ire, as it reinscribes the indigenous (numbat substitute human) characters as hapless victims, passively waiting to be rescued.

Whilst I agree with Collins-Gearing and Osland (2010) that the narrative reinscribes the colonialist binaries in ways that inadvertently reconfirm the 'natural' dominance of the whites invaders, I also appreciate the ways in which Tan's queer artistic sensibilities contribute so much more complexity to this text, and also hint at some of the less comfortable aspects of common worlds. Although the narrative's rehearsal of the hegemonic 'rape script' (as Gibson-Graham, 2006, calls those discourses that perpetuate victim/oppressor relationships) could well have counterproductive and disenabling effects, Tan's strange visual juxtapositions and hybridized figurations also confound and subvert its binary logic. In short, they transform a potentially didactic script into an interestingly layered book, full of knotty contradictions. Unlike *The Hidden Forest*, there is no happy ending. The images raise questions about co-habitation in a strangely reconstituted, realigned and reassembled common world – the confounding legacy of different worlds colliding, which definitely does not offer the reassuring 'telos of a final peace' (Haraway, 2008a: 301). These entangled histories raise important questions to discuss with children – not how to return to an imagined perfect past, or how to launch a heroic rescue mission, but how to grapple with the knotty dilemmas we inherit in our thrown together common worlds. Recognizing and responding to the wonders of more-than-human difference, as Ben did, is one of the key features of living in common worlds – but so is 'staying with the trouble' (Haraway, 2010; Potts and Haraway, 2010: 327) and dealing with the mess.

Common worlds ethics and politics

Over the last couple of years, Miriam Giugni and I have been drawing upon the trans-disciplinary theoretical works I have outlined above to assemble a common worlds conceptual framework. Our purpose has been to simultaneously reconceptualize inclusion and environmental education in early childhood communities (see Taylor and Giugni, 2012). Our efforts have been underpinned by a shared belief that the human-centric and happy pluralist version of inclusion – which celebrates children's and families' cultural, ethnic and gender diversities – is not nearly enough. We have both had enough experience living and working in culturally diverse and Indigenous Australian educational contexts to know that inclusion and the question of belonging (particularly, but not only, in the post-colonial settler context) might sound benevolent, but is a highly charged and contested political field (see Giugni and Mundine, 2011; Taylor, 2007; Taylor, Fasoli and Giugni, 2009; Taylor and Richardson, 2005b). Inclusive rhetorics and good intentions alone are not enough, particularly if there is little critical reflection upon the questions of who get to do the including, who gets included and what exactly they are being included into. Neither are we convinced that the recent interest within early childhood education to include more nature activities (coded as 'outdoor') and to care for the environment is hitting the mark when it emphasizes the ways in which nature's aesthetic, wondrous and educational qualities can enrich and ennoble human lives. Having also mulled over the complicated implications of our own significant more-than-human relations – namely with our close kin cats and dogs (vale Hen and the Waf); smelly wombats (mostly road-kill); rent-a-chooks (commercial Australian caged chickens); caterpillar desert landforms; rivers (dry and flooding); accessories and bags (mostly Miriam's); wool and indoor fires (while knitting in front of); the food we eat; the weather (increasingly wild); clay; prehistoric limestone caves (still dripping); earthquakes; and rocks on the move – we have become increasingly convinced that common worlds offer children far more than the best intentions for inclusive (exclusively) human communities and staged nature experiences.

Our collaborations (see also Taylor, Blaise and Giugni, 2012) have sought to push bounded understandings about inclusion and environmental education beyond a celebration of individual children's differences and individual children's experiences of awe and wonder, and beyond the framing discourses of (exclusive) human agency and enrichment. This involves two main shifts. The first is a shift away from thinking about inclusive communities as ones that incorporate and celebrate (exclusively) human diversity and 'manage' individual differences – towards thinking about common worlds (or common worlding) as dynamic collectives of humans and more-than-humans, full of unexpected partnerships and comings together, *which bring differences to bear on the ways our lives are constituted and lived*. The second and related shift moves us from thinking about these inclusive (but separate) human communities as caring for the environment (or non-human nature) to thinking about the ongoing ethics and politics of living in heterogeneous (human and more-than-human) common worlds and of *collectively responding* to the challenges that they thrown up.

The common worlds optic is also my way of refocusing on the 'elsewhere' of nature. As Haraway (2004b: 90) points out, 'the world is precisely what gets lost' when we separate nature from the human world (otherwise known as society) in order to objectively know about it and/or to valorize it. Bringing the world back into the mix is my broader motivation for reconstituting the natures of childhood 'elsewhere' – an 'elsewhere' where children's lives are inseparably bound up with all manner of other lives, other forces and other things. These entwined worlds, like the tangled world of weeds that Ben at first only fishes above and then swims within, are full of (unknown until sought out) wonders (Baker, 2000), but they are also messy worlds of co-implicated histories, uneven power relations and ethical challenges, as the colliding Australian worlds of numbats and techno-culture rabbits confrontingly reveal (Marsden and Tan, 1998).

The addition of the commons to these worlds resonates with western philo-sophical traditions. Plato was one of the first to consider when and why it is important to set aside individual interests in order to attend to the 'common good' of the social collective (Brown, 2010). Quite recently, Michael Fielding and Peter Moss (2011) have brought the idea of the 'common good' back into the educational lexicon, offering a vision of 'radical education', based on the principles of participatory democracy, within 'a common school' context (see also Theobald, 1997). Their 'common school' promotes an ethics of care and operates as a kind of 'collective workshop' whereby the (public) school takes responsibility for pursuing 'collective purposes and projects of collective interest and benefit' (2011: 53, 57). The idea of the 'common good' has also been extended beyond the social fabric. For instance, the 'global commons' is a contemporary notion that offers an ecological perspective on collectivity and ethics. Adopting the notion of the 'global commons', environmentalists call for people across the world to take collective responsibility to ensure the sustainability, rather than the exploitation, of the world's unowned natural resources, such as Antarctica, outer space and the earth's atmosphere and oceans (Buck, 1998).

When Latour (2004: 98) makes reference to the commons in his common world politics, he is only partly referring to the collective's responsibility for attending to the common good that Plato spoke of. Plato's common good presupposes an already-assembled social collective with already-established shared interests. Beyond this exclusively human set of common interests and responsi-bilities, Latour proposes a common world ethics that requires us to remain radically open to the changing, uneven and above all generative *composition* of these worlds. At times, territorial interests and political tensions can deter our openness to the composition of worlds, leading to denial, suppression or oblit-eration of difference. This is the point being made in *The Rabbits* (Marsden and Tan, 1998), a book that not only forces its readers to engage with the ethics and politics of cultural dispossession and environmental degradation within the making of colonized worlds, but also of living with the strange new hybrid formations that materialize 'when very different worlds collide' (Tan, 1999). The mutual composition of common worlds effectively takes shape when we act on our curiosity to find out more about where we are, and who and what is there with us. This is well illustrated in *The Hidden Forest* (Baker, 2000), when Ben immerses himself in the underwater world he had only previously known as a source of fish. His encounters with complexities and differences within this new world, and in particular his face-to-face meeting with the whale, provokes him to assume a new kind of ethical responsibility for this newly expanded common world of human and sea creatures.

In reconfiguring the natures of childhood as common worlds, I adopt Latour's (2004) understanding of the collective as an ongoing process of collecting, and his associated generative and emergent notion of a common world. This means never foreclosing on who or what kinds of entities and differences might be assembled in children's common worlds, but attending, instead, to the practice of continually tracing, unfolding and collecting them. This sounds like the kind of work that a bricoleur might be well equipped to do and implies that we might approach children's common worlds as a process – a process of common worlding. It also sounds like the kind of work that requires unfolding understandings of ethical responsibilities and political implications as we find out more about where we are, and who or what is there with us. Common worlding pushes us beyond a singular ethics of care of the self (Foucault, 1986); an exclusively human-focused ethics of care of the 'other' (Levinas, 1969); and an ethics of care of an externalized environment (Marshall, 2002; Martins, 2007). Within common worlds, an ethics of 'care for self, other and environment' (Ritchie et al., 2010) becomes an inseparable 'relational ethics' (Whatmore, 2002).

Heterogeneous relations in common worlds

There are two baseline tenets that I want to recap. First, children's common worlds are not separated, pure and natural utopic spaces. They are mixed up worlds in which all manner of things co-exist – including the manufactured and the organic, the living and the inert, entities and forces, and humans young and old. Second, humans are not the only ones making or assembling the common worlds – doing the common worlding. Common worlds are produced through the heterogeneous relations between all of these things. In other words, children's common worlds are impure and emerging worlds, produced through ongoing heterogeneous relations that take place within and between a whole host of actors (living beings) and actants (things and non-living forces) (Latour 2004, 2005). Children's picture books and films (including all the texts that I have made reference to in this and the previous section) are just some of the material/discursive entities within this heterogeneous array of relations that produce children's common worlds. At the same time, the texts themselves can be seen as the product of heterogeneous discursive/material relations. And occasionally, some of these books, like *The Hidden Forest* and *The Rabbits*, will draw children's attention to the relational ethics of living in common worlds.

So, for example, *The Hidden Forest* can be reconsidered as not only Baker's work (contrary to citation conventions), but as having been produced through the relations between the real place it represents, Baker's art collages and script, the printed books, the publishers' requirements, the commercial contract, the discourses of nature and gender that inform it, and the images of a boy, a girl, fish, fish-traps, diving masks, seaweed, a whale, crustaceans, rocks, sand, waves, sea water, currents, a dinghy and sunshine that Baker has crafted, at least partly from her own corresponding experiences of such things. In an interview that is published on her website, Baker (2012) gives us more insight into the actancy of the actual place in the productive process. She explains that *The Hidden Forest* book was inspired by a number of visits she has made to the east coast of Tasmania and the dives she has made into the giant kelp forests in that area. On another section of her website, Baker describes how her collages often include real materials, like sand, shells and preserved pieces of seaweed. In this case, not only did her encounters with the place give her the idea for the book, but it also gave the book some of its material form. Although produced in entirely different circumstances, *The Rabbits* (Marsden and Tan, 1998) is also the product of a complicated heterogeneous array of relations – and in fact has colonial relations of power as its overt referent. This book has been made by the relations between real life events (including violent and violating acts), (white) anti-colonialist discourses about these events, an artist and a writer, literary and art tropes (including intertextual visual references) and narrative and visual representations of hybrid and apocalyptic post-colonial Australian figures and landscapes.

Both of these children's texts and the wider children's worlds that they help to shape are specific constellations of assembled heterogeneous relations, which in turn produce very specific kinds of children's common worlds. These worlds (and worlds within worlds) are the product of the comings together, the intra- and inter-actions and relations of all these entities and forces, living and inert (Barad, 2007). Haraway describes the generative nature of heterogeneous relations as a kind of perpetual 'dance of relating', in which '[a]ll of the dancers are remade through the patterns they enact' (2007: 25). She goes on to declare that these relationships 'are the smallest possible units for analysis; the partners and actors are their still ongoing products. It is all very prosaic, relentless, mundane, and exactly how worlds come into being' (2007: 26). Apart from offering new tools for analyzing children's texts, and for elucidating how and why children's common worlds might be best thought of as a common worlding process, Haraway's relational ontology, and her descriptions of this never-ending mutually transformative 'dance of relating' between actors (human and non-human), provoke many questions for early childhood educators. What kinds of heterogeneous common world relations make and remake childhoods? What kinds of dance patterns weave between children, educators, texts, the curriculum, pedagogical materials, the architecture of the early learning environment, families and the wider world? How might we rechoreograph these patterned relations to reshape common worlds? How might we pedagogically engage children with the making and reshaping of their own common worlds? What kind of ethical dilemmas might children encounter in the dance of relating, especially in relating across difference? How can we best support them to respond to these ethical dilemmas and to co-exist with difference?

A queer relational ethics and ontology

Learning to live ethically with difference (human and more-than-human) in heterogeneous worlds is one of our biggest challenges, and the central concern of common worlds pedagogies. Haraway has a number of useful conceptual tools for thinking through the challenges and the affordances of common world relations and I offer them here as a way of queering the ways we might think about the ontologies, the ethics and the politics of these relations.

'Queer kin' is one of my favourite Haraway concepts, and one I find particularly helpful for reconfiguring the natures of childhood within common worlds. She uses it liberally and consistently (for instance in Haraway, 1991, 1994, 1997, 2003, 2004d, 2004e, 2008a, 2008b, 2010, 2011). In order to pave the way for understanding queer kin, I recall Haraway's statement that '[A]ctual encounters are what make beings' (1997: 67). This statement reminds us that ontologies are relational – that things (including books, childhoods and all manner of odd but still significant relationships) come into being in the process of relating. Riding on the back of relational ontology, Haraway's notion of queer kin gives an alternative way of thinking about procreation and intimacy outside of the normative 'blood lines' of the heterosexual human family. Queer kin is a deliberatively irreverent and counter-essentialist notion, which expands our familial networks, allows all sorts of odd bedfellows and other kinds of strange partners to come together, and gives new status to the significant nonhuman others in our common worlds. For Haraway, it has become a generic term to describe all kinds of boundary-crossing significant relationships, including relations that produce hybrid forms (like cyborgs), the relations that humans have with technologies (for instance, children's relations with their mobile phones), and companion species relations. I find it particularly pertinent for honouring the prevalence and significance of children's close relations with other species. In the nomenclature of queer kin, Haraway offers us a way to rename and reframe the important relations between children and their nonhuman living companions. Dogs, cats, rabbits, guinea pigs, and so on, need no longer be demeaned as children's 'pets', and children are spared the onus of 'mastering' human 'ownership'. Queer kin encapsulates the possibility of sustaining relations with unlikely and very different but nevertheless significant others in common worlds, in ways that resist the temptation to minimize, negate, sentimentalize, anthropomorphize, or assimilate these relations (see Taylor and Giugni, 2012).

Let me make it very clear that queer kin common world relations are not synonymous with harmonious Disney nature worlds, worlds of happy (cross-species) pluralism, in which cute and innocent children and animals only ever frolic together as equals. Queer kin relations are close relations forged across difference, but, as Haraway points out in relation to cross-species queer kin relations, they are 'almost never symmetrical' (2008a: 74) and therefore they require us to 'live responsively' in 'questioning relationships' (2008a: 71). She repeatedly stresses that queer kin relations compel us to keep 'grappling' with the 'sticky knots' that are thrown up when we commune with differences. The process of continual questioning is central to any ethics, but in a common worlds relational ethics, queer kin relations, with all their unlikely intimacies, predictable asymmetries and radical differences, pose significant challenges for living together. Queer kin relations require continual grapplings without the promise of a resolution. In the face of these challenges, Haraway urges us to 'stay with the trouble' and to 'inhabit this question [of difference] uncomfortably and non-innocently' (in Potts and Haraway, 2010: 322, 327).

Haraway's visions of queer kin and of staying with the trouble in questioning relationships are simultaneously playful, ethical, political and hopeful. They offer us a welcome alternative to the ubiquitous romanticization of Nature's Child and the aestheticization of children's relationships with animals and nature, which prevail in popular media and in educational discourses. In the face of the seductive appeal of such discourses, Haraway's queering ethics helps us to resist oversentimentalizing and thus depoliticizing children's relations with the more-than-human world. It helps us to reframe children's common worlds around a relational ethics. On the one hand, this relational ethics retains hope in the generative possibilities of children's relations with more-than-human others. On the other hand, it appreciates the political imperative to grapple with the dilemmas and tensions that inevitably arise when we co-inhabit with differences.

Equipped with Haraway's notion of queer kin, and the associated encouragement to grapple with sticky knots and stay with the trouble, it is now possible to politically fortify the generative notion of common worlding and retain its inclusive impulses, but also overlay these with an extended understanding of a queer kin relational ontology (becoming with others in our common worlds) and of a queer kin relational ethics (grappling with encounters of difference in common worlds). This queer common worlding (Haraway, 2008b) is precisely what I intend to do in the next chapter.

Chapter 5

Enacting common worlds

... cobbled together pastpresent symbiogenetic doings are what make critters of all kinds to be kin, most often through something other than linear genetic descent, intentional acts, or cybernetic informational exuberance. To be kin ... is to be responsible to and for each other, human and not.

(Haraway, 2010: 54)

Traditional societies do not live in harmony with nature, they are unacquainted with it.

(Latour, 2004: 232)

The common worlds of child–animal relations are the subject of this chapter. Far from rehearsing the perfect coupling of children and animals as one of nature, purity and innocence (as the Romantics would have us believe), I set out to rearticulate child–animal relations as queerly situated naturecultures (Instone, 2004). Both the children and the animals in my enactments are co-shaped by their entangled relations with each other, but also by the very specific geo-historical common worlds in which they are enmeshed and embedded. Drawing from feminist, ecological and post-human philosophies, hybrid geographies and non-western world-views, my common world child–animal rearticulation or enactments interrupt taken-for-granted humanist and developmentalist understandings about the 'nature' of the individual child, the 'nature' of animals in children's lives, the 'nature' of human nature and the 'nature' of kinship. Reconfigured within the common worlds of naturecultures, child–animal relations become completely mixed up affairs.

Children, pets and the menageries of childhood

In *After Nature*, an anthropology of English kinship in the late twentieth century, Marilyn Strathern (1992: 11–15) starts to muddy the waters of human–animal (nature-culture) differences, when she makes the point that middle-class

English notions of kinship are not framed by biology (nature) alone. They are also distinguished by the cultural tradition of valuing individualism – of professing the unique individuality of each offspring child. Strathern predictably links this perception of the special or unique individual child with the self-evident circumstances of late marriage, low birth rates and isolated small nuclear family structures – but also quite unexpectedly with the English sentimental regard for the family pet, as a kind of substitute child. If this muddling of human–animal boundaries and exclusively biological notions of kinship is not queer enough, Strathern (1992: 12) points out that this petted animal–child cultural tradition has a long history. She cites Alan Macfarlane's (1978) tracings of the origins of English individualism back to medieval times, when the practice of fussing over or 'petting' prized animals, who were regarded as luxury possessions, in turn led to the petting of human children as 'superior pets'. From the Enlightenment on, children became similarly fussed over or petted and concomitantly highly valued as unique and special human individuals. The little known fact that this peculiarly English tradition of petting animals underpins the sacrosanct notion of the individual children as special and unique foreshadows child–animal relations as a potentially fertile ground for queering and reconfiguring the natures of childhood.

Strathern and Macfarlane are not the only ones in the Anglophone world to comment upon this tendency to regard and/or treat pets as children and children as pets. North American child psychologist Gail Melson (2005) makes similar observations in her book *Why the Wild Things Are: Animals in the Lives of Children* – although she does not historically locate this interchangeable child–animal petting within classed English cultural traditions. Her long-term US study of children's relationship with animals confirms that pets are often equated with children. The English traditions have clearly travelled. For instance, she relates the findings that in the US, pets are almost universally regarded as a part of the family (2005: 37–8), that pets are seen as 'cute' like human babies, and their 'babyface' cuteness stirs human nurturing feelings (2005: 38–9), that children often refer to family pets as their siblings (2005: 39–41) and that pets are often centrally incorporated within family narratives and are seen as key players in family dramas (2005: 41–3). These same (English) cultural traditions of regarding pets as family members are also evident in Australia (Franklin, 2006) and as Blaise notes (in Taylor, Blaise and Giugni, 2012), the 'petting' of dogs in Chinese families is becoming increasingly popular within the Hong Kong ex-British colonial context.

In her sensory description of the discursive and material ways that animals are interwoven within the fabric of children's lives, Melson (2005: 189) observes:

> … how thickly animal threads run through children's everyday lives. There are the pets, of course, and the farm animals. There is the wild animal life wriggling, chirping, squeaking, and scurrying underfoot, at arm's reach, and overhead. In children's imaginations, more creatures take up residence.

Monsters roar in dreams, humanoid animals tell story-book tales, and furry and feathered 'pals' wisecrack on their own Web sites.

Another US child developmental psychologist, Gene Meyers (1998), shares this unusual academic interest in children's relations with animals. He describes young children's worlds as menageries, 'saturated by animal presences' (1998: 1) which take real-life physical, imaginary and narrative forms. In fact, animal presences are so ubiquitous in children's lives, so natural and normal, that the fondly regarded and actively encouraged affinity between children and animals and the menageries of childhood rarely attract the focused attention of childhood 'experts' beyond some specific special circumstances (such as animals as therapy for children with special needs). As Meyers (1998) and Melson (2005) separately note, there is virtually no interest within child developmental discourses in engaging with the significance of child–animal relationships. Their empirical studies of children and animals set out to tackle this disregard (Meyers, 1998; Melson, 2005). Both these authors point out that when children's relationships with animals are acknowledged, they are usually cast as immature but useful rehearsals for the 'real thing' – as preparing children for those 'all important' human-to-human relations that are commonly referred to as social relationships. Children's (socially endorsed and encouraged) interest in animals is most commonly regarded as a training ground for the development of empathy and as a way of 'inculcating care and responsible *social* behavior' (Meyers, 1998: 1; my italics).

The resolutely anthropocentric (or human-centric) gaze of developmental theory, which is concerned with nothing beyond the social, affords little space for considering children's relations with more-than-human others beyond their use value for exclusively human concerns and values. Moreover, developmental theory's fixation upon rationality as the ultimate 'arrival point' of human maturation supports the assumption of human exceptionalism, and, in turn, the 'hyper-separation' of (rational and mature) humans from other animals (Plumwood, 1993, 2002). The implication of all this is that developmental theory not only positions early childhood as a pre-rational (or immature) stage of human development, but also inadvertently naturalizes the close association of young children with nonhuman animals, who are permanently consigned to the inferiorized status of those less evolved species who will never have the capacity to reason. Perceived as sharing a lack of rationality and maturity, young children and animals are lumped together as natural innocents – at least until children mature, fulfil their predestined human capacity to reason, 'outgrow' their animal affinities, graduate into adult society and leave their animal 'siblings' behind.

Myers (1998) and Melson (2005) also identify developmentalism's anthropocentrism and its privileging of human reason as the two main obstacles to taking child–animal relations seriously. However, because they are positioned within the same humanist (and human-centric) paradigm that they are challenging, they struggle to think beyond the deep-seated developmentalist preoccupation with the agentic 'becoming rational' individual child that inexorably re-enacts anthropocentrism. For instance, when Meyers (1998: 170) suggests that young children's connections to nonhuman animals develop a sense of belonging to and being responsible for the environment – a sense that he describes as an 'ecological self' – he is refuting the idea that humans are separate from nature. But even while stressing our connections with the environment, he ultimately defaults back to the primacy of the agentic and 'becoming rational' individual child, who can understand and act on this realization of connection by becoming an environment steward – another heroic human narrative. Melson (2005: 189) is similarly constrained when she critiques developmentalism's anthropocentrism:

> In an anthropocentric take on development, [the] childhood animal world buzzes, squeals, and purrs only as a background music to the central dramas of human relationships. At most, childish fascination with animals is a scaffolding that falls away as the edifice of maturity rises. In a biocentric view, by contrast, the animal connection is the foundation of the building *that children construct of their lives.*

> (Melson, 2005: 189; my italics)

Her shift of emphasis – from animals-as-temporary-scaffolding to animal connections-as-permanent-foundations upon which children build their lives – consolidates the importance of animals in children's lives, without displacing the baseline assumption of the child's ultimate autonomous agency. Even in Melson's expanded 'biocentric view', it appears inevitable that children will still get on with the job of being in charge of their own lives. Although Melson (2005) and Meyers (1998) both revalue the significance of animals in children's lives by putting them centre stage in their development narratives, and their respective scripts promote enriched, more insightful, more connected and less self-centred human lives, they fall short of troubling the premise of an already-constituted (if still developing) and autonomously agentic individual child. With only the masters' tools at hand, they cannot derail the anthropocentrism (nor its associated child-centrism) that underpins the great progress narrative of human development.

Reconfiguring child–animal relations

My somewhat perilous intention is to completely change tack – to use my common worlds conceptual tools to reconfigure child–animal relations in ways that *refuse the centrisms of the individual child and foreground the enmeshed and heterogeneous common worlds that children inherit and inhabit.* To do this, I quickly set to felting the thick 'animal threads' that Melson (above) observes to 'run through children's everyday lives' (2005: 189). I matt them together to confound the reading of animal presences as simply threads that enrich the warp and weft of children's lives, and to counter moves to temporarily stitch animals and young children together in complicit innocence and simplicity. By robust matting, child and animal become *mutually* embroiled in their common worlds, reconfigured as *queer kin relations that matter*. They cannot be [hyper-] separated out. As a part of this matting process, I attend to the 'pastpresent symbiogenetic doings' that Haraway (above) asserts 'make[s] critters of all kinds to be kin', and most importantly 'be responsible to and for each other' (2010: 54). By matting (and mattering) these child–animal queer kin relations, I enact a relational ontology, emphasizing how children's and animals' lives are *co-shaped* through the entangled historical legacies they inherit and the mutually enmeshed geographical presents that they cohabit.

Common worlds provide the locus for these matted and entangled child–animal lives – and their multispecies historical and geographical convergences. In an increasingly mixed-up global world, characterized by rapid change, hybrid natureculture and technonatureculture forms, border crossings (human and more-than-human), past–present and local–global articulations and political place events that are the effects of 'throwntogetherness' (Massey, 2005), mixed-up child–animal common worlds are anything but natural and innocent and anything but worlds that revolve around (already constituted) individual children's lives. To the contrary, all of these lives (human and more-than-human) are mutually constituted within complex sets of contested histories and spaces, messy inheritances, asymmetrical relations and the ensuing politics of belonging.

The common worlds that children inherit and inhabit are always unsettled, and productively so. They are full of the ongoing grapplings that are part and parcel of cohabiting. Child–animal common worlds are leaky, messy, challenging, dynamic and transforming. They are about as far you can get from the hermetically sealed, pure and perfect child–animal worlds manufactured by Disney Dreamworld Studios. They not only take children's real-world relations with animals seriously (as do Melson, 2005, and Myers, 1998), but they seriously consider the geo-historical specificities that constellate to produce queerly heterogeneous and configured child–animal common worlds in particular times and places – common worlds that are characterized by their own distinctive political and ethical challenges.

The two child–animal common worlds that I enact in this chapter are very different but nevertheless co-implicated and distinctively Australian. They are both very familiar to me. The first of these is the Arrernte common world of Yeperenye (caterpillar) children in Mparntwe country, in the central Australian desert (where all of the Arrernte children and all of the Yeperenye caterpillars live). The second is the common world of immigrant setttler Australian children and wombats, constellated mainly around the south-eastern part of the country (where the greatest concentration of wombats and immigrant children live). Because of my own past-present cohabitations with immigrant and Arrernte children, wombats and caterpillars, I have an investment in these particular common worlds. I care about them. So I enact them here in the hope of 'fruitfully informing [more] liveable politics and ontologies' (Haraway, 2003: 4);

promoting more 'hospitable multispecies environment[s]' (Tsing, 2011: 19); and advocating for 'the flourishing of significant otherness' (Haraway, 2003: 3).

Australian landscapes

For those unfamiliar with the Australian milieu, in this section and the next I survey the geo-historical landscapes upon which contemporary Yeperenye childhoods and immigrant child–wombat common worlds unfold. This involves marking some of the significant events that have constellated to produce entangled contemporary Australian (human and more-than-human) landscapes, but which are not specifically about children. The result is a snapshot of the heterogeneous 'throwntogetherness' of place (Massey, 2005) that is now called Australia. An appreciation of the 'throwntogetherness' of the heterogeneous Australian landscape also throws light on the contested grounds of Australian belongings that children and nonhuman animals inherit and co-inhabit. As well as providing the geo-historical and political landscapes for my idiosyncratic Indigenous and non-indigenous child, wombat and caterpillar stories, this section and the next underscore the fact that *all children's worlds are enmeshed and embedded worlds*. This means that childhoods, just like natures, cannot be separated from the broader landscapes of these worlds.

The events that I select are from the contemporary Indigenous and immigrant post-colonial Australian landscapes. Australian worlds are post-colonial in the sense that the legacies of the still-quite-recent colonial past reside in all post-colonial local Australian presents. These colonialist legacies are never far from the surface. Mutually entangled colonial histories, discourses and practices infuse the relations between contemporary Indigenous and non-indigenous Australians. Their effects can be witnessed in the national statistics, which reveal significant and entrenched inequities between Indigenous and non-indigenous Australians in health and life expectancy, educational outcomes, access to housing, participation in the workforce, and in the disproportionately high representation of Indigenous Australians in the criminal justice system (Australian Human Rights Commission, 2012). The colonizers' settlement of the land is also materially imprinted upon the landscape (for example, through urban development, fencing, massive forest clearances, introduced species, pastoral grazing) and all of this has directly impacted upon the flora and fauna, as *The Rabbits* (Marsden and Tan, 1998) makes painfully clear. The biodiversity of Australia's unique species is rapidly diminishing, in what Deborah Bird Rose (2011) refers to as the 'age of extinction'. In the most recent biodiversity audit, the Australian government reported across-the-board rises in the number of threatened species, including listings of 426 threatened animal species, 1324 threatened plant species and 46 threatened ecological communities (or entire groups of plants and animals) (Australian Bureau of Statistics, 2010).

In terms of human habitation, the post-colonial Australian landscape is a predominantly immigrant one. Almost all Australians can trace their immediate ancestry back to at least one other country. According to figures from the 2011 population census (Australian Bureau of Statistics, 2012a, 2012b), and just 223 years after British colonization, Australia has a 97.5 per cent non-indigenous and hence immigrant population and 46 per cent of these are first- or second-generation immigrants. As a direct consequence of colonization, Indigenous Australians now comprise a mere 2.5 per cent of the total population in their own land. Tracing a lineage through hundreds of different Indigenous language groups across the country, Indigenous Australians are the descendants of the world's oldest living cultures. According to the palaeontologists, their ancestors have been living on this island continent for at least the last 50,000 years. According to their own oral histories, Aboriginal people have always been and will always be this country's traditional owners and custodians, a legal fact that has only recently been recognized by the Australian government in the Native Title Act (1993). Notwithstanding this belated legal recognition, for millennia this country has been inscribed by the traditional stories and shaped by the traditional practices of its original pre-colonial inhabitants, and according to their own stories, *the country, in turn has shaped them* (Rose, 2000, 2002, 2004; Rubuntja and Green, 2002; Turner, 2010). The specific Australian child–animal common worlds that I reconfigure in this chapter are constituted by these national demographics, entangled Indigenous/non-indigenous geo-histories, contested post-colonial politics of belonging, and by the county itself, with all its living and non-living entities, including the animals.

Animal–human entwined lives: The Australian story

Both prior to and ever since colonization, Australian animals have been entwined with humans in the life and death embodied relations of cohabiting – of living (surviving, eating) and killing (or being killed). As ethnographer Levi-Strauss once famously observed and Franklin (2006: 6) reiterates, 'animals are not only good to eat, they are "good to think with"', so Australian animals, like all others, have also been of key symbolic significance to us humans (Aboriginal and immigrant). Not only do most of us eat them and live with them, but we also use them to think about who we are and where we fit (see also Oliver, 2009). Accordingly, since colonization, Australian animals have centrally figured within the fraught, contested and often contradictory post-colonial politics of belonging. In the earliest days of the colonial invasion and encounter, otherwise known as 'discovery', Australian animals were measured against the established Linnaean system of classification as soon as the British colonists set eyes on them.

Confoundingly, they did not fit within any of the established categories. Mammals with pouches (koalas, possums, kangaroos, wallabies and wombats) were weird enough, but some of these even hopped on two legs, and the hybrid mammalian, egg-laying, duck-billed (platypus) and spikey (echidna) creatures were completely baffling. These unintelligible animals, which did not resemble any of the familiar northern hemisphere species, immediately gained the reputation of being exotic oddities, 'freaks of nature' (Franklin, 2006: 26) and inferior aberrations. Upon visiting the colonies to see these unruly natures for himself, the great evolutionary theorist, Charles Darwin, wrote: 'A disbeliever in everything beyond his own reason might exclaim: "surely two distinct creators must have been at work"' (Darwin, 1836, cited in Franklin, 2006: 26).

In his detailed study of animals in the project of Australian nation building, Adrian Franklin (2006) connects the colonists' derisions of the newly 'discovered' misfit animals with the stigma of the penal colony.

> Australian animals that existed outside of European taxonomic conventions seemed conveniently to mirror the 'reject', 'deviant' and 'undeserving' status of the convict colony, and such thoughts encouraged the notion of Australia as a failed experiment of the Great Creator, or even a poorly realised afterthought.
>
> (2006: 26)

Further and more explicit connections can be made between the colonists' low regard for these 'torpid, senseless creatures' (Perry, 1811, cited in Franklin, 2006: 36) and their disconcertion with the original human inhabitants – who were widely regarded as belonging to some kind of subhuman 'missing link' racial category, positioned somewhere between the primate animal and human worlds and destined, therefore, for extinction (see Anderson, 2007).

In considering the material and semiotic significance of Australian animals within the unfolding nineteenth-century colonial geo-historical events, I stress the mutually determining entanglements of human–animal and Aboriginal–immigrant relations. It is possible to trace these interconnections by following any of the threads, but I start here with the very knotty thread of Aboriginal dispossession via the British colonial legal fiction of 'terra nullius' – or land belonging to no one. This legal fiction justified the physical removal of Aboriginal people from their (unrecognized) traditional lands, and steadily opened up the country for the great colonial land grab of the British (settler) immigrants. Land grants were forthcoming for 'free settlers' and convicts with 'tickets of leave', but were conditional upon the clearing and fencing of the country. So settler immigrants steadily replaced the native trees, shrubs and grasses with the imported pastures that were palatable to the European sheep and cattle that they brought with them. These rich new pastures, in turn, attracted increasing numbers of native grazing animals – such as kangaroos, wallabies and emus. As Aboriginal people were systematically purged from the encroaching frontier (either killed by the settlers, or European diseases, or removed to missions and reserves), these native animal populations ceased to be monitored and controlled by traditional burning and hunting practices. The rapidly multiplying 'freakish' native animals, but in particular the grass-loving and fence-hopping kangaroos, were quickly declared to be 'vermin' (a reputation they still hold in many parts of rural Australia), as they were seen as the main grazing competitors of the European livestock and hence a threat to the survival of the settler immigrants. Native animals had always been hunted – either for 'sport', food, or their skins – but the mass slaughter of these despised native animals climaxed by the end of the nineteenth century when the NSW Pastures and Stock Protection Act of 1882 called for the 'destruction' of kangaroos and other grass-eating marsupials thgough ambushing 'kangaroo drives' and mass poisonings (Dawson, 1995: 148).

By the early twentieth century, Aboriginal–settler and human–animal relations were reconstellating around a shifting material–semiotic landscape. In 1901, the colonies became states within a rapidly urbanizing and newly federated Australian nation. As one of its first pieces of legislation, the new federal parliament passed the Immigration Restriction Act (1901) to ensure 'the purity of the white Australian race', effectively establishing a white Australia policy that was not superseded until the early 1970s (Anderson and Taylor, 2005). In line with the white Australian policy, Aboriginal people were explicitly excluded from the nation's constitution, and were not to gain citizenship in their own country for another six decades. This legally secured the complete exclusion of Aboriginal people from 'white' Australia, having already been physically segregated from the main areas of settlement by their internment on remote missions and reserves. In the most highly populated areas, Aboriginal people were literally 'out of sight' and 'out of mind' of the brave new nation and its 100 per cent 'white settler' (immigrant) citizenry.

Native animals, on the other hand, began to attain new profile and status in the recently constituted nation (albeit not fully embraced in all sectors). They were, as Franklin (2006: 138) puts it, effectively 'enrolled … into the constitution of Australia itself'. This favourable foregrounding of (assumed to be simple and innocent) Australian animals also coincided with the backgrounding of disenfranchized (and by now conveniently absented) Indigenous Australian people. In 1908, the kangaroo and the emu took pride of place on the Australian Coat of Arms – symbolically conferring native status to this new, 'white' Commonwealth nation. Even as bush-dwelling or rural (white settler) Australians continued to hunt down, shoot, trap, poison and fence out the kangaroos, emus, wallabies, possums and wombats (all classified as 'vermin' until well into the late twentieth century), these same Australian native animals were rapidly becoming the symbolic sentimental focus for the newly constituted nation. Franklin (2006) points out that this was the moment at which 'bushland creatures' became the 'metaphors and metonyms for Australia' (2006: 114), 'conservation-mindedness for indigenous species' began to be linked with 'good citizenship' (2006: 113), and native animals themes started to emerge as a form of nationalism in Australian children's literature.

The emerging body of early twentieth-century Australian children's literature enthusiastically embraced the role of fostering the national identity of the first generation of young (immigrant) white Australians, and of cultivating them as worthy Australian citizens. For the first time, Australian children's narratives were based on securing their close identification with the distinctive Australian flora and fauna, in addition to the farmhouse (European) gardens, dogs, horses and sheep that featured in the bush legendary of colonial art and literature. No longer cast as 'freaks of nature' (Franklin, 2006: 26), Australian plants and animals were sentimentally portrayed as cute, loveable and proud mascots of authentically Australia childhoods. By identifying Australian childhoods with native plants and animals, children were encouraged to think differently about their relationships to and responsibilities for the Australian bush. Often this was quite explicit. For example, in her preface to the enduring Australian children's classic, *Snugglepot and Cuddlepie*, which features the bush adventures of flowering gum nut baby characters, author May Gibbs (1918) pleads, 'Humans, Please be kind to all Bush creatures and don't pull flowers up by the roots.' And, of course, Ethel Pedley's (1997 (1906)) story of *Dot and the Kangaroo*, which I discussed in some detail in Chapter 2, is overtly structured around an environmental stewardship agenda, as encapsulated in her preface: 'To the children of Australia in the hope of enlisting their sympathies for the many beautiful, amiable and frolicsome creatures of their fair land, whose extinction, through ruthless destruction, is being surely accomplished.'

Now that I have offered a snapshot of entangled post-colonial Australian relations, it is time to turn to my collection of child–animal stories and to reconfigure some of the co-shaped child–animal geo-histories that make up these worlds. Far from generic or generalizable, these are very *situated* stories that grapple with ordinary encounters between sometimes unlikely (queer kin) child–animal partners in distinctive circumstances. These child–animal imbroglios carry high stakes. They highlight the importance of learning how to inherit in the *post-colonial* Australian settler-immigrant and indigenous common worlds that I have just outlined, by facing 'the living – and killing – past … in order to take the present serious, [and] in order to be able to move toward multi-species [Indigenous and non-indigenous] reconciliation' (Haraway, 2011: 106).

Yeperenye childhoods

The Yeperenye childhood stories that I recount here include both pre-colonial Aboriginal Dreaming (or creation) stories, and embroiled post-colonial Aboriginal and non-indigenous stories. Both sets of stories are past-present stories of inheritance that shape the lives of the Yeperenye children of Mparntwe, or Alice Springs, in the Northern Territory of Australia. Recounted together, these pre- and post-colonial stories bear witness to colonization's profound effects upon Yeperenye children and offer a window into their complexly layered common worlds.

The child–animal relations within the Yeperenye Dreaming stories are of a radically different kind to those considered by Meyers (1998) and Melson (2005). They bear no resemblance to western child-centred stories that feature (often sentimentalized) children's relationships with animals. Dreaming stories are inherited Aboriginal 'culture country' stories (Rubuntja, in Rubuntja and Green, 2002: 161), handed down from generation to generation through oral storytelling, song, dance and artworks. They explain how all the different parts of the country and its inhabitants (humans, mountains, rocks, rivers, plants and animals) came into being. No two Dreaming stories are the same, because they relay the defining totemic relations and characteristics of particular places. However, they do share common forms, purposes and themes. Like all other Dreaming stories, the Ayeparenye[1] Altyerre – or Yeperenye Dreaming stories – articulate a relational ontology, within which the very *being* of Yeperenye children and animals is co-determined within a natureculture imbroglio, and is inseparable from the country (see also Rose (2000), *Dingo Makes Us Human*).

Yeperenye Dreaming stories belong to and emanate from Mparntwe country. This is red desert country in the geographical centre of Australia, flanked by the imposing rocky escarpments of the ancient MacDonnell Ranges. Mparntwe is midway along these ranges, which run in an east–west direction for over 600 kilometres. The West MacDonnell National Park, abutting Alice Springs, is an international tourist destination, renowned for its spectacular rocky-red chasms and gorges and deep water holes. The other major landform in Mparntwe country is Lhere Mparntwe (otherwise known as the Todd River) – a usually dry river that cuts through a gap in the ranges at a place called Ntaripe (or Heavitree Gap). 'The Gap' (as it is locally known) also functions as the southern road and rail entry point into the township of Alice Springs.

For millennia, Yeperenye Dreaming stories have been passed between the custodians of Mparntwe country – the Central Arrernte people – and other

Figure 5.1 Mparntwe Country. 'I love living in Alice Springs. See these hills. That's the Yeperenye Dreaming.' Shanika Cole from *Listen Up* (2012). Image by Dylan McDonald. Reproduced by permission of CAAMA Productions.

Indigenous groups in this Central Desert region. They are stories of 'culture country' continuity. By contrast, the relatively recent post-colonial stories of Yeperenye children are modern survival stories, in the face of dispossession and dispersal. They are the product of hugely impactful colonial encounters and ongoing and fraught post-colonial relations between the custodial Arrernte people and the Indigenous and non-indigenous immigrants to Mparntwe country. My life story first intersected with these Yeperenye stories in the mid-1980s. At this time, I had come to Alice Springs to work as a teacher. My employers were the local Arrernte council of elders, who set up Yipirinya School in the late 1970s to cater for the Aboriginal town camp children who were not receiving any schooling at that time. Yipirinya School is still operating and is still run by a council of local Aboriginal elders (Yipirinya School Council, 2012), although most of the founding elders that I worked with have now passed away and the culture programme has been significantly reduced and adversely affected by funding cuts (Rhonda Inkamala,[2] 2012, personal communication).

Almost nothing that I learnt in my teacher education course back on the east coast was relevant to the task of teaching at Yipirinya School. Although I had a strong sense of myself as a political ally in a starkly racialized and often violently racist town, my initial ignorance about this resolutely relational (human and more-than-human) Arrernte world made it almost impossible to be an effective teacher. I had an enormous amount to learn. My struggles to understand the significance of these complex relations quickly unravelled any western conceits I may have held about the universality of the individual child, the appropriateness of child-centred learning and the panacea of catering for children's individual learning needs. It was only due to the patient perseverance of my Arrernte mentors,[3] who inducted me into the layered meanings of 'two way learning', that I managed to gain any insight into this inherently relational world, in which 'Country is nothing else but culture' (Rubuntja, in Rubuntja and Green, 2002: 161) and the source of children's collective identities and kin relations.

As a direct consequence of the (white) settlement of the Alice Springs region, there has been a steady loss of cultural practice and knowledge associated with the Yeperenye Dreaming story. Instead of being regularly enacted through customary ritual practice, the totemic Yeperenye caterpillar has become a memorialized figure in the township of Alice Springs. In the public domain, it has become a kind of town mascot. Yeperenye is the name of the main shopping mall and the tourist industry-sponsored 'Grand Circle Yeperenye' is a giant metal sculpture in the arts precinct. The big Yeperenye sculpture now functions as an Aboriginal tourist monument, but was designed and constructed as a community arts project involving key local Arrernte elders and the children from Yipirinya School. The elders' and children's narratives and artworks adorn the inside of the structure, telling the travel stories of three different kinds of caterpillars that converged on Mparntwe from the north, south, east and west, creating the landforms (the ranges, the nearby waterholes) as well as the rocks, trees and the people of Mparntwe. Mparntwe is described in the signage (by an unnamed

Figure 5.2 Yeperenye Sculpture, Araluen Art Centre, Alice Springs. Author's photograph.

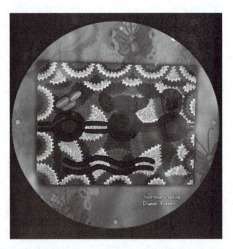

Figure 5.3 Dianne Furber's Yeperenye Dreaming painting on inside of Yeperenye sculpture. Author's photograph.

author) as 'the epicentre of caterpillar culture'. However, the focus is upon the main protagonists – the Yeperenye caterpillars who belong to the ayepe vine (or sticky tarvine) of Mparntwe. As one of the founding elders of Yipirinya School, Kwementyaye[4] E. Rubuntja explains (on the signage), 'Arenye means belong. Ayepe – arenye.' He also refers to the ways in which this Yeperenye belonging story has been passed on from generation to generation: 'People got to tell him and sing him. How they travel.'

The Yeperenye sculpture is one kind of telling – specifically designed to welcome tourists to Mparntwe country and to educate them about the significance of the totemic Yeperenye caterpillar. An unnamed traditional owner on the Yeperenye sculpture signage reassures the visitors that the story itself has not been erased with the building of Alice Springs township: 'the story is still here. Under the houses the same story from the old people. From the beginning.' But elders do worry that if the story is not properly passed on to Yeperenye children, it might eventually become dormant: 'This story ... must be kept for the future ... so all the grandchildren can get the proper true story' (Rubuntja, in Rubuntja and Green, 2002: vii). They worry that without enough knowledge of this story, Yeperenye children might lose their all-important connections with country and their full sense of 'ayepe – arenye' – their caterpillar belonging.

In *The Town Grew Up Dancing* (Rubuntja and Green, 2002), the prominent Arrernte lore man[5] and artist, Kwementyaye W. Rubuntja, provides a window into the ways in which the Ayeparenye Altyerre was passed on to him through regular ritual practice. He recounts memories of his childhood, growing up in the township of Alice Springs in the early twentieth century:

> ... lots of people used to come in from all over the place. Different languages ... They used to worship the little *ayeparenye* caterpillar all the time. They used to worship them... They danced the *altherte* for the *ayeparenye* caterpillar. The *arntalye – arntalye*. That *altherte* ceremony belonged to Mparntwe – *arenye* people [Alice Springs people] ... When we were small ones we used to dance. The little boys danced – and when the little girls danced they would really go for it ...

> (2002: 48)

Having been actively involved in Ayeparenye ceremonies in his childhood, Kwementyaye W. Rubuntja not only had a keen sense of the spiritual significance of this Dreaming story, but was able to provide intricate details about the routes that the ancestral Yeperenye caterpillars travelled and the exact geophysical features that they created in the Mparntwe landscape (see also Brookes, 2007). In this abridged excerpt from his book, it is still possible to get a sense of the intricate knowledge about the Yeperenye story that was passed on to him from childhood:

> ... the *ayeparenye* caterpillar was always in Mparntwe country. That *ayeparenye* caterpillar came straight from Urlatherrke ... and went straight to Anthwerrke ... It climbed in this direction, then others came from Arturle to Thararle Tneme ... All of those shady river trees ... are another group of *ayeparenye* caterpillars ... They came from Apmakwend ... From there to Mpwetyerre – where there is that little rock lying there, where the Casino is built ... The *ayeparenye* went past two sand hills and then they went towards Heavitree Gap, where the *ayeparenye* beetle was. The *arlperenye* beetle

[stinky green beetle] chopped [all their heads off], and then they went on to Apanparle-irreke … That's why it's everybody's four corners, everybody's four corners.

(Rubuntja, in Rubuntja and Green, 2002: 156)

Kwementyaye W. Rubuntja stresses that the Yeperenye Dreaming is one of convergence, that it brings different people together – 'everybody's four corners'. As well as being a story of converging caterpillar ancestors, the 'four corners' is also a reference to the Arrernte kinship system, which is based upon two intergenerational groups (moieties), each of which contains four skin groups. All Yeperenye children belong to a skin group as well as carrying the Yeperenye totem, and these 'belongings' are interconnected. The kinship relations not only determine the forms and patterns of *social* relationships and responsibilities, but also establish patterns of responsibility for particular parts of the *country* (Rubuntja and Green, 2002: 162).

In Arrernte onto-epistemologies, even though children are recognized as having distinctive personalities, this is always mediated through the 'acts of relatedness' that they must practice within a dense field of kinship relations (Austin-Broos, 2009: 159–65). As well as ensuring children's collective sense of identity and belonging, kinship relations must be acted upon. It is never just a matter of children *being* themselves, and expressing their individuality as encouraged in western societies. The emphasis is on them learning how to *practise* who they are within the collective and complex set of reciprocal relations and responsibilities that they inherit along with their skin group. The 'growing up' of children, which is often seen to be the primary responsibility of the grand-parent generation (the other moiety), not only involves teaching children where they fit in, but also how to act in order to take care of the kinship world that they inherit. It is the very *practice* of 'ayepe – arenye', or belonging to totemic Yeperenye country, that is under threat in the contemporary lives of Yeperenye children. This was one of the most compelling reasons for providing 'two-way learning' at Yipirinya School.

In the late 1980s, a mural of Yeperenye children and their Arrernte elders was painted on the entrance wall to the newly-built Yipirinya School. It represents an ideal imaginary of Yeperenye children's past-present post-colonial common worlds, blending ancient Aboriginal cultural lore and practices with contemporary western knowledge and technologies. The images of Yeperenye children contemporaneously belonging to traditional and modern culture signify the 'two-way learning' philosophy that underpins the school's curriculum (Yipirinya School Council, 2012). In more general terms, these images bear witness to what anthropologist Diane Austin-Broos (2009: 265) describes as the 'shifting imaginaries' of Arrernte people as they negotiate the possibilities of '"hunter-gatherer" modernity'. The mural co-locates the elders (or grandparents) with Yeperenye children at this site of learning – indicating the pedagogical importance of alternate generation kinship relations and the pedagogical significance

Figure 5.4 Yipirinya School mural, Alice Springs. Author's photograph.

of past-presents. It clearly situates both generations (moieties) of Yeperenye children and elders within this red desert Mparntwe country. It shows how Yeperenye childhoods are temporally and spatially interconnected worlds in which the entwined responsibilities for inherited kinship and country must somehow coexist with the learning of whitefella culture.

In order to bring these aspirational 'two-way' worlds into being, it is critical for Arrernte people to be able to imagine or dream up '"hunter-gatherer" modernity'. Dreaming always has its present performative aspects as well as its originary pasts. Materializing the 'two-way' dream was Yipirinya School's original mission. But it is also incredibly hard to realize. For as well as inheriting ancient cultural traditions and stories that connect them to the ancestral caterpillars of Mparntwe country, Yeperenye children have also inherited the devastating colonialist legacies of racism, dispossession, welfare dependence and, in the worst cases, complete social anomie. Such crippling legacies threaten their full enculturation into their Yeperenye Dreaming, as well as making their whitefella education and acculturation a daunting task.

Moreover, there is very little that is ideal about the modern world that Yeperenye children now inhabit. Most Yeperenye children live on the urban fringes in the town camps of Alice Springs, where the locational marginality mirrors their cultural marginality from both traditional Aboriginal and modern western worlds. The actualities of Yeperenye children's common worlds are far removed from Rousseau's romantic fantasies of noble savagery and New-Ageist appropriative interests in 'authentic' spiritual wisdom. They are in-between worlds, where the stressful everyday realities of belonging to a small and vulnerable group of disenfranchised people are most acutely felt.

The town camps are an historical phenomenon associated with the earliest days of colonial settlement of Alice Springs and notorious for their overcrowding, material squalor and alcohol-related violence. From the beginning, these camps have been reviled by the white settler community as an eyesore and a public disgrace, and there have been many unsuccessful attempts to disband, demolish and relocate them (Coughlan, 1991). These efforts came to a climax in 2007, when the Alice Springs town camps were targeted as key sites within the Australian government's 'Northern Territory Emergency Response Intervention'. This full-scale mobilization (involving the Australian army) to 'stabilise and normalise' Aboriginal communities was taken in response to allegations of child sexual abuse within the *Little Children are Sacred* report (Anderson and Wild, 2007). This 'Intervention' still continues, and is highly controversial in the affected Aboriginal communities, as well as in the public debate involving both Indigenous and non-indigenous commentators (see Altman and Hinkson, 2010).

Central Arrernte people have always lived in and around Mparntwe country and Aboriginal people from other parts of Central Australia have always been regular visitors to this country for Yeperenye ceremonies. This pattern began to change in the late nineteenth century, when Alice Springs was first established as a remote telegraph station and a service centre for the outback pastoral industry. At this time, Aboriginal people from other areas started to set up camps in and around the township. Most of them came to Alice Springs seeking 'rations' in exchange for labour, when their hunting and gathering practices on the pastoral stations were no longer sustainable (Coughlan, 1991; Rubuntja and Green, 2002). Until the 1960s, Alice Springs town camps were also impacted by the policy of forced removal of Aboriginal children of mixed descent from their families and placement in 'half-caste institutions'. These children are often referred to as the 'stolen generations', and many now regard this forced assimi-lation policy as a strategic form of cultural genocide (Van Krieken, 1999). In the Central Australian area, 'stolen generation' children were taken to Alice Springs and placed in a 'half-caste' home for children called the Bungalow (MacDonald, 1995). This in turn led to increasing numbers of Aboriginal families moving into the town camps to be close to their children. As a result, Yeperenye children are quite a mixed-up bunch – or in Kwementyaye W. Rubuntja's (2002: 49) words, they are 'mixed up together just like spiders and ants and flies and all'. All of these post-colonial migrations add yet another historical layer to the Yeperenye story of convergences upon Mparntwe from the 'four corners'.

The removal of Aboriginal children from their families did not stop at the end of the forced removal era. In 2010, the national rate of Indigenous Australian children in out-of-home care was nearly ten times the rate of non-indigenous children, and in the Northern Territory (the location of Alice Springs), close to 75 per cent of children in care were Indigenous children (Australian Institute of Health and Welfare, 2011: 54). The main difference in recent years is that the removals are based on 'at risk' assessments, and as far as possible, Indigenous children are placed in nearby Indigenous families and communities.

Such is the story of seven-year-old Ricco Japaljarri Martin, which is told in the documentary *Wirriya: Small Boy* by Aboriginal film-maker Beck Cole (2004).

Figure 5.5 Ricco Japaljarri Martin at Hidden Valley Town Camp, 2004.
Photograph by Beck Cole. Reproduced by permission of Beck Cole
and CAAMA Productions.

Ricco is a Warlpiri boy, originally from Tennant Creek (north of Alice Springs), but who came to live in Hidden Valley town camp, on the outskirts of Alice Springs when 'the Welfare' took him away from his mother and gave him to one of the grandmothers who often take in foster children. After introducing his nine dogs by name, Ricco introduces his foster mother as his 'nanna' and his 'three sisters' (none of them blood relatives). He has only good things to say about his family: 'They're helpful. They share, you know. Share a feed.' And his nanna confirms: 'We just all mixed up tribe living here. We just live together, friendly way.' This is not an unusual situation, as she notes: 'There's a lot of grandmothers looking after children. Yeah. Big problem.' Ricco says he has no story to tell about his mother, but his nanna tells the story of Ricco's mother drinking and fighting with her boyfriend, and Ricco laying on top of his mother to protect her from being killed: ' "Leave my mother alone, leave my mother alone. You kill me too," he said.' Ricco's nanna describes him as 'clever boy' and we see him going to Yipirinya School. He is an enthusiastic learner, who is interested in other countries as well as his own. He goes to Warlpiri language and culture classes to learn more about his skin group. Ricco wants to get an education so he can work when he grows up and care for his nanna. He wants to be a policeman, so he can 'lock up all those people' who are fighting, 'those drunken people'. The only thing he does not like about school is when the teacher 'growls' at him. I'm not a 'naughty boy' he insists. Sometimes he skips school with his older sisters, despite his nanna's frustrated efforts to convince him that he should go every day.

Ricco's dogs seem to be particularly important to him and he is proud of the fact that he looks after them so well. He also loves to go hunting for lizards in the hills behind the camp. He is looking forward to being old enough to 'be a gun shooter' like his uncle and 'go for kangaroo'. Aboriginal people have always kept dogs – as companions, for hunting and for keeping warm in the cold desert nights (Wingfield and Austin, 2009: 14). Dogs are especially prized if they are good hunters. Eastern Arrernte elder M. K. Turner likens dogs to guns – 'only better, because they knew how to catch a goanna or a perentie, without ripping anything, without tearing them apart' (2010: 168). All animals have Dreamings too and must be treated with respect. Even those that are eaten, like kangaroos, emus and lizards must be talked about 'the right way ... then they're satisfied' (Wingfield and Austin, 2009: viii). As well as the Yeperenye Dreaming, there is also a Dog Dreaming associated with Alice Springs, and some sacred dog sites around town that all the children at Yipirinya School know about. The fact that Mparntwe has a Dog Dreaming can make it hard to control dogs in the camps. Sometimes they get out of hand, they get 'cheeky' and attack people. They can also pose a health threat to the children when they pass on parasites and scabies.

In all their natureculture layerings of prosaic material and heightened symbolic significance, the child–animal relations in these Yeperenye stories cannot be separated from thinking, knowing and acting on a sense of relatedness. As M. K Turner puts it, 'we're part of the animals that live there, and birds ... We're part of the water there, we're part of the grasses, the medicines, the fruits' (2010: 114). Even the practice of eating animals cements these kin relations: 'The bush meat comes from the Land, and that was our meat [kere], and that kere is part of us ... We really relate to all those animals because they're part of us ...The eaters get eaten. That eats this and you eat that. Same like arrwe' [rock wallaby] (Turner, 2010: 165, 166). As well as serving to connect children to the ancient Dreaming past, Yeperenye child–animal relations are also firmly enmeshed within the violent post-colonial histories and reconfigured geographical presents that have brought extraordinary challenges to the disrupted and 'throwntogether' lives of Aboriginal children living in Mparntwe today. As a testament to the adaptive capacity of Arrernte culture, and hence to its survival, these same child–animal relations produce newly constellated kinship relations and contribute to the creation of continually reimagined past-present modern 'hunter gatherer' subjectivities, lifestyles and practices.

Common worlds of settler children and wombats

My common worlds story of immigrant settler child and wombats[6] begins in Micalong Creek – 2,500 kilometres from Mparntwe country. This is the place that I write this book. Micalong Creeks runs into the Goodradigbee River, in the Wee Jasper valley at the northern edge of Australia's high country in the south-east of the continent. It is not that far from Canberra, the national 'bush' capital of Australia. This is Ngunnawal country. Although there have not been any

Figure 5.6 The wombats of Micalong Creek. Artwork by Ruby Elliott. Reproduced with her permission.

Ngunnawal people living in the Wee Jasper area since the valley was cleared for farming in the mid to late nineteenth century, the Ngunnawal people and their ancestors have been the traditional custodians of this country for at least 50,000 years. For similar millennia, this hilly limestone and granite bushland country has been a bountiful home for the species *Vombatus Ursinus*.

The name given to this animal by the Ngunnawal people is no longer known, but since early colonial days, it has been commonly referred to as a wombat. Wombat is an English adaptation of a word from an Aboriginal language, but not from the Ngunnawal language. The accounts are sketchy, but it believed to have passed into the English language as 'whom-batt' via an ex-convict who lived with Indigenous people in the mountains west of Sydney (Simons, 2008: 14–15). The 'whom-batt' was described by the governor of the Sydney Cove settlement in 1798 as 'a large animal between a bear and a badger' (Hunter, cited by Woodford, 2001: 43), but it is, in fact, the world's largest burrowing marsupial and herbivore. Wombats are hefty vegetarians, weighing in at around 30–35kgs and measuring up to 1.4 metres long and 70cm high. They eat a lot of grass, do a lot of poos and dig very big burrows. They are different from other marsupials, as their pouch openings are reversed, making it possible for them to dig without burying their resident joeys. As the immigrant settlers were eventually to realize, there are three distinctive species of wombats, living in different parts of the country.

The wombats of Micalong Creek are of the Bare-nosed Wombat or Common Wombat variety, descendants of the giant marsupial mega fauna, Nototherium, that survived the Ice Age, and whose fossilized remains have been found in one of the local limestone caves (Barton, 2011: 320). With such deep-time ancestry, Common Wombats are indisputably the longest surviving permanent resident mammals of Micalong Creek and amazingly they are still very common. They flourish in this moist mountain river country, which is permanently dotted with their bountiful droppings – not so surprising once you know that one wombat averages 100 poos per night (French, 2005: 95). The country is also well marked by their mighty burrows. The wombats share their country with humans – with the campers who flock to the area for river camping, fishing, caving and bushwalking; with the local farmers; and with some semi-permanent bush dwellers, such as me.

Last year, during exceptionally wet weather, a very large wombat dug an equally large burrow under the shelter of my small raised house on the banks of Micalong Creek. Since then, we have been regular part-time cohabitants. My wombat messmate, like others of her species, is a secretive, solitary and nocturnal animal, so I rarely see her. But I constantly see the markings of her never-ending but impressive burrow extensions, the scratchings around her holes in the fence and the plentiful fresh droppings she leaves on top of small rocks and logs to mark her nightly passage around the neighbourhood and down to the creek. I also hear her 'hmmphing' grunts, her whining squeals, her scratchings and scrapings and I smell the pungent wombat aroma that wafts up from her burrow on a hot day. She has a very earthy presence, and as wombats rely heavily on their sense of smell, I am sure she is very familiar with my scent too.

My relatively new living arrangements kindled my curiosity about other wombat–settler relations in the local area. It turned out that many of my neighbours spend a considerable amount of time trying to stop wombats (with very little success) – to stop them from excavating under sheds and houses; to stop them from digging holes in their freshly ploughed paddocks; to stop them from wreaking havoc in the vegetable gardens; and to stop them from breaking through their rabbit-proof wire fences. The ancient wombats of Micalong Creek, as elsewhere in rural Australia, are most commonly referred to as 'mangy pests'. Not only are they widely regarded as destructive animals, but because they are not good to eat and their (often patchy) fur is bristly and not worth skinning, they are regarded as useless creatures, dead or alive. In fact, up until the mid-twentieth century, wombats were declared a 'noxious' species in many parts of the country and farmers were legally bound to kill them (Woodford, 2001: 188–9). In all areas they were routinely culled until declared a protected species in the early 1970s. However, farmers can still obtain licences to cull quotas of wombats as mitigation against property damage. In the Wee Jasper and Micalong Creek areas, present-day wombat killings, although no longer rife, are neither unheard of nor regarded as particularly out of the ordinary.

Since colonial days, children growing up in the Australian bush have not only lived in close companionship with many native and farm animals, but have been inducted into the practices of trapping, poisoning and shooting many of the local animals, including wombats. This is still the case in the relatively isolated

Wee Jasper valley (white settler) community, in which the business of multi-species cohabitation and subsistence living and dying is an unsentimental and unremarkable reality of everyday life. For generations, young children in this isolated mountain valley have routinely undertaken their share of animal 'chores', including milking cows, feeding chickens, ducks and lambs, collecting eggs and skinning rabbits (Barton, 2011: 151). But hunting has always been the stand-out favourite animal activity. All Wee Jasper children learn to fish as soon 'as they can hold a fishing rod', but I have also heard tales of young children hunting rabbits with ferrets and air-guns and of older children shooting foxes and wild pigs, even 'wrestling wombats' by hauling them out of their burrows.

Perhaps the most legendary story of real-life child–wombat encounters is that of the 'wombat boy' – Peter Nicholson – and the wombats of Taungurong country, which is recounted by James Woodford in *The Secret Life of Wombats* (2001). Peter grew up in Canberra in a family and community of high-profile Australian scientists. He first became interested in wombats as a young boy, when he saw them in the Brindabella Mountains that abut the Wee Jasper valley. But his intimate relationship with wombats flourished in 1960, when he was a young teenager attending Timbertop, a remote boarding school in the mountain ranges of north-east Victoria. It all started when Peter took to sneaking out of the dormitory at night to 'study' the wombats by exploring their burrows and tracking their nocturnal journeys across the high country.

At the time, there was almost no scientific knowledge about the underground life of wombats. This was possibly because no scientists had dared to climb down a wombat burrow, and the 'critter cams' that are used today had not been invented. Wombats are well known as fierce protectors of their underground lairs, especially when they have young, and have clawed and crushed to death many unfortunate dogs who have unwisely ventured into their holes. Incredibly, Peter spent hundreds of hours over a period of months crawling around in cold, dark wombat tunnels wearing his specially fortified wombat trousers, with a ball of string (to chart and measure his passage), a torch (to find his way) and a small shovel (to dig his way out of tricky situations). He was never attacked.

Although Peter was well schooled by his parents in the scientific practices of observation, measuring and recording, he taught himself the most important skill of all – how to practise wombat etiquette when entering wombat worlds. From his careful observations of the ways in which wombats greeted each other, he learnt how to mimic wombat calls – 'hhhmmmmpph, hhhhmmmmppph' – and he took pains to make a 'slow respectful approach' as he ventured into the burrows (Woodford, 2001: 20). In short, he learnt how to 'do' wombat. Schoolboy Peter wrote about his time underground with wombats:

> Soon I learned that they were usually friendly and very inquisitive but not until second term did I start in earnest to try to make friends with one. I picked a fairly young wombat and spent an hour each day with it. This time was never wasted as he usually gave me some demonstration of

digging or burrow life. I always had a torch with me but never pointed it directly at him ... For quite long periods the torch was off so that he could examine me. Occasionally he would come up to me and sniff my arms and examine my face and hair inquisitively while I imitated his friendly grunt ... you cannot say positively what such an intelligent animal will do. He will have certain habits but, as he is at least as intelligent as a dog, he is unpredictable ... After about three months of knowing me he followed me out of the burrow as I was leaving it. I sat down near his sit and he in it. The day was overcast and very dull. He then came up to me and examined me very closely, putting his forepaws on my legs and sniffing up and down my legs. After this he would usually follow me out on a dull day. I never attempted to feed him and it seemed he was only inquisitive. He gave the impression of being an intelligent, one-track-mind person. He used to love to be scratched.

(Nicholson, cited in Woodford, 2001: 31, 32, 37)

Convivial human–wombat interspecies friendships such as these are rare but not unknown (see French, 2005; Plumwood, 2005). However, there are no others that I know of that have been forged underground – inside wombat terrain, so to speak – and on wombat terms. In the earliest possible sense, young Peter's and the wombat's most unusual 'dance of encounters' offer a vignette of immigrant child and nonhuman animal 'become worldly with' each other, as Haraway (2008a: 3–4) might say. Put simply, Peter and the wombat reshaped each other's lives, they made each other different, they expanded each other's worlds. Not only can we characterize Peter as a 'wombat boy', but if we take account of these relational encounters as mutual ontological acts, we can regard the young wombat 'that loved to be scratched' as a 'boy wombat'. This 'real' queer kin story shows us that it is possible for human nature and wombat nature to be experienced as an interspecies relationship.

As an addendum to this story, with his parent's encouragement, Peter wrote up his study and it was published in a scientific journal in 1961, when he was just 15 years old. It remains the only one of its kind and has attained a kind of cult status. Nicolson's article is still regularly cited by those who study wombats, including Barbara Trigg, one of Australia's foremost wombat 'experts' (Trigg, 1988). She refers to Nicholson's work as 'one of the most useful "in depth" studies of wombats that has been published' (Trigg, 1988, cited in Woodford, 2001: 30). Interestingly, its usefulness and depth is built upon its queer kin relational integrity as much as, if not more than, the validity of its 'objective' scientific observations and measurements.

For a number of reasons, Peter Nicholson's wombat encounters were quite exceptional. The majority of immigrant/settler Australians never cross paths with a live wombat, and if they do, it is most likely to be at the wildlife park or the zoo. Even though wombat markings on the landscape continue to pose a 'problem' for many farmers, and the occasional wombat is sighted by human campers and

Figure 5.7 Wombat road-kill event. Photograph by Miriam Giugni. Reproduced with her permission.

rural dwellers while out on its nightly forays, by and large they remain elusive animals. Sadly, most human–wombat encounters are fleeting but deadly events. They are most likely to occur when night drivers run over and kill wombats that are grazing on the verges of country roads, or when day-time motorists speed past their roadside carcasses. These grizzly road-kill events are the most common of all settler–wombat encounters.

In sharp contrast to the harsh reality of real-life road-kill encounters, and to their unsentimental reputation as useless 'mangy pests' within many rural bush communities, in the sanitized white settler national imaginary wombats occupy a benign and affectionate space that is closely aligned with a nostalgic regard for Australian childhoods. This is not because many immigrant Australian children are likely to have formed convivial relationships with real-life wombats (like Peter Nicholson did) but because wombats are easy to caricature as harmless and unsophisticated animal characters – and thus seen as perfect literary companions for innocent children. Comical, anthropomorphized and bear-like wombat characters abound in Australian children's literature. The most famous of these is Ruth Park's (1994 (1962)) red-coated 'muddle headed wombat'. There is even a Wee Jasper wombat children's picture book story, called *Wombat Pooh* (Barton, 2012), that tells the story of the elusive wombat, whose droppings are everywhere, but is never actually seen. These loveable wombat characters (some of which bear an uncanny resemblance to Winnie-the-Pooh, Paddington Bear or Yogi Bear) also perpetuate the animal nation theme that promotes the national identification and naturalization of immigrant Australian children.

Figures 5.8 and 5.9 Dairy of a Wombat. Illustrations by Bruce Whatley, author Jackie French. Reproduced by permission of HarperCollins Publishers.

Diary of a Wombat is a wombat children's story of a somewhat different ilk. It is a co-production of wombat–immigrant human convivial, if at times testing, relations. Not only was it written by Jackie French (2002), but as she puts it, it was written 'with wombats as my muse' (French, 2005: 155). The story is based on French's real-life experiences of cohabiting with many Common Wombats, including Mothball, the main character in this book (French, 2005, 2011). The story details a week in Mothball's life. Mothball is a cute and very determined wombat, whose daily routines of sleeping, scratching, eating and digging are conducted at very close quarters with a human family. French and illustrator Bruce Whatley humorously convey the ways in which the wombat seeks to train its humans to feed it more carrots, and conversely, how Mothball's entrenched digging and scratching habits simultaneously amuse, inconvenience and infuriate her human companions.

More often than not, wombats that hang around humans are the grown up progeny of road-kill victims. Taken from their dead mother's pouches as small joeys, they are reared by human 'wildlife rescuers' and released back into their bush habitats when grown. However, not all of the released wombats make a complete transition. Having been fed by humans, some habituated wombats develop an appetite beyond their staple native grasses and seek out human companionship. Like Mothball, they prefer to stay close to the human source of provision – the vegetable garden and the farmhouse kitchen. Wildlife rescue wombats battering down kitchen doors for carrots give a whole new meaning to the concept of 'pester power', and wombats digging burrows under humans' houses puts a whole new slant on 'moving back in' not to mention 'co-sleeping'.

Notwithstanding its whimsical appeal, *Diary of a Wombat* is more than an innocent tale of a cute wombat. It is not like the more standard children's stories that feature anthropomorphized wombats doubling as infantilized humans in furry suits. And it is definitely not a domestication story that celebrates human mastery of nature. It is a common worlds queer kin story of knotty wombat–immigrant coexistence of an unexpected and opportunistic kind. It is a post-colonial story about cross-species relational grapplings that are the direct consequence of immigrant/settler practices that disturb and endanger wombats' lives. By offering children the paradoxically mundane, yet unusual, details of such daily wombat–human grapplings, this story also prompts them to ask 'What else is going on here?' It encourages curiosity about the specific circumstances that bring wombats and humans together as hybridized families or queer kin in the first place. It creates a space for children to think about how they live with the differences of more-than-human others in their own common worlds.

Like Nicolson, French (2005) acknowledges how much she has learned from her relationship with wombats and being privy to their 'secret world'. In fact she claims that 'everything I know in life I owe to wombats' (2005: 165). From this basis, and in the tradition of posing Australian animals as mentors for immigrant Australian children, which Ethel Pedley (1997 (1906)) set a century earlier in *Dot and the Kangaroo*, French offers her wombat-gleaned wisdom to Australian children: 'be determined ... be *very* determined ... know your land, and love it'. She goes on to elaborate: 'When a wombat "sees" the land, it can smell yesterday as well as today ... and maybe last year, too. Try to see the world like a wombat does. Know your land well enough to look at the past and try to see the future too' (2005: 165). This is advice that some immigrant Australian adults might also well heed.

By paying particular attention to the past and the future, my final post-colonial immigrant child–wombat common worlds tale of unexpected kin and kind poses many serious questions, grapplings and ethical dilemmas. It features a young human child from the 'technoculture generation', a 'speculative confabulation' (Haraway, 2011) or chimeric creature (Orgaz and Piccinini, 2007) and *Lasiorhinus Kreftii*, the Northern Hairy-nosed Wombat. However, it also evokes the carnage of colonization, the work of human wildlife rescuers and the everyday realities of rural children's animal cohabitations in which 'human and non-human ways of living and dying are at stake' (Haraway, 2008a: 295). It is the creation of Patricia Piccinini, a high-profile Australian artist, whose provocative work has pushed me to think hard about the connections between wombat–settler relations, Australian children and the ethics and politics of common worlds inheritance, kinship and cohabitation that are my central concern.

'Undivided' is a hyperrealist figurate silicon sculptural installation made by Piccinini in 2004, as part of a larger exhibition called 'Natures Little Helpers' (Piccinini, 2012). The material semiotics of this installation narrate a poignant scene of cohabiting multispecies difference – of a young settler-descendent human child curled up asleep in a blue-sheeted bed with an older sci-fi non-human, but strangely humanoid, creature. The child and creature are cupped closely together, suggestive of a tranquil, close and nurturing relationship. The child is wearing starry blue pajamas and the creature is bare. The faces of both human child and enigmatic creature are very peaceful. The combination of their very differently aged and formed bodies and their physical closeness evokes what

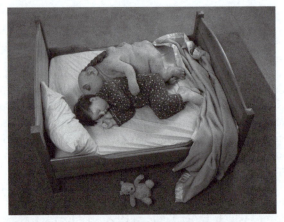

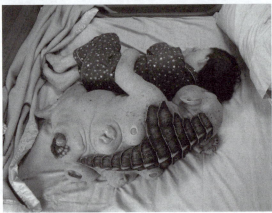

Figures 5.10 and 5.11 Undivided. 2004 Silicone, fibreglass, human hair, flannelette, mixed medium. 101 x 74 x 127 cm. Courtesy of the artist, Haunch of Venison, Tolarno Galleries and Roslyn Oxley9 Gallery. Photographer Graham Baring.

Piccinini describes as a deliberatively 'strange combination of innocence and disquiet' (in Orgaz and Piccinini, 2007).

The technoculture creature is called Surrogate and is one of a number of helper creatures from Piccinini's 'Natures Little Helpers' series. Surrogate is helping nature by gestating and suckling three pairs of Northern Hairy-nosed Wombat joeys in two rows of parallel dorsal pouches running down the spine of her armour-plated back. The joeys are at different stages of development. The smallest pair, in the two highest pouches, are still foetal. Below them nestle a pair of slightly larger, but still hairless, joeys. The two largest furry wombat joeys are popping out of the lowest pouches. They appear to be capable of living independent lives and to be on the brink of leaving the pouch.

The Northern Hairy-nosed Wombat is one of the most vulnerable and endangered mammal species on earth. In fact, there are only about 25 breeding females left. The surviving members all live in Epping Forest National Park in central Queensland, a dedicated sanctuary that has been fenced off to protect the wombats from dingo predators (Woodford, 2001) However, it was not the dingos that originally triggered the chain of events that resulted in these marsupials facing extinction. It was the early immigrant settler colonists, who planted African buffel grass to feed their sheep and cattle, and introduced pasture that rapidly invaded the native grasslands that for countless millennia had sustained the Northern Hairy-nosed wombats (Australian Government, Department of Sustainability, Environment, Water, Population and Communities, 2011).

'Undivided' not only alerts its audiences to the plight of the Northern Hairy-nosed Wombat, but it confronts us with the ways in which technocultural and ecological dilemmas, or sticky knots, become inseparably entwined. Piccinini (in Orgaz and Piccinini, 2007) reminds us that '[i]n the western world we have a long history of looking to new technologies to find a rapid fix to a difficult problem'. Indivisible technocultural/ecological knots intensify when the 'problems' caused by the 'throwntogtherness' (Massey, 2005) of heterogeneous species in colonized common worlds prompt scientific solutions, which subsequently themselves create new problems and ethical dilemmas. To add even more layers of complexity to this conundrum, 'Undivided' (like many of Piccinini's other artworks) highlights children's apparent ease and trusting relationship with new technologies – a relationship that Piccinini (2012) tells us she both loves and finds slightly disconcerting. The installation provides no solutions, but it raises a plethora of interconnected grapplings and questions. Can technologies solve environmental problems? Should we be worried or encouraged by the fact that young children seem to be so at ease with technoculture? Who is responsible for redressing the life and death consequences of invasive colonialist legacies? How might we best respond and encourage children to respond? How will our responses impact upon future generations of human and more-than-human species?

The questions seem endless, but of central interest to me are those that are provoked by the unsettling intimate relations of the child, the technoculture Surrogate creature and the endangered wombats – relations that force us to reconsider matters of post-colonial settler inheritance, kinship and cohabitation. The co-presence of these unlikely bedfellows immediately speaks to the fact that immigrant Australian children, just like Yeperenye children, are already entangled in post-colonial hybrid common worlds and all of their inherent challenges, *not by their choosing but because of their inheritance*. By its titling, its semiotics and its materiality, 'Undivided' hammers home that white settler Australian children's lives are inextricably embroiled in messy common worlds. These children cannot be singled out or separated from the messed-up post-colonial worlds they have inherited and now share with a whole host of other heirs – of human, animal and other hybrid kinds. This is where they all lie – alongside each other on the surface of an inherited post-colonial landscape, on which the colonial past is always present.

The child's uncanny relationship to the Surrogate figure also requires us to confront the tensions and challenges of cohabiting with radical differences in an increasingly mixed-up, thrown together and interdependent world. For instance, it is hard to resist imagining whether or not the child will be frightened by the creature's very different body when s/he awakes, and wondering whether or not this relationship might dispose her/him to be more at ease with difference than we are, as discomforted adult viewers of this scene. Despite the deliberately disquieting aspects of this relationship, the Surrogate appears to be the child's queer kin carer as well as the surrogate parent of the joey wombats, making the human and wombat infants queer kinder-kin. This raises additional questions about responsibility and care for their mutually-enmeshed futures. How will the child respond to the plight of its endangered wombat kinder-kin? Will they play together and share a common future?

Conclusion

This troubled and troubling queer kin 'Undivided' relationship reminds me that it is not only Indigenous Australian children who have inherited the challenging legacies of colonization and who bear the responsibility for caring for the country. Although the specificities of the challenges they inherit in their particular common worlds are radically uneven and do not by any means equate, all Australian children – settler, immigrant and Indigenous – are linked through the kinship of their interconnected post-colonial inheritance. They are all confronted by the dilemmas and challenges of figuring out how to co-inhabit with their human and more-than-human kin and compatriots, and to accommodate difference in their mixed up, messy and co-implicated post-colonial Australian worlds. How to make these common worlds 'more liveable' (Haraway, 1994: 60) is the overarching challenge for all.

In all their idiosyncrasies, these enacted common worlds of Yeperenye children and settler children and wombats address the question of how we might do nature otherwise in childhood studies. By situating Australian children and animals within their common worlds, I have reconfigured nature as an imbroglio of mutually entangled and inseparable relations – as naturecultures. This reconfiguration reveals the mess and non-innocence of common worlds relations, shattering the illusion of childhood as existing in an other-worldly utopic space of pure nature. Of course, this is not a new way of thinking for indigenous people worldwide, including the Arrernte people of Central Australia. As Latour (2004: 232) points out:

> Non-western cultures *have never been interested in* nature; they have never adopted it as a category; they have never found a use for it. Westerners were the ones who turned nature into a big deal, an immense political diorama,

a formidable moral gigantomachy, and who constantly brought nature into the definition of their social order.

In lieu of making nature 'a big deal', as it is in the more conventional western way of ordering and doing childhood, in this chapter I have offered some reconfigurations of nature in the form of natureculture child–animal relations. These Yeperenye and wombat childhood relations are clearly not a blueprint for all children everywhere – they are specific to the geo-historical circumstances and materialities of their production. I have offered them not as a basis of generalization, nor by way of suggesting that we should all adopt Indigenous Australian onto-epistemologies, but to demonstrate how it is possible, even for those of us schooled in western traditions, to think relationally about childhood and nature and to do childhood 'otherwise'. The pedagogical implications of these common worlds reconfigurations are the subject of the next, and concluding, chapter.

Notes

1 Yeperenye, ayeparenye and yipirinya are alternative spellings of the same word. These variations are the result of different anthropologists and linguists working with different groups of Arrernte (Aranda) people.
2 Rhonda Inkamala is Yipirinya School's former Cultural Principal.
3 I am especially indebted to Kwementyaye L. Raggett for taking me into her world, humouring me, putting up with my stupid questions and being my most patient teacher.
4 Kwementyaye is a generic name of respect, which is used as a substitute for the given name of a deceased person.
5 A lore man is someone who has been ceremonially initiated into Aboriginal lore, gaining access to deeper levels of knowledge about the country.
6 An abridged version of this story appears in Taylor, Blaise and Giugni (2012).

Conclusion

Towards common worlds pedagogies

We must find another relationship to nature besides reification, possession, appropriation, and nostalgia ... all the partners in the potent conversations that constitute nature must find a new ground for making meanings together.

(Haraway, 2004c: 158)

The shift from Nature's Child to children's common worlds

It is simply not possible to 'find another relationship to nature' (Haraway, 2004c: 158) and thereby to childhood, without making a sizeable conceptual and difficult emotional shift. Nevertheless, from the start of this book I have suggested that there is more to gain than to lose if we can shift from the seductively simple and natural Romantic coupling of childhood and nature that I outlined in Part 1, to the messy and complicated queer kin common worlds of childhood that I reconfigured in Part 2.

This is by no means an easy move. One of the main reasons for this is that the authority of Romantic nature is so powerful that it makes questioning feel counter-intuitive, irreverent and, indeed, 'un-natural'. This sense of un-naturalness is only heightened when we try to disengage from our emotional investments in Romantic Nature's Child. In the western world, it just feels like 'second nature' to maintain a tight grip on natural childhood as a preordained state of innocence and purity and to want to preserve it. In fact, protecting childhood's natural purity and innocence becomes a highly charged obligatory task in which, as Daston and Vidal (2004: 14) put it, '"[d]oing what comes naturally" holds out the dream of the self-enforcing rule'. The change in our relationship to nature that Haraway entreats is a tough call.

Unlike the seductive appeal of singular valorized Nature, common worlds do not provide a utopic and pure 'other space' that can be divided from the imperfect world in which we live. Common worlds do not ensure a perfect safe haven for pure and innocent children. They posit none of the moral certitudes of 'nature knows best' prerogatives, no reassuringly simple escape route from the excesses of the digital era, no heroic rescue of 'disadvantaged' or 'deficit' childhoods and no miraculous antidote for postmodern childhood disorders (Louv, 2008). These warts-and-all, always messy, queerly reconfigured, mixed up and 'Undivided' (Piccinini, 2012) nature-culture common worlds seem only to offer baffling liaisons and daunting complexities. Articulating childhoods within common worlds and tracing the interconnecting semiotic and material threads is quite daunting and troubling conceptual work. Even as I have undertaken it, these intertwined common worlds have presented more and more confronting challenges. So why would I bother, or expect others to be convinced that they might also make this shift?

There are actually many reasons why, and I summarize them here by way of concluding this book. The first is obvious. Just as it is impossible to neatly carve nature out from culture, it is also impossible to carve children's lives out from the worlds in which they are embroiled with a whole host of others – human and more-than-human. Children are not only inextricably enmeshed within their common worlds, but as I have shown in Chapter 5, the specificities of their lives are shaped by the idiosyncratic geo-historical (earthly and cultural) convergences of these worlds. As the Arrernte people of Central Australia already know, children *are* their worlds. It is the particularities and distinctive features of these worlds that make children who they are. So it is not only impossible but also nonsensical to imagine that we could separate them out in order to 'protect' or 'save' them. This is not about abandoning children to an unforgiving world, but recognizing where they come from, in order to be able to make some useful response.

On the ground, rather than in the Disney fantasy, there is no going back and nowhere to go back to. Even if we could extricate children from the mixed-up worlds in which they are embedded, there is nowhere else to send them. As I was concerned to point out in Chapters 1 and 2, the imagined pure and perfect other world of nature – separate from human tampering or cultural interference – does not actually exist. Neither does Rousseau's Nature's Child who is associated with it and has been reiterated in a number of formations over the last few centuries. Nature's Child is a modern western fantasy, produced through the fatally flawed logic of the nature/culture divide, and dependent upon the futile (and ideologically suspect) maintenance work of purification (Latour, 2004). My primary purpose in reconfiguring childhoods within a common worlds framework is to carefully reconsider the possibilities inherent in childhoods embedded in natureculture. This is not about jettisoning down-to-earth nature or denying its significance for childhood, but about firmly situating both earthy (and unsanitized) nature and childhood within the natureculture imbroglio and more fully appreciating the ethical, political and pedagogical significance of this situatedness.

A relevant shift

By shifting our relationship to nature through resituating childhoods within down-to-earth natureculture common worlds, we are not just making our lives hard and condemning children to live with their lot. Instead, we are making a shift that is congruent with and has direct relevance to the rapidly globalizing twenty-first-century landscape that children inherit and inhabit, and is therefore ultimately useful to them.

There are arguably two central ethical challenges facing twenty-first-century children. The first is the challenge of living peacefully within an increasingly complex, interconnected, mixed-up, boundary-blurring, hybrid and radically uneven world characterized by difference (human and more-than-human). The second is the challenge of ensuring the sustainability of this ecologically inter-dependent and yet human-dominated and damaged planetary environment. A common worlds approach is directly relevant to both of these present-future scenarios. It centrally addresses the questions of cohabiting with entangled 'throwntogether' differences (Massey, 2005), and of grappling with the ethical and political 'sticky knots' thrown up by these differences (Haraway, 2008a). It also underscores the inter-determining effects of entwined human and more-than-human relations within the wider natureculture world. In terms of sustainability, these inter-determinations are perhaps most profoundly and disturbingly played out within the macro natureculture event of human-induced global warming. This is the world that we bequeath to children. I am arguing that we have some responsibility to equip them, as well as we can, to deal with it.

In Chapter 3, I noted that contemporary nature-based education empha-sizes the correlation between young children's embodied experience of and connections with the natural world and their dispositions to become future environmental stewards (see Chawla, 2006, 2009; Kahn, 2002; Kellert, 2002; Louv, 2008; Orr, 2004; Pyle, 2002; Sobel, 2008; Warden, 2010). These relationships of responsibility are premised upon the child learning 'in' and 'from' nature, not just 'about' it (Sobel, 1996, 2008; Pyle, 2002) and upon the developmentalist belief that childhood is the critical life stage for bonding with nature. The notion of the timely immersion of the child in nature is framed by a double dualism, with spatial as well as temporal dimensions. Not only is the child taken from the cultural domain (where Rousseau's 'education of Man' takes place) and handed over to the uncontaminated space of nature (where Nature is Teacher), but this handover must take place when the child is still in the pre-rational and primarily sensory stage of life, in order to prepare her/him for the ultimate heroic (and cultural) task of championing nature as a fully rational and agentic adult. As well as being framed by the nature/culture and child/adult divides, these calls for nature education as the precursor for environmental stewardship are also construed within the overarching paradigm of humanism. Humanism invests the (rational adult) human with the exclusive capacity for intentional agency and identifies the autonomous individual as the fundamental unit for exercising this agency (for being self-determining and for saving the world).

Within humanist developmental discourses, the concomitant emphases upon the developing (and thereby becoming rational, autonomous and agentic) individual child, upon child-centredness, and upon the primacy of their individual needs, might be good for growing consumers and capitalist entrepreneurs, but it does little to prepare children to deal with the already entangled and increasingly interconnected, boundary-blurring and hybridizing global world that carries the challenges that I have identified above. Humanist developmental discourses, even those that dovetail with environmental educational discourses and enlist nature to nurture and teach budding young environmental stewards, inevitably reinforce human exceptionalism and individual acts of heroism. Whether or not we are speaking about Nature's Child, the orthodox child-centred focus upon the child's individuality and their developing autonomous agency (even their agency to protect nature) runs completely counter to the task of appreciating that no one stands or acts alone, that all human lives are inextricably enmeshed with others (human and more-than-human) and that all human actions are implicated with and have implications for others (including nonhuman others).

My point is that *twenty-first-century children need relational and collective dispositions*, not individualistic ones, to equip them to live well within the kind of world that they have inherited. If they are to peacefully coexist in this hetero-geneous world, with differences that often pose ethical dilemmas, and if they are to do so without seeking to dominate, assimilate or appropriate these differences, they will need a firm sense of shared belonging and shared responsibility within the natureculture collective of their immediate common worlds. If they are to effectively respond to the big picture challenges of coexisting sustainably in an already disturbed planetary ecology, they will need to be able to build upon a foundational sense of connectivity to this same natureculture collective. Such dispositions and capacities will never be fostered through the application of a child-centred and hyper-individualistic developmental framework, nature-loving or not.

An inclusive shift

It is my interest in inclusivity and justice that also drives my efforts to shift our relationship to nature. A desire to practise inclusion in new ways and upon expanded grounds not only motivates me to shift far beyond individual conceptu-alizations of Nature's Child, but also beyond the notion of children as embedded in their socio-cultural contexts (Vygotsky, 1978). It has been my intention, in writing this book, to stretch the bounds of inclusivity to encompass the common worldly vision of 'a collective of humans and non humans' (Latour, 2009). As I set out to demonstrate in my Chapter 4 common worlds assemblage and in my subsequent Chapter 5 natureculture enactments (Law, 2004), children's common worlds are human and more-than-human collectives or 'whole-lot' worlds. They are not selective and depoliticized worlds that only admit nature's good, beautiful, innocent, pure and enriching qualities. They require us to relinquish protectionism and separatism and to open up to the whole lot – including reconfigured technoculture kin and interspecies relations (Haraway, 2004d), often discomforting geo-historical legacies, proliferating nature–culture hybrids (Latour, 2004), new technologies, uneven power relations and challenging knotty dilemmas. To make this shift, we must first resist the urge to sequester childhood in a natural enclave (as Rousseau would have us do) and then step out into the less-than-perfect but worldly world to actively collect, encounter, acknowledge and include all of the significant other players (or actants) in children's entangled lives.

Early childhood education is a field that prides itself on being inclusive. It works hard at respecting diversity and making all children feel that they belong – through welcoming their families; being attuned to the significance of their gendered, classed, religious and cultural backgrounds and their special needs; and building their relationships with key people in the local communities (Bernard van Leer Foundation, 2007; Friendly and Lero, 2002). This is all very important, but rarely does the understanding of diversity and inclusion extend beyond the exclusively human or social domain (see Elliott and Davis, 2008). At the same time, it is also significant that in a field that has from its inception invested heavily in the ideal of natural education, early childhood educators rarely frame nature-related or environmental concerns within an ethos of inclusion and justice. This is because the nature/culture divide, or what Latour (1993) calls the 'Great Divide', ensures that we approach the social world and the natural environment as separate projects conducted in separate domains. It is always an either/or scenario. By resituating childhood within the common worlds of blended naturecultures we dispense with these separations, blend the projects and widen the scope of possibilities for inclusion and for justice.

A common worlds approach includes the whole lot because it recognizes the entanglement of human and more-than-human relations. Like Piccinini's (2012) 'Undivided' sculptural installation of the co-sleeping child, technoculture surrogate and endangered joey wombats that I discussed in Chapter 5, a common worlds approach recognizes that children inherit messy, mixed-up and inseparable relations that they must ultimately respond to. Beyond the stock-in-trade human-centric understandings of social inclusion and early childhood communities, a common worlds framework includes all of children's significant and worldly relations – chosen and inherited, human and more-than-human – as worthy of our careful and considered attention.

The more-than-human others in the worldly collective include (but are not restricted to) nonhuman living and nonhuman-made inert entities and elements that are typically separated into the valorized and exteriorized 'nature' camp – such as other animals, plants, weather, water and 'natural' materials. These are also the kinds of natures that have been the focus of 'natural' education since Rousseau's (2003 (1762)) *Emile* treatise that I discussed in Chapter 1. However, instead of restoring and/or enhancing childhood by extending the amount of time that children spend in valorized external nature (for instance by taking children 'outdoors' to play in all weathers, or taking them into the forest), bringing in natural materials (for instance clay instead of play dough, wood instead of plastic) and constructing opportunities for children to interact with plants and domesticated animals (for instance gardening, keeping chicks or guinea pigs in cages), the inclusive scope of a common worlds perspective attends to the members of the natureculture collective that are *already integral to and constitutive of* children's lives. These are not carefully chosen or selected for their value-adding qualities or educational benefits to children – they are included because they are already matted into the geo-historical trajectories of children's situated discursive and material natureculture collective worlds. They are the already-entangled cohabitants and unlikely partners, including the 'queer kin' (Haraway, 2004d, 2004e, 2008a, 2008b, 2011) that have already shaped particular children's lives and been shaped by them. In the idiosyncratic common worlds that I enacted in Chapter 5, these already-entangled partners included caterpillars, dogs, mountain ranges and wombats – not because they seemed like the right kinds of value-adding natural entities to offer up as suitable companions for children, but because these queer compatriots were the already-there and already-significant players and kin within these particular natureculture entanglements.

A pedagogical shift

A common worlds framework not only offers a new relationship to nature and childhood, but also portends a shift in understandings about the 'nature' of learning and gestures towards some new pedagogical possibilities. The prospect of new pedagogical possibilities should appeal to those early childhood educators who are interested in being inclusive of the more-than-human world (including 'nature', 'technology' and hybrid formations of both) and tackling the real world challenges facing twenty-first-century children (such as cohabiting peacefully with difference and ecological sustainability), without been entrapped in the 'established disorders' (Haraway, 2004a: 47) of the 'Great Divide' (Latour, 1993) and seduced by the sentimental appeal of the Nature's Child narratives that I traced in the first part of this book.

In Chapter 3, I noted that nature's pedagogical affordances have featured quite centrally in the trajectory of early childhood education, courtesy of Rousseau and his followers. At the same time I argued that when conceptualizations of nature are partitioned within the Romantic nature/culture divide, nature-based pedagogical endeavours are fraught with contradictions and can produce unintended consequences. For instance, many nature-based pedagogies rehearse the human-centric traps that Haraway implies in the opening quotation to this Conclusion, and which flow from the 'Great Divide'. These include: reifying nature (treating nature as Nature – as a fixed, singular and often personified entity); possessing it (claiming nature as the providence of science and/or the state of childhood); appropriating it (using nature to authorize essentialist or universalist 'truths' – including 'truths' about childhood and learning); and investing it with wistful, sentimental and nostalgic adult projections (positioning nature as desirable exotic otherness).

As an alternative to this entrapment, an understanding of common worlds as entangled naturecultures affords an embedded, emplaced and above all *relational* understanding of diverse childhoods and natures. This, in turn, fashions new sets of pedagogical possibilities. For if we can first recognize our common worlds and then utilize them as the collective 'new ground for meaning making together' that Haraway (2004c: 158) talks about, we will inadvertently make a pedagogical shift – away from knowing *about* nature, or even *in* nature and towards learning *with* those others with whom we are already entangled (see also Giugni, nd). We will be tapping into the pedagogical opportunities inherent in the imbroglio of common worlds relations and on our way to inventing all kinds of emergent collective and collaborative (human and more-than-human) pedagogical ventures.

Although pedagogies that draw upon human–more-than-human relations are far from the norm, I would like to acknowledge a few initiatives that have already tapped into the possibilities of 'changing our relations to nature' and 'making meaning together' (Haraway, 2004c: 158). For instance, Miriam Giugni (in Taylor, Blaise and Giugni, 2012) writes about a 'companion species curriculum' (following Haraway, 2003, 2008b) that unfolded in an urban Australian early childhood education centre. This curriculum emerged from educators and children grappling with some of the dilemmas, or 'sticky knots' thrown up by cohabiting in the centre, first with caged rented chooks[1] and then with the chooks once they were released from their cage and allowed to roam free. Her 'companion species curriculum' taps into the possibilities of learning with others that is enabled by such grapplings.

Margaret Somerville (2011) reports on a place pedagogy in which primary school children living in a highly industrial mining area in Australia engaged with frogs in nearby constructed wetlands. In ways reminiscent of the 'wombat boy' in Chapter 5, the children formed relationships with frogs that operate on a number of different levels. Not only did they establish scientific relationship with frogs, by learning how to be junior frog scientists – counting, observing, recording and classifying frogs – but they also constructed an emplaced and embodied relationship with frogs based upon their actual encounters with frogs in frog worlds. Drawing upon Deleuze's and Guattari's (1987) writings on 'becoming' and Grosz's (1994) dynamic conceptualization of human and non-human body connectivities as central to these becomings, Somerville identifies the most interesting aspects of this place pedagogy as the children's embodied process of 'becoming frog'. She describes the multi-sensorial ways in which the children were corporeally engaged with non-human wetland bodies and elements during regular 'Community Frog Watch' evenings – engaged with the moonlight, the wind, the frog call noises, and so on. Drawing upon these embodied and emplaced experiences of frog worlds, children enacted what it is like to be frogs by emulating frog movements and performing frog dances to the frog-call music that they recorded during the wetland visits.

Another initiative was the large research project in ten Aotearoa/New Zealand early childhood centres, conducted by Jenny Ritchie, Iris Duhn, Cheryl Rau and Janita Craw (2010), which set out to establish a 'culture of ecological sustainability' in everyday early childhood pedagogical practice based upon the enactment of an 'ethics of care for self, others and the environment' and an 'ethics of place'. Although the project unfolded quite differently in the different centres, it was built upon some common principles that challenged the standard separations between the human and more-than-human world. Most significantly, it incorporated kaupapa Māori onto-epistemologies about the productive interrelationships between people and place and related Māori ecological tenants, including kaitiakitanga, or guardianship, and manaakitanga, or care. The Māori perspectives underpinning this project, together with its focus upon the pedagogical affordances of place, ensured a distinctively local and ethical pedagogical approach.

As this small selection of 'making meaning together' pedagogical projects indicates, there are no prescribed road maps or blueprints for making the shift from learning about nature to learning with others in the human and non-human collective. What unfolds is always new and often surprising. It is always the product of the specific constellations of thrown together relations that exist within specific common worlds. Like all 'learnings-with', the unfolding children's learnings with neighbourhood wetlands and frogs; with indigenous ecological onto-epistemologies and ethical practices; and with rented chooks in the examples above were determined by the composition of their particular natureculture collectives. Even though it is not possible to predict or pin down the ways in which learning-with will unfold in different common world contexts, there are a number of key concepts and principles that I assembled in Chapter 4 and enacted in my child–animal common worlds stories in Chapter 5 that might provide some useful scaffolding to support such pedagogical unfoldings.

Pedagogical principles

Attending to children's relations in common worlds

An understanding that relations are central to everything would be the first guiding principle. Flowing from this, an attendance to children's enmeshed relations with others in their worlds would be the focus of any common worlds pedagogy. This is in line with what Karen Martin[2] (2007) refers to as the centrality of 'relatedness' in Aboriginal Australian onto-epistemology. Martin urges early childhood educators to take account of the mutually constituting relationships between children and the world around them when thinking about teaching and learning. She explains that in her Quandamoopah people's cultural traditions, children's growing up is seen as a process of building 'ever-increasing sets of relatedness ... to people, plants, animals, waterways, climate, land and skies' (2007: 18). This is very different from the modern western teleological view of childhood as the first stage in the process of becoming a (rational) adult. While I am not suggesting that educators everywhere should simply adopt Martin's Aboriginal world-views, I do want to stress that the location of individual children within registers of human development is neither a universal practice nor the only way to structure pedagogy. It is relations that constitute common worlds, not sets of individual developmental trajectories. By relocating children within common worlds, the relations themselves become the locus of pedagogical attention (see also Lenz-Taguchi, 2010).

Relations of difference would be of particular interest within common worlds pedagogies – including the queer kin relations that children form with more-than-human others. The focus on relations of difference would support children to directly engage with the heterogeneity of their common worlds and to face the challenges of coexisting peacefully with others who are not necessarily like them. Along with this focus comes the acknowledgement that relations of difference are often asymmetrical and infused with power. The asymmetry of power relations, based upon difference, requires an ethical response. Children would be supported to reflect upon the uneven valuing of differences in their common worlds – between humans and between humans and other species – and upon the responsibilities that come with being implicated within such asymmetrical relations. This would be an important aspect of a common worlds pedagogical process. It would require fostering a reflective and questioning disposition and a sense of collective, not just individual, responsibility. In other words, children would not only be encouraged to recognize and celebrate human difference (as they often already are), but to respond to the dilemmas that are thrown up by coexisting with a whole host of different co-inhabitants, not all of whom are equally valued. By encouraging children to question the relations they have inherited as well as chosen, and to reflect upon the best ways of coexisting with relations of differences, early childhood educators would be supporting children to practise what Sarah Whatmore (2002), along with others, refers to as a 'relational ethics'.

Attending to children's emplacement in common worlds

Children's relations take place on the grounds of common worlds. Like all relations, they are produced and enacted in particular times and places. They are situated and emplaced relations. The generative or productive nature of place, as well as time, is another key principle for common worlds pedagogies. Most people view place as fixed and static (a backdrop or stage on which human actions take place) and see history as the active and dynamic determinant. However, as Foucault (1980) observed, not enough attention is paid to the spatialities of power in history, or to the ways in which geography (space and place) disperses history. The seemingly banal fact that things turn out differently in different places (Philo, 1992) helps us to recognize the productive significance of place, and by association, of common worlds. An appreciation of the ways in which geometries of power are constellated in local places (Massey, 1993) alerts us to the political and uneven grounds of common worlds. The concept of places as 'spatio-temporal events' (Massey, 2005: 130) replete with power relations is key to understanding the significance of children's common worlds and to designing learning-with pedagogies. As we attend to the pedagogical significance of children's emplacement in their common worlds, we need to appreciate that places are productive and also non-innocent grounds.

A number of educational scholars have promoted the pedagogical affordances of place (Greunewald and Smith, 2008; Sobel, 2004; Somerville, 2010 and 2011), but Iris Duhn (2012) offers a concept of place-as-assemblage that is synonymous with common worlds and that elucidates its principles. Duhn urges early childhood educators to view place as a 'lively' assemblage of human and more-than-human others, in which agency is exercised by all matter (not just humans) and as a kind of routine maintenance work. Conceived of this way, agency is no longer restricted to a series of exclusively human (and often heroic) interventions. She argues that a pedagogy of place-as-assemblage, in which agency is distributed beyond the human, has the potential to blur the distinction between knowing (human) subjects and known-about objects that characterizes and limits western pedagogy. In the same way, common worlds pedagogies would endeavor to circumvent children-as-subjects learning about nature-as-object. An early childhood pedagogy that emplaces children in their common worlds, and emphasizes their entangled relations within this world, would follow the principle of learning with or becoming worldly with the others in the collective.

Using collective inquiry

It is not possible to appreciate the pedagogical opportunities of children's common worlds without being curious about their human and more-than-human composition and without undertaking some form of collective inquiry into the connective threads that constitute these natureculture worlds. Collective inquiry would be the method of a common worlds learning-with pedagogy. It would be the way of enacting its guiding principles and impulses.

This collective inquiry would involve educators and children learning with a whole host of others (human and more-than-human) to find out more about the worlds in which they are already located and embroiled. The first task would be to exchange perspectives on where they are, who and what is there with them, how they all got to be there, the different kinds of lives that are lived and stories that are told there, and where they and others fit within these interconnected lives and stories. What they find and where it might lead would depend on the natureculture composition and affordances of their particular common worlds.

To add an ethical dimension to this pedagogical inquiry, early childhood teachers would support children to grapple with the challenges of inheritance and coexistence that are thrown up in their common worlds. They would encourage inquiring questions about the different regard for differences and the asymmetry of relations related to these unequally valued differences. They would ask children to reflect upon the overarching ethical questions of how best to deal with the uneven grounds of their inheritance and how to cohabit in ways that allow all differences (human and more-than-human) to flourish.

In acting upon these principles, the collective inquiry method would foster children's dispositions to include all members of their common worlds nature-culture collective, to trace threads of connection between themselves and others in their common worlds, to be curious about the differences of others in these common worlds, and to work on the challenges and opportunities thrown up by these relations of difference. This kind of pedagogy would encourage children to situate themselves within the real worlds in which they live. It would show them ways of acting together with the others with whom they share these worlds, to ensure that they collectively create the best possible enmeshed future.

Towards common worlds pedagogies

Throughout this book I have argued that the ways in which we know, or figure, nature determines how we do it, and concomitantly how we do 'natural' childhood. Following the geo-historical trajectories of Rousseau's twin figures of Nature's Child and Nature as Teacher in Part 1, I traced a number of representational and educational doings or performances of children's special relationship with nature. I highlighted the paradoxes inherent in trying to maintain the epistemological purity of these natural figures via their cultural performances or enactments. In Part 2, I offered some different ways of knowing, or reconfiguring, and doing nature and childhood by articulating them within the collective of hybrid naturecultures that I have been calling common worlds. My academic enactments are only preliminary steps in shifting our relations to nature and thus to childhood. I have made them in the hope of envisioning and supporting more liveable common worlds and futures for twenty-first-century children. I look forward to seeing what kinds of on-the-ground doings might be enabled by such a shift towards common worlds pedagogies.

Notes

1   Chook is an Australian colloquialism for chicken
2   Karen Martin is an early childhood education scholar and a Quandamoopah Aboriginal woman from Queensland, Australia.

Bibliography

References

Adams, A. (2010). Ansel Adams Gallery website. Retrieved from: www.anseladams. com/
—(2000). 'Nature schools'. *Resurgence*, 199: 44.
Aitken, S. C. (2001). *Geographies of Young People: The Morally Contested Spaces of Identity*. London and New York: Routledge.
Alaimo, S. and Hekman, S. (eds) (2008). *Material Feminisms*. Bloomington and Indianapolis, IN: Indiana University Press.
Altman, J. and Hinkson, M. (eds) (2010). 'Culture Crisis: Anthropology and Politics in Aboriginal Australia'. Sydney: UNSW Press.
Anderson, K. (1995). 'Culture and nature at the Adelaide Zoo: At the frontiers of "human" geography'. *Transactions of the Institute of British Geographers* New Series, 20 (3): 275–94.
—(2001). The nature of 'race', in N. Castree and B. Braun (eds), *Social Nature: Theory, Practice and Politics*. Malden, MA, and Oxford: Blackwell, pp. 64–83.
—(2007). *Race and the Crisis of Humanism*. London and New York: Routledge.
Anderson, K. and Taylor, A. (2005). 'Exclusionary politics and the question of national belonging: Australian ethnicities in "multiscalar" focus'. *Ethnicities*, 5 (4): 460–85.
Anderson, P. and Wild, R. (2007). *Ampe Akelyernemane Meke Mekarle: 'Little Children are Sacred'*. Report of the Northern Territory Board of Inquiry into the Protection of Aboriginal Children from Sexual Abuse, 2007. Retrieved from: www. inquirysaac.nt.gov.au/pdf/bipacsa_final_report.pdf
Änggård, E. (2010). 'Making use of "nature" in an outdoor preschool: Classroom, home and fairyland'. *Children, Youth and Environments*, 20 (1): 4–25.
Austin-Broos, D. (2009). *Arrernte Present Arrernte Past: Invasion, Violence and Imagination in Indigenous Central Australia*. Chicago, IL and London: University of Chicago Press.
Australian Bureau of Statistics (2010). 'Biodiversity'. ABS Australia's Environment: Issues and Trends, Jan. 2010 Website. Retrieved from: http://www.abs.gov.au/AUSSTATS/abs@.nsf/Lookup/4613.0Chapter105Jan+2010
Australian Bureau of Statistics (2012a). '2011 Census of population and housing: Counts of Aboriginal and Torres Strait Islander peoples'. ABS website. Retrieved from: http://www.abs.gov.au/ausstats/abs@.nsf/Lookup/2075.0main+features32011

—(2012b). '2011 Census of population and housing'. ABS website. 'Cultural diversity in Australia. Reflecting a nation: Stories from the 2011 census'. ABS website. Retrieved from: http://www.abs.gov.au/ausstats/abs@.nsf/Lookup/20 71.0main+features902012-2013

Australian Government, Department of Sustainability, Environment, Water, Population and Communities (2011). Threatened Species and Ecological Communities publications website. 'Northern hairy-nosed wombat' (Environment Australia 1998). Retrieved from: www.environment.gov.au/biodiversity/ threatened/publications/northern-hairynosEdhtml

Australian Human Rights Commission (2012). 'A statistical overview of Aboriginal and Torres Strait Islander People in Australia, 2008'. Aboriginal and Torres Strait Islander Social Justice website. Retrieved from: http://www.hreoc.gov.au/social_ justice/statistics/index.html

Australian Institute of Health and Welfare (2011). 'Child protection Australia, 2009–2010'. Child Welfare Series, No. 51. Cat. no. CWS 39. Canberra: AIHW. Retrieved from: http://www.aihw.gov.au/publication-detail/?id=6442475448&tab=2

Baker, J. (2000). *The Hidden Forest*. London, Boston, MA, Sydney and Auckland: Walker Books.

—(2012). 'Exploring a hidden forest: Hayden Washington interviews Jeannie Baker'. Jeannie Baker website. Retrieved from: http://www.jeanniebaker.com/ focus_web/exploring_a_hidden_forest.htm.

Barad, K. (2003). 'Posthumanist performativity: Toward an understanding of how matter comes to matter'. *Signs*, Spring 2003: 801–31.

—(2007). *Meeting the Universe Halfway: Quantum Physics and the Entanglement of Matter and Meaning*. Durham, NC: Duke University Press.

—(2008). 'Queer causation and the ethics of mattering', in N. N. Giffney and M. J. Hird (eds), *Queering the Non/Human*. Burlington, VT and Hampshire: Ashgate, pp. 311–38

—(2011). 'Nature's queer performativity'. *Qui Parle: Critical Humanities and Social Sciences*, 19 (2): 121–58.

Barton, J. (2011). *You Can't Eat Scenery: Life in Wee Jasper 1850–1970*. Self-published with editing and design by K. Howarth. Kingston, ACT: Kainos Print.

—(2012). *Wombat Pooh*. Self-published. Kingston, ACT: Kainos Print.

Bentsen, P., Mygind, E. and Randrup, T. (2009). 'Towards an understanding of udeskole: education outside the classroom in a Danish context'. *International Perspectives on Outdoor and Experiential Learning, Education 3–13*, 37 (1): 29–44.

Bernard van Leer Foundation (2007). *Early Childhood Matters: Promoting Social inclusion and Respect for Diversity in the Early Years*. Number 108. Retrieved from: http://www.bernardvanleer.org/Promoting_social_inclusion_and_respect_for_ diversity_in_the_early_years

Bhabha, H. K. (ed.) (1990). *Nation and Narration*. New York and London: Routledge.

Blair, D. (2009). 'The child in the garden: an evaluative review of the benefits of school gardening'. *Journal of Environmental Education*, 40 (2): 15–38.

Blaise, M. (2005). *Playing it Straight: Uncovering Gender Discourses in the Early Childhood Classroom*. New York and London: Routledge.

Blaise, M. and Taylor, A. (2012). 'Using queer theory to rethink gender equity in early childhood education'. Research in Review, *Young Children*, January 2012: 88–97.

Blyton, E. (2010 (1942)), *Five on Treasure Island*. E-book edition. London: Hodder Children's Books.

Braidotti, R. (2006). *Transpositions*. Malden, MA and Cambridge: Polity Press.

Braun, B. (2002). *The Intemperate Rainforest: Nature, Culture and Power on Canada's West Coast*. Minneapolis, MN: University of Minnesota Press.

Braun, B. and Castree, N. (eds) (1998). *Remaking Reality: Nature at the Millenium*. London and New York: Routledge.

Bredekamp, S. (ed.) (1986). *Developmentally Appropriate Practice*. Washington, DC: NAEYC.

Brookes, D. for the Mparntwe people (2007). *A Town like Mparntwe: A Guide to the Dreaming Tracks and Sites of Alice Springs*. Alice Springs: Jukurrpa Books, IAD Press.

Brosterman, N. (1997). *Inventing Kindergarten*. New York: Harry N. Abrams Inc.

—(2002–3). 'Fröebel and the gifts of kindergarten'. *Cabinet Magazine* Special Issue on *Childhood*, 9. Retrieved from: http://cabinetmagazine.org/issues/9/brosterman.php

Brown, E. (2010). 'Plato's ethics and politics in *The Republic*', in E. N. Zalta (ed.), *The Stanford Encyclopedia of Philosophy* (Winter Edition). Retrieved from: http://plato.stanford.edu/archives/win2010/entries/plato-ethics-politics/.

Brown, H. S., Perez, A., Mirchandani, G. G., Hoelscher, D. and Kelder, S. H. (2008). 'Crime rates and sedentary behavior among 4th grade Texas school children'. *International Journal of Behavioural Nutrition and Physical Activity*. Online publication. Retrieved from: www.ncbi.nlm.hih.gov/pmc/articles/PMC2412913/.

Brown, W. H., Pfeiffer, K. A., McIver, K. L., Dowda, M., Addy, C. L. and Pate, R. R. (2009). 'Social and environmental factors associated with preschoolers' nonsedentary physical activity'. *Child Development*, 80 (1): 45–58.

Buck, S. J. (1998). *The Global Commons: An Introduction*. Washington, DC: Island Press.

Buckingham, D. (2000). *After the Death of Childhood: Growing up in the Age of Electronic Media*. Cambridge: Polity Press.

Butler, J. (1990). *Gender Trouble: Feminism and the Subversion of Identity*. New York and London: Routledge.

—(1993). *Bodies that Matter: On the Discursive Limits of 'Sex'*. New York and London: Routledge.

Cannella, G. S. and Kincheloe, J. K. (eds) (2002). *Kidworld: Childhood Studies, Global Perspectives and Education*. New York: Peter Lang.

Cannella, G. S. and Soto, L. D. (eds) (2010). *Childhoods: A Handbook*. New York, Washington, DC, Bern, Frankfurt, Berlin, Brussels, Vienna and Oxford: Peter Lang.

Cannella, G. S. and Viruru, R. (2004). *Childhood and Postcolonization: Power, Education and Contemporary Practice*. New York: RoutledgeFalmer.

Carson, R. (1998 (1956)). *The Sense of Wonder*. New York: HarperCollins.

Castaneda, C. (2002). *Figurations: Child, Bodies, Worlds*. London: Duke University Press.

Castree, N. (2001). 'Socializing nature: Theory, practice and politics', in N. Castree and B. Braun (eds), *Social Nature: Theory, Practice and Politics*. Malden, MA, and Oxford: Blackwell, pp. 1–21.

—(2005). *Nature*. New York: Routledge.

Castree, N. and Braun, B. (1998). 'The construction of nature and the nature of construction: analytical and political tools for building survivable futures', in B. Castree, N. and Braun, B. (eds) (2001). *Social Nature: Theory, Practice and Politics*. Malden, MA, and Oxford: Blackwell.

Chawla, L. (1990). 'Ecstatic places'. *Children's Environments Quarterly*, 7 (4): 18–23.

—(1998). 'Significant life experiences revisited: A review of research on sources of environmental sensitivity'. *The Journal of Environmental Education*, 29 (3): 11–21.

—(2002). 'Spots of time: Manifold ways of being in nature in childhood', in P. H. Kahn Jr and S. R. Kellert (eds), *Children and Nature: Psychology, Sociocultural and Evolutionary Investigations*. Cambridge, MA, and London: MIT Press, pp. 199–226.

—(2006). 'Learning to love the natural world enough to protect it'. *Barn*, 2: 57–8.

—(2009). 'Growing up green: Becoming an agent of care for the natural world'. *Journal of Developmental Processes*, 4 (1).

Childhood and Nature Network (2012). 'Childhood and Nature Network' website. Retrieved from: www.childrenandnature.org/

Cixous, H. (1976). 'The Laugh of the Medusa'. Trans. K. Cohen and P. Cohen. *Signs*, 1 (4): 875–93.

Cobb, E. (1977 (1959)). *The Ecology of Imagination in Childhood*. New York: Colombia University Press.

Collins–Gearing, B. and Osland, D. (2010). 'Who will save us from the rabbits?: Re-writing the past allegorically'. *The Looking Glass: New Perspectives on Children's Literature*, 14 (2). Online journal. Retrieved from: http://www.lib.latrobe.edu.au/ojs/index.php/tlg/article/view/227/225

Cole, B. (2004). *Wirriya – Small Boy*. Film documentary from Nganampa Anwernehenhe Series, Central Australian Aboriginal Media Association (CAAMA), Producations, Alice Springs. Distributed by Ronin Films, Canberra.

—(2012). *Listen Up*. Film documentary. Central Australian Aboriginal Media Association (CAAMA) Productions, Alice Springs.

Corsaro, W. A. (2005). *The Sociology of Childhood* (2nd edition). Thousand Oaks, CA, London and New Delhi: Pine Forge Press.

Coughlin, F. (1991). 'Aboriginal town camps and Tangentyere Council: The battle for self-determination in Alice Springs'. Unpublished Masters of Arts thesis. La Trobe University, Bundoora, Victoria.

Coveney, P. (1982). 'The image of the child', in C. Jenks (ed.), *The Sociology of Childhood, Essential Readings*. London: Batsford, pp. 42–7.

Cranston, M. (1991). *The Noble Savage: Jean-Jacque Rousseau 1754–1762*. Chicago, IL: University of Chicago Press.

Cronon W. (1996). 'In search of nature', in W. Cronon (ed.), *Uncommon Ground: Rethinking the Human Place in Nature*. New York: W. W. Norton, pp. 23–68.

—(1998). 'The trouble with wilderness, or, getting back to the wrong nature', in J. B. Callicott and M. P. Nelson (eds), *The Great New Wilderness Debate*. Athens, GA, and New York: University of Georgia Press, pp. 471–99.

Cuddon, J. A. and Preston, C. (1998). *A Dictionary of Literary Terms and Literary Theory* (4th edition). Malden, MA, and Oxford: Blackwell.

Dahlberg, G. and Moss, P. (2005). *Ethics and Politics in Early Childhood Education*. London and New York: RoutledgeFalmer.

Dahlberg, G., Moss, P., and Pence, A. (1999). *Beyond Quality in Early Childhood*

Education and Care: A Postmodern Perspective. London and New York: RoutledgeFalmer.

Daston, L. (2004). 'Attention and the values of nature in the enlightenment', in L. Daston and F. Vidal (eds), *The Moral Authority of Nature.* Chicago, IL, and London: University of Chicago Press, pp. 100–26.

Daston, L. and Vidal, F. (2004). 'Introduction: Doing what comes naturally', in L. Daston and F. Vidal (eds), *The Moral Authority of Nature.* Chicago, IL, and London: University of Chicago Press, pp. 1–20.

Dau, E. (ed.) (2005). *Taking Early Childhood Education Outdoors.* Croydon: Tertiary Press.

Davis, J. and Elliott, S. (2003). *Early Childhood Environmental Education: Making it Mainstream.* Canberra: Early Childhood Australia.

Dawson, T. J. (1995). *Kangaroos: Biology of the Largest Marsupials.* New York: Cornell University Press.

Day, A. (1996). *Romanticism.* London: Routledge.

Deleuze, G. and Guattari, F. (1987). *A Thousand Plateaus: Capitalism and Schizophrenia.* Trans. B. Massumi. Minneapolis, MN: University of Minnesota Press.

Denzin, N. (1977). *Childhood Socialization.* San Francisco, CA: Jossey-Bass.

Derrida, J. (1976). *Of Grammatology.* Trans. G. C. Spivak. Baltimore, MD, and London: Johns Hopkins University Press.

—(2005 (1978)). 'Structure, sign and play in the discourse of the human sciences', in *Writing and Difference*, University of Chicago (trans.). New York and London: Routledge, pp. 351–70.

Dewey, J. (1997 (1938)). *Experience and Education.* New York: Free Press.

—(2009 (1916)). *Democracy and Education: An Introduction to the Philosophy of Education.* New York: WLC Books.

Doyle, M. E. and Smith M. K. (2007). 'Jean-Jacques Rousseau on education'. *The Encyclopedia of Informal Education.* Retrieved from: www.infEdorg/thinkers/et-rous.htm

Duhn, I. (2012). 'Places for pedagogies, pedagogies for places'. *Contemporary Issues in Early Childhood Education*, 13 (2): 99–107.

Edelglass, W., Hatley, J. and Diehm, C. (eds) (2012). *Facing Nature: Levinas and Environmental Thought.* Pittsburg, PA: Duquesne University Press.

Elliott, S. (ed.) (2008). *The Outdoor Playspace – Naturally – For Children Birth to Five Years.* Castle Hill, NSW: Pademelon Press.

Elliott, S. and Davis, J. (2004). 'Mud pies and daisy chains: Connecting young children and nature'. *Every Child*, 10 (4): 4–5.

—(2008). 'Introduction. Why outdoor playspaces?', in S. Elliott (ed.), *The Outdoor Playspace – Naturally – For Children Birth to Five Years.* Castle Hill, NSW: Pademelon Press, pp. 1–14.

Faber Taylor, A. and Kuo, F. E. M. (2011). 'Could exposure to everyday green spaces help treat ADHD? Evidence from children's play settings'. *Applied Psychology: Health and Well-Being*, 3 (2): 281–303.

Fielding, M. and Moss, P. (2011). *The Common School: A Democratic Alternative.* London: Routledge.

Fjørtoft, I. (2001). 'The natural environment as a playground for children: The impact of play activities in pre-primary school children'. *Early Childhood Education Journal*, 29 (2): 111–17.

—(2004). 'Landscape as playscape: the effects of natural environments on children's play and motor development'. *Children, Youth and Environments*, 14 (92): 21–44.

Foltz, B. V. and Frodeman, R. (eds) (2004). *Rethinking Nature: Essays in Environmental Philosophy*. Bloomington and Indianapolis, IN: Indiana University Press.

Foucault, M. (1972). *The Archaeology of Knowledge and the Discourse of Language*, Trans. A. M. Sheridan Smith. New York: Pantheon Books.

—(1980). 'Questions on geography', in C. Gordon (ed.), *Power/Knowledge: Selected Interviews and Other Writings 1972–77*. New York: Pantheon Books, pp. 63–77.

—(1982). 'The subject and power', in H. L. Dreyfus and P. Rabinow (eds), *Michel Foucault: Beyond Structuralism and Hermeneutic*. Hertfordshire: Harvester Press.

—(1986). 'Of Other Spaces'. *Diacritics*, 16: 22–7.

—(1990). *The History of Sexuality. Volume 1: An Introduction*. New York: Vintage Books; London: Penguin.

Franklin, A. (2006). *Animal Nation: The True Story of Animals and Australia*. Sydney: University of New South Wales Press.

French, J. (2002). *Diary of a Wombat*. Illustrated by B. Whatley. Sydney: Angus and Robertson.

—(2005). *The Secret World of Wombats*, Illustrated by B. Whatley. Sydney: Angus and Robertson.

—(2011). 'The story behind Diary of a Wombat'. Jackie French's website: http://www.jackiefrench.com/wombat.html

Friendly, M. and Lero, D. S. (2002). *Social Inclusion Through Early Childhood Education and Care*. Laidlaw Foundation. Online publication. Retrieved from: http://www.offordcentre.com/VoicesWebsite/library/reports/documents/laidlaw/lero.pdf

Fröebel, F. (1912a (1826)). *Fröebel's Chief Writings on Education: Part One: The Education of Human Nature*. Trans. S. S. F. Fletcher and J. Welton. London: Edward Arnold. University of Roehampton digital library. Retrieved from: http://core.roehampton.ac.uk/digital/froarc/frochi/

—(1912b (1838–1840)). *Fröebel's Chief Writings on Education: Part Two: The Kindergarten*. Trans. S. S. F. Fletcher and J. Welton. London: Edward Arnold. University of Roehampton digital library. Retrieved from: http://core.roehampton.ac.uk/digital/froarc/frochi/

Fuchs, E. (2004). 'Nature and *bildung*: Pedagogical naturalism', in L. Daston and F. Vidal (eds), *The Moral Authority of Nature*. Chicago, IL, and London: University of Chicago Press, pp. 155–81.

Gabriel, M. and Goldberg, E. (directors) (1995). *Pocahontas*. Animated feature film. Los Angeles, CA: Disney/Pixar Film Productions.

Gibbs, M. (1916). *Gumnut Babies*. Sydney: Angus and Robertson.

—(1918). *Snuggle Pot and Cuddle Pie*. Sydney: Angus and Robertson.

Gibson-Graham, J. K. (2006). *A Postcapitalist Politics*. Minneapolis, MN, and London: University of Minnesota Press.

Gill, T. (2005). 'Let our children roam free'. *The Ecologist*. Retrieved from: www.theecologist.org/archive_detail.asp?content_id=481

Giugni, M. (nd). 'Inclusion through relatedness: Learning "with"'. Inclusion Support Facilitators encountering the Early Years Learning Framework. Online publication of the ACT Inclusion Support Agency. Retrieved from: www.cscentral.org.au/support/pdf/inclusion_through_relatedness.pdf

Giugni, M. and Mundine, K. (eds) (2011). *Talkin' Up, Speakin' Out: Aboriginal and Multicultural Voices in Early Childhood Education.* Castle Hill, NSW: Pademelon Press.

Grant Bruce, M. (1910). *A Little Bush Maid.* London: Ward Lock.

Gregory, D. (2001). '(Post)colonialism and the production of nature', in N. Castree and B. Braun (eds), *Social Nature: Theory, Practice and Politics.* Malden, MA, and Oxford: Blackwell, pp. 84–111.

Griffin, S. (1978). *Women and Nature: The Roaring Inside Her.* New York: Harper and Row.

Gross, Y. (director) (1977). *Dot and the Kangaroo.* Animated feature film. Sydney: Yoran Gross Films. DVD version. Hen's Tooth Video.

Grosz, E. (1994). *Volatile Bodies: Towards a Corporeal Feminism.* Sydney: Allen and Unwin.

Gruenewald, D. A. and Smith, G. A. (eds) (2008). *Place-based Education in the Global Age.* New York: Taylor and Francis.

Gura, P. F. (2007). *American Transcendentalism: A History.* New York: Hill and Wang.

Hand, D. (director) (1942). *Bambi.* Animated feature film. Los Angeles, CA: Disney Film Productions.

Haraway, D. (1985). 'Manifesto for cyborgs: science, technology and socialist feminism in the 1980s'. *Socialist Review,* 80: 65–108.

—(1989). *Primate Visions: Gender, Race and Nature in the World of Modern Science.* New York and London: Routledge.

—(1991). *Simians, Cyborgs and Women: The Reinvention of Nature.* New York: Routledge.

—(1994). 'A game of cat's cradle: Science studies, feminist theory, cultural studies'. *Configurations,* 2 (1): 59–71.

—(1997). *Modest_Witness@Second_Millenium.FemaleMan©_Meets_OncoMouse.* London and New York: Routledge.

—(2003). *Companion Species Manifesto: Dogs, People and Significant Otherness.* Chicago, IL: Prickly Paradigm Press.

—(2004a). 'Ecce homo, ain't (ar'n't) I a woman and inappropriate/d others: the human in a post-human landscape', in *The Haraway Reader.* New York and London: Routledge, pp. 47–62.

—(2004b). 'The promises of monsters: A regenerative politics for inappropriate/d others', in *The Haraway Reader.* New York and London: Routledge, pp. 63–124.

—(2004c). 'Otherworldly conversations; terran topics; local terms', in *The Haraway Reader.* New York and London: Routledge, pp. 125–50.

—(2004d). 'Cyborgs to companion species: Reconfiguring kinship in technoscience', in *The Haraway Reader.* New York and London: Routledge, pp. 295–320.

—(2004e). 'Cyborgs, coyotes, and dogs: A kinship of feminist figurations' and 'There are always more things going on than you thought: Methodologies as thinking technologies'. 'An interview with Donna Haraway conducted in two parts by Nin Lykke, Randi Markussen, and Finn Olesen'. In *The Haraway Reader.* New York and London: Routledge, pp. 321–42.

—(2008a). *When Species Meet,* Minneapolis, MN, and London: University of Minnesota Press.

—(2008b). 'Forward: Companion species, mis-recognition and queer worlding', in

N. N. Giffney and M. J. Hird (eds), *Queering the Non/Human*. Burlington, VT and Hamphshire: Ashgate Publishing Ltd, pp. xxiii–xvi.

—(2010). '*When Species Meet*: staying with the trouble'. *Environment and Planning D: Society and Space*, 28 (1): 53–5.

—(2011). 'Speculative Fabulations for Technoculture's Generations: Taking Care of Unexpected Country'. *Australian Humanities Review*, 50: 95–118.

Haraway, D. and Harvey, D. (1995). 'Nature, politics, and possibilities: a debate and discussion with David Harvey and Donna Haraway'. *Environment and Planning D: Society and Space*, 13 (5): 507–27.

Harris, W. T. (2003 (1892)). 'Editor's preface', in J.-J. Rousseau, *Emile: Or Treatise on Education*. Trans. W. H. Payne. New York: Prometheus Books, pp. vii–xvi.

Harrison, S., Massey, D. and Richards, K. (2006). 'Complexity and emergence (another conversation)'. *Area*, 38 (4): 465–71.

Harrison, S., Massey, D., Richards, K., Magilligan, F. I., Thrift, N. and Bender, B. (2004). 'Conversations across the divide'. *Area*, 36: 435–42.

Harrison, S., Pile, S. and Thrift, N. J. (eds) (2004). *Patterned Ground: Entanglements of Nature and Culture*. London: Reaktion Books.

Harvey, D. (1996). *Justice, Nature and the Geography of Difference*. Cambridge, MA: Blackwell.

Higonnet, A. (1998). *Pictures of Innocence: The History and Crisis of Ideal Childhood*. London: Thames and Hudson.

Hinchcliffe, S. (2005). 'Nature/Culture', in D. Atkinson, P. Jackson, D. Sibley and N. Washbourne (eds), *Cultural Geography: a Critical Dictionary of Key Concepts*. London: I. B. Taurus.

—(2007). *Geographies of Nature: Societies, Environments, Ecologies*, Los Angeles, CA, London, New Delhi and Singapore: Sage Publications.

Holloway, S. and Valentine, G. (2000). 'Children's geographies and the new social studies of childhood', in S. Holloway and G. Valentine (eds), *Children's Geographies: Learning, Living, Learning*. London and New York: Routledge, pp. 1–28.

Hultqvist, K. and Dahlberg, G. (eds) (2001). *Governing the Child in the New Millennium*. New York and London: Routledge.

Hutton, D. and Connors, L. (1999). *A History of the Australian Environment Movement*, Cambridge: Cambridge University Press.

Inkamala, R. (2012). Personal communication. Alice Springs.

Instone, L. (1998). 'The coyote's at the door: Revisioning human–environmental relations in the Australian context'. *Ecumene*, 5 (4): 452–67.

—(2000). 'Dancing with dingos: Humans, animals and the Australian landscape'. *UTS Review*, 6: 165–75.

—(2001). *Lines Across the Land*. Unpublished PhD thesis. Monash University, Melbourne.

—(2004). 'Situating nature: On doing cultural geographies of Australian nature'. *Australian Geographer*, 35 (2): 131–40.

Jack, G. (2010). 'Place matters: The significance of place attachments for children's well-being'. *British Journal of Social Work*, 40 (3): 755–71.

James, A., Jenks, C. and Prout. A. (1998). *Theorizing Childhood*. Oxford: Polity Press.

James, A. and Prout, A. (1990). *Constructing and Reconstructing Childhood: Contemporary Issues in the Sociological Study of Childhood*. London and New York: Routledge.

Jemielniak, D. (2012). *The New Knowledge Workers*, Cheltenham: Edward Elgar Publishing.

Jenks, C. (2005). *Childhood* (2nd edition). London and New York: Routledge.

Jones, O. (2000). 'Melting geography: Purity, disorder, childhood and space', in S. Holloway and G. Valentine (eds), *Children's Geography: Living, Playing, Learning*. London: Routledge, pp. 29–47.

Kahn Jr, P. H. (1999). *The Human Relationship with Nature*. Cambridge, MA: MIT Press.

—(2002). 'Children's affiliations with nature: Structure, development, and the problem of generational amnesia', in P. H. Kahn Jr and S. R. Kellert (eds), *Children and Nature: Psychology, Sociocultural and Evolutionary Investigations*. Cambridge, MA, and London: MIT Press, pp. 92–116.

Kahn Jr, P. H. and Kellert, S. R. (eds) (2002). *Children and Nature: Psychology, Sociocultural and Evolutionary Investigations*. Cambridge, MA, and London: MIT Press.

Kaplan, R. and Kaplan, S. (2011). 'Well-being, reasonableness and the natural environment'. *Applied Psychology, Health and Well-Being*, 3 (3): 304–21.

Kehily, M. J. (ed.) (2004). *An Introduction to Childhood Studies*. Oxford and New York: Open University Press.

Kellert, S. R. (1997). *Kinship to Mastery: Biolphilia in Human Evolution and Development*. Washington, DC: Island Press.

–(2002). 'Experiencing nature: Affective, cognitive and evaluative', in P. H. Kahn Jr and S. R. Kellert (eds), *Children and Nature: Psychology, Sociocultural and Evolutionary Investigations*. Cambridge, MA, and London: MIT Press, pp. 117–52.

Kendall, K. (2008). 'The face of a dog: Levinasian ethics and human/dog co-evolution', in N. N. Giffney and M. J. Hird (eds), *Queering the Non/Human*, Burlington, VT and Hamphshire: Ashgate Publishing Ltd, pp. 185–204.

Knight, S. (2009). *Forest Schools and Outdoor Learning in the Early Years*. London: Sage Publications.

Kollner, S. and Leinert, C. (1998). *Waldkindergarten/Forest Kindergartens*. Augsburg: RIWA-Verlag.

Koonce, C. (2010). *Thinking Towards Survival*. Bloomington, IN: I-Universe.

Langton, M. (1996). 'What do we mean by wilderness? Wilderness and Terra Nullius in Australian Art'. *The Sydney Papers*, 8 (1): 10–31.

Latour, B. (1993). *We Have Never Been Modern*. Cambridge, MA, and London: Havard University Press.

—(2004). *The Politics of Nature: How to Bring the Sciences into Democracy*. Trans. C. Porter. Cambridge, MA, and London: Harvard University Press.

—(2005). *Reassembling the Social: An Introduction to Actor Network Theory*. Oxford and New York: Oxford University Press.

—(2009). 'A collective of humans and non humans: Following Daedalus's labyrinth', in D. M. Kaplan (ed.), *Reading in the Philosophy of Technology*. Maryland and Plymouth: Rowman and Littlefield, pp. 156–72.

Law, J. (2004). 'Enacting naturecultures: A note from STS'. Published by the Centre for Science Studies, Lancaster University, Lancaster LA1 4YN, UK. Retrieved from: http://www.comp.lancs.ac.uk/sociology/papers/law-enacting-naturecultures.pdf.

Lee, N. (2001). *Childhood and Society: Growing Up in an Age of Uncertainty*. Buckingham: Open University Press.

Lenz-Taguchi, H. (2010). *Going Beyond the Theory/Practice Divide in Early Childhood Education: Introducing an Intra-Active Pedagogy*. London and New York: Routledge.

Levinas, E. (1969). *Totality and Infinity: An Essay on Exteriority*. Trans. A. Lingis. Pittsburgh, PA: Duquesne University Press.

Levi-Strauss, C. (1966). *The Savage Mind*. London: Weidenfeld and Nicolson.

Little, H. and Wyver, S. (2008). 'Outdoor play – does avoiding the risks reduce the benefits?' *Australian Journal of Early Childhood*, 33 (2): 33–40.

Louv, R. (1990). *Childhood's Future*. Boston, MA: Houghton Mifflin.

—(2008). *Last Child in the Woods: Saving Our Children from Nature-Deficit Disorder* (2nd edition). Chapel Hill, NC: Algonquin Books.

MacDonald, R. (1995). *Between Two Worlds: The Commonwealth Government and the Removal of Aboriginal Children of Part Descent in the Northern Territory*. Alice Springs: IAD Press.

MacNaughton, G. (2005). *Doing Foucault in Early Childhood Studies: Applying Poststructural Ideas*. London and New York: Routledge.

Marsden, J. and Tan, S. (1998). *The Rabbits*. Sydney: Lothian.

Marshall, A. (2002). *The unity of nature*. London: Imperial College Press.

Martin, K. (2007). 'Ma(r)king Tracks and Reconceptualising Aboriginal early childhood education: an Aboriginal Australian perspectiv'. *Childrenz Issues*, 11 (1): 15–20.

Martins, P. (2007). 'Caring for the environment: Challenges from the notions of caring'. *Australian Journal of Environmental Education*, 23: 57–64.

Massey, D. (1993). 'Power-geometry and a progressive sense of place', in J. Bird, B. Curtis, T. Putnam, G. Robertson and L. Tickner (eds), *Mapping the Futures: Local Cultures, Global Change*. London: Routledge, pp. 60–70.

—(2005). *For Space*. London: Sage Publications.

Maynard, T. (2007). 'Forest schools in Great Britain: An initial exploration'. *Contemporary Issues in Early Childhood*, 8 (4): 320–31.

McCurdy, L. E., Winterbottom, K. E., Mehta, S. S. and Roberts, J. R. (2010). 'Using nature and outdoor activity to improve children's health'. *Current Problems in Pediatric and Adolescent Health Care*, 40 (5): 102–17.

Melson, G. F. (2005). *Why the Wild Things Are: Animals in the Lives of Children*. Cambridge, MA, and London: Harvard University Press.

Merchant, C. (1980). *The Death of Nature*. London: Wildwood House.

Meyers, G. (1998). *Children and Animals: Social Development and Our Connection to Other Species*. Boulder, CO, and Oxford: WestviewPress.

Mies, M. and Shiva, V. (1993). *Ecofeminism*. London: Zed Books.

Miklitz, I. (2001). *The Forest Kindergarten*. Berlin: Luchterhand.

Milne, A. A. (1994 (1928)), *The Complete Tales of Winnie-the-Pooh*. New York: Duttons Children's Books.

Mindstretchers (2012). 'Nature Kindergartens' webpage. Retrieved from: www.mindstretchers.co.uk/naturekindergartens.cfm

Montessori, M. (1912). *The Montessori Method: Scientific Pedagogy as Applied to Child Education in "The Children's Houses"*. Trans. A. E. George. New York: Stokes.

—(1946). *Education for a New World*. Madras: Kalakshetra Publications.

Moore, R. C. and Cooper Marcus, C. (2008). 'Healthy planet, healthy children: Designing nature into the daily spaces of childhood', in S. Kellert, J. Heerwagen and M. Mador (eds), *Biophilic design: Theory, science and practice*. Hoboken, NJ: John Wiley and Sons, Inc., pp. 153–203.

Moss, S. (2012). *Natural Childhood*. National Trust Report. Retrieved from: www.nationaltrust.org.uk/servlet/file/store5/item789980/version2/natural_childhood.pdf

Muñoz, S-A. (2008). 'Children in the outdoors: A literature review'. Sustainable Development Research Centre, Horizon Scotland. Retrieved from: http://www.abdn.ac.uk/crh/uploads/files/Children%20in%20the%20Outdoors%20%20A%20literature%20review%20%20Munoz%20S.pdf

Myers, G. (1998). *Children and Animals: Social Development and Our Connection to Other Species*, Boulder, CO: Westview Press.

Nabhan, G. P. and Trimble, S. (1994). *The Geography of Childhood: Why Children Need Wild Places*. Boston, MA: Beacon Press.

O'Brien, L. and Murray, R. (2005). 'Forest schools in England and Wales: woodland space to learn and grow'. *Environmental Education*, Autumn: 25–7.

—(2007). 'Forest School in England: an evaluation of three case study settings'. *Environmental Education*, Spring: 8–9.

Oliver, K. (2009). *Animal Lessons: How They Teach Us To Be Human*, New York: Columbia University Press.

O'Loughlin, M. and Johnson, R. (eds) (2010). *Imagining Children Otherwise: Theoretical and Critical Perspectives on Childhood Subjectivity*. New York, Washington, DC, Bern, Frankfurt, Berlin, Brussels, Vienna and Oxford: Peter Lang.

Ong, A. D. and Peterson, C. (2011). 'The health benefits of nature: introduction to the special section'. *Applied Psychology, Health and Well-Being*, 3 (3): 229.

Orgaz, L. F. and Piccinini, P. (2007). 'The naturally artificial world: A conversation between Patricia Piccinini and Laura Fernandex Orgaz'. *Tender Creatures* exhibition catalogue, Artium, Spain. Retrieved from: http://www.patriciapiccinini.net/essays/29

Orr, D. (2004). *Earth in Mind: On Education, the Environment and Human Prospect*. Washington, DC: Island Press.

Park, R. (1994 (1962)). *The Muddle Headed Wombat*, Illustrated by N. Young. Sydney: Angus and Robertson.

Passey, R. and Waite, S. (2011). 'School gardens and forest schools', in S. Waite (ed.), *Children Learning Outside of the Classroom: From Birth to Eleven*. London: Sage Publications, pp. 162–75.

Payne, W. H. (2003 (1892)). 'Introduction by the translator', in J.-J. Rousseau, *Emile: Or Treatise on Education*. Trans. W. H. Payne. New York: Prometheus Books, pp. xvii–xlv.

Pedley, E. C. (1997 (1906)). *Dot and the Kangaroo*. Sydney: Angus and Robertson. Reproduction of original Angus and Robertson 1906 print edition prepared by Sydney University liberary, 1997. Retrieved from: http://setis.library.usyd.edu.au/ozlit/

Philo, C. (1992). 'Foucault's geography', *Environment and Planning D: Society and Space*, 10: 137–61.

Piaget, J. (1928). *The Child's Conception of the World*, London: Routledge and Kegan Paul.

—(1952). *The Origins of Intelligence in the Child*, New York: International University Press.

Piccinini, P. (2012). 'Natures Little Helpers'. Patricia Piccinini website. Retrieved from: http://patriciapiccinini.net/natureslittlehelpers/index.php?show=cv&subtype=cv&textfile=nlh.htm.

Pierce, P. (1999). *The Country of Lost Children – An Australian Anxiety*. Cambridge: Cambridge University Press.

Plumwood, V. (1993). *Feminism and the Mastery of Nature*. London and New York: Routledge.

—(2002). *Environmental Culture: The Ecological Crisis of Reason*. London and New York: Routledge.

—(2005). 'Decolonising Australian gardens: Gardening and the ethics of place'. *Australian Humanities Review*, 36. Eco-humanities Corner on-line publication. Retrieved from: http://www.australianhumanitiesreview.org/archive/Issue-July-2005/09Plumwood.html

Postman, N. (1982). *The Disappearance of Childhood*. New York: Delacourt Press.

Potter, B. (2002 (1902)). *The Tales of Peter Rabbit*. London: Fredrick Warne and Penguin Group.

Potts, A. and Haraway, D. (2010). 'Kiwi chicken advocates talks with Californian dog companion'. *Feminism and Psychology*, 20 (3): 318–36.

Prout, A. (2005). *The Future of Childhood: Towards the Interdisciplinary Study of Children*. Abingdon, Oxon and New York: RoutledgeFalmer.

Pyle, R. M. (1993). *The Thunder Tree: Lessons from an Urban Wildland*. Boston, MA: Houghton Mifflin.

Pyle, R. M. (2002). 'Eden in a vacant lot: Special places, species, and kids in the neighborhood of life', in P. H. Kahn Jr and S. R. Kellert (eds), *Children and Nature: Psychology, Sociocultural and Evolutionary Investigations*. Cambridge, MA, and London: MIT Press, pp. 305–28.

Qvortrup, J. (1993). *Childhood as a Social Phenomenon*. Vienna: European Centre.

Renold, E. (2005). *Girls, Boys and Junior Sexualities: Exploring Children's Gender and Sexual Relations in the Primary School*. London and New York: Routledge.

Ridgers, N. D. and Sayers, J. (2012). 'Encouraging play in the natural environment: A child-focused case study of Forest school'. *Children's Geographies*, 10 (1): 49–65.

Ritchie, J., Duhn, I., Rau, C. and Craw, J. (2010). *Titiro Whakamuri, Hoki Whakamua – Caring for Self, Other and the Environment in Early Years' Teaching and Learning*. Final Report to the Teaching Learning Initiative. Wellington, NZ: TLRI/New Zealand Council for Educational Research.

Rivkin, M. (1995). *The Great Outdoors: Restoring Children's Rights to Play Outside*. Washington, DC: NAEYC.

—(1998). 'Happy play in grassy places: The importance of outdoor environment in Dewey's educational ideal'. *Early Childhood Education Journal*, 25 (3): 199–202.

Robertson, J. (2008). 'I Ur och Skur "Rain or Shine": Swedish Forest Schools'. Report. Creative Star Learning Company. Retrieved from: www.friluftsframjandet.se/c/document_library/get_file?folderId=39265&name=DLFE-5521.pdf

Robinson, K. H. (2005). 'Childhood and sexuality: Adult constructions and silenced children', in J. Mason and T. Fattore (eds), *Children Taken Seriously in Theory, Policy and Practice*. Philadelphia, PA and London: Jessica Kingley, pp. 66–78.

Rose, D. B. (2000). *Dingo Makes Us Human*. Cambridge: Cambridge University Press.

—(2002). 'Dialogue with place: toward an ecological body'. *Journal of Narrative Theory*, 32 (3): 311–25.

—(2004). *Reports from a Wild Country: Ethics for Decolonization*. Sydney: University of New South Wales Press.

—(2011). *Wild Dog Dreaming: Love and Extinction*. Charlottesville, VA, and London: University of Virginia Press.

Rousseau, J.-J. (2003 (1762)). *Emile: Or Treatise on Education*. Trans. W. H. Payne. New York: Prometheus Books.

—(2007 (1755 and 1762)). *The Social Contract and Discourses*. Trans. G. D. H Cole. Nashville, TN, BN Publishing.

Rubuntja, W. and Green, J. (2002). *The Town Grew Up Dancing: The Life and Art of Wenton Rubuntja*. Alice Springs: Jukurrpa Books, IAD Press.

Ryan, S. and Grieshaber, S. (eds) (2005). *Practical Transformations and Transformational Practices. Globalization, Postmodernism and Early Childhood Education: Advances in Early Education and Day Care*. Stamford, CT: JAI Press.

Safran, H. (director) (1976). *Storm Boy*. Feature film. Adelaide: South Australian Film Corporation.

Salten, F. (1998 (1928)). *Bambi: A Life in the Woods*. New York: Simon and Schuster.

Simons, J. (2008). *Rossetti's Wombat: The Pre-Raphaelites and Australian Animals in Victorian England*. London: Middlesex University Press.

Smith, N. (1991). *Uneven Development: Nature, Capital and the Production of Space*. Cambridge, MA: Blackwell, Publishing.

Sobel, D. (1996). *Beyond Ecophobia: Reclaiming the Heart in Nature Education*. Nature Literacy Series. Great Barrington, MA: The Orion Society.

—(2002). *Children's Special Places: Exploring the Role of Forts, Dens, and Bush Houses in Middle Childhood*. Detroit, MI: Wayne State University Press.

—(2004). *Place-based Education: Connecting Classrooms and Communities*. Nature Literacy Monograph Series No. 4. Great Barrington, MA: The Orion Society.

—(2008). *Children and Nature: Design Principles for Educators*. Portland, ME: Stenhouse Publishers.

Somerville, M. (2010). 'A place pedagogy for global contemporaneity'. *Journal of Educational Philosophy and Theory*, 42 (3): 326–44. Retrieved from: http://dx.doi.org/10.1111/j.1469-5812.2008.00423.x

—(2011). 'Becoming-frog: Learning place in primary school', in M. Somerville, B. Davies, K. Power, S. Gannon and P. de Carteret, *Place Pedagogy Change*. Rotterdam: Sense Publishing, pp. 65–80.

Soper, K. (1995). *What is Nature?* Oxford: Blackwell Publishing.

Spence, M. D. (1999). *Dispossessing the Wilderness: Indian Removal and the Making of the National Park*. New York: Oxford Press.

Stabb, M. (2009). 'An introduction: Simply walking'. *The Thoreau Reader*. EServer, Iowa State University. Retrieved from: www.http://thoreau.eserver.org

Staempfli, M. B. (2009). 'Reintroducing adventure into children's outdoor play environments'. *Environment and Behavior*, 41 (2): 268–80.

Steiner, R. (1996 (1906–11)). *The Education of the Child: And Early Lectures on Education*, Barrington, MA: Anthroposophic Press.

Strathern, M. (1992). *After Nature: English Kinship in the Late Twentieth Century*. Cambridge, New York and Melbourne: Cambridge University Press.

—(2004). *Commons and Borderlands: Working Papers on Interdisciplinarity, Accountability and the Flow of Knowledge.* Oxon: Sean Kingston.

Sutton, L. (2008). 'The state of play: disadvantage, play and children's well-being'. *Social Policy and Society,* 7 (4): 537–49.

Tan, S. (1999). 'Rabbiting On: A conversation about *The Rabbits*'. Interviewer N. Strathopoulos. Retrieved from: http://www.shauntan.net/images/essay%20 Rabbits%20interview.html

Taylor, A. (2007a). 'Playing with difference: The cultural politics of childhood belonging'. *International Journal of Diversity in Organisations, Communities, Nations,* 7 (3). Retrieved from: http://ijd.cgpublisher.com/product/pub.29/prod.526

—(2007b). 'Innocent children, dangerous families and homophobic panic', in G. Morgan and S. Poynting (eds), *Outrageous: Moral Panics in Australia.* Hobart: Australian Clearinghouse for Youth Studies, pp. 210–22.

—(2008). 'Taking account of childhood excess: Bringing the elsewhere home', in B. Davies (ed.), *Judith Butler in Conversation: Analyzing the Texts and Talk of Everyday Life.* New York and London: Routledge, pp. 195–216.

—(2010a). 'Troubling childhood innocence: Reframing the debate over the media sexualisation of children'. *Australian Journal of Early Childhood,* 35 (1): 48–57.

—(2010b). 'Disciplining young desire: Young children, schools and the media', in Z. Millei, T. R. Griffith and R. J. Parkes (eds), *Retheorising Discipline in Education: Problems, Politics and Possibilities.* New York, Washington, DC, Bern, Frankfurt, Berlin, Brussels, Vienna and Oxford: Peter Lang, pp. 120–30.

—(2011). 'Reconceptualising the "nature" of childhood'. *Childhood: A Journal of Global Childhood Research,* 18 (4): 420–33.

Taylor, A., Blaise, M. and Giugni, M. (2012). 'Haraway's "bag lady story-telling": Relocating childhood and learning within a "post-human landscape"'. *Discourse: Studies in the Cultural Politics of Education,* 34 (1): DOI:10.1080/01596306.2 012.698863

Taylor, A., Blaise, M. and Robinson, K. (2007). 'Making trouble. A conversation about departing from the straight and narrow in early childhood'. *International Journal of Equity and Innovation in Early Childhood,* 5 (2): 32–46. Retrieved from: http://www.edfac.unimelb.edu.au/ceiec/members/IJEIEC/nonmembers/ IJEIECNonVol5No2.htmlo

Taylor, A., Fasoli, L. and Giugni, M. (2009). 'Three Sisters: Final Report'. Canberra: DEEWR. Retrieved from: http://www.deewr.gov.au/Earlychildhood/Policy_ Agenda/Documents/ThreeSistersFinalReport2009.pdf

Taylor, A. and Guigni, M. (2012). 'Common worlds: Reconceptualising inclusion in early childhood communities'. *Contemporary Issues in Early Childhood Education,* 13 (2): 108–20.

Taylor, A. and Richardson, C. (2005a). 'Queering home corner'. *Contemporary Issues in Early Childhood,* 6 (2): 163–74.

—(2005b). 'Home renovations, border protection and the hard work of belonging'. *Australian Research in Early Childhood,* 12 (1): 93–100.

Theobald, P. (1997). *Teaching the Commons: Place, Pride and the Renewal of Community.* Boulder, CO: Westview Press.

Thiele, C. (1964). *Storm Boy.* Sydney: New Holland Publishers.

Thoreau, H. D. (2009 (1854)). 'Walden'. *The Thoreau Reader.* EServer, Iowa State University. Retrieved from: www.http://thoreau.eserver.org

—(2009 (1862)). 'Walking'. *The Thoreau Reader.* EServer, Iowa State University. Retrieved from: www.http://thoreau.eserver.org

Thrift, N. (2007). *Non-Representational Theories: Space, Politics, Affect.* London: Routledge.

Tilley, E. N. (2007). *White Vanishing: A Settler Australian Hegemonic Textual Strategy, 1789–2006.* PhD thesis, School of English, Media Studies and Art History, University of Queensland. Retrieved from: http://espace.library.uq.edu.au/view/UQ:158427

Tilley, E. (2009). 'A natural(ised) home for the Lintons: Lost children and indigenising discourse in Mary Grant Bruce's and John Marsden's young adult fiction'. *Australasian Victorian Studies Journal Australia.* Retrieved from: http://www.nla.gov.au/openpublish/index.php/australian-studies/article/view/1574

Trigg, B. (1988). *The Wombat: Common Wombats in Australia.* Kensington, NSW: University of New South Wales Press.

Tsing, A. for the Matsutake Worlds Research Group (2011). 'Arts of inclusion, or how to love a mushroom'. *Australian Humanities Review,* 50: 5–21. Retrieved from: http://epress.anu.edu.au/apps/bookworm/view/Australian+Humanities+Review+-+Issue+50,+2011/5451/ch01.xhtml

Turner, M. K. (2010). *Iwenhe Tyerrtye – What it Means to be an Aboriginal Person.* Alice Springs: IAD Press.

Uhrmacher, P. B. (1995). 'Uncommon schooling: A historical look at Rudolf Steiner, Anthroposophy and Waldorf Education'. *Curriculum Inquiry,* 25 (4): 381–406.

UNESCO (2012). 'Education for Sustainable Development (ESD'. United Nations Educational, Scientific and Cultural Organization, Education Themes website. Retrieved from: http://www.unesco.org/new/en/education/themes/leading-the-international-agenda/education-for-sustainable-development/

Valentine, G. (1996). 'Angels and devils: Moral landscapes of childhood'. *Environment and Planning D: Society and Space,* 14: 581–99.

Van Den Berg, A. and Van Den Berg, C. (2011). 'A comparison of children with ADHD in a natural and built setting'. *Child: Care, Health and Development,* 37 (3): 430–9.

Van Krieken, R. (1999). 'The "Stolen Generations" and cultural genocide: The forced removal of Australian Indigenous children from their families and its implications for the sociology of childhood'. *Childhood,* 6 (3): 297–311.

Vygotsky, L. S. (1978). *Mind in Society: The Development of Higher Mental Processes.* Cambridge, MA: Harvard University Press.

Waite, S. (ed.) (2011). *Children Learning Outside of the Classroom: From Birth to Eleven.* London: Sage.

Walkerdine, V. (1988). *The Mastery of Reason: Cognitive Development and the Production of Rationality.* London: Routledge.

Walsh, M. (2007). *May Gibbs, Mother of the Gumnuts.* Sydney: University of Sydney Press.

Warden, C. (2010). *Nature Kindergartens: An Exploration on Naturalistic Learning within Nature Kindergartens and Forest Schools.* Perthshire: Mindstretchers Ltd.

Whatmore, S. (1999). 'Hybrid geographies: Rethinking the "human" in human geography', in D. Massey, J. Allen and P. Sarre (eds), *Human Geography Today.* Cambridge: Polity Press, pp. 22–39.

—(2002). *Hybrid Geographies: Natures, Cultures and Spaces*. London: Sage Publications.

Whitescarver, K. and Cossentino, J. (2008). 'Montessori and the mainstream: A century of reform on the margins'. *Teachers College Record*, 110 (12): 2571–600.

Whitley, D. (2008). *The Idea of Nature in Disney Animation*. Burlington, VT and Hampshire: Ashgate Publishing.

Willems-Braun, B. (1997). 'Buried epistemologies: The politics of nature in (post-) colonial British Columbia'. *Annals of the Association of American Geographers*, 87 (1): 3–31.

Williams, R. (1983). *Keywords* (revised edition). New York: Oxford University Press.

Wilson, A. (1991). *The Culture of Nature: North American Landscape from Disney to Exxon Valdez*. Cambridge, MA, and Oxford: Blackwell.

Wilson, E. O. (1984). *Biophilia*. Cambridge, MA, and London: Harvard University Press.

—(1993). 'Biophilia and the conservation ethic', in S. R. Kellert and E. O. Wilson (eds), *The Biophilia Hypothesis*. Washington, DC: Island Press.

—(1997). *In Search of Nature*. Washington DC: Island Press.

Wilson, R. A. (1993). *Fostering a Sense of Wonder During the Early Childhood Years*. Columbus, OH: Greyden Press.

—(1995). 'Let nature be your teacher'. *Early Childhood Education Journal*, 22 (3): 31–4.

—(2007). *Nature and Young Children: Encouraging Creative Play and Learning in Natural Environments*. London: Routledge.

—(2008). 'The wonders of nature: Honoring children's ways of knowing'. *EarlychildhoodNEWS*. Retrieved from: www.earlychildhoodnews.com/earlychildhood/article_view.aspx?ArticleID=70

—(2011). 'Becoming whole: Developing an ecological identity'. *Wonder*, May/June edition of Newsletter of Nature Action Collaborative for Children. Retrieved from: www.ccie-media.s3.amazonnews.com/nacc/wonder_may11.pdf.

Wingfield, E. W. and Austin, E. M. (2009). *Living Alongside the Animals – Anangu Way*. Illustrated by B. McKenna. Alice Springs: IAD Press.

Wolch, J., Jerrett, M., Reynolds, K., McConnell, R., Chang, R., Dahmann, N., Brady, K., Gilliland, F., Su, J. G. and Berhane, K. (2010). 'Childhood obesity and proximity to urban parks and recreational resources: A longitudinal cohort study'. *Health & Place*, 17 (1): 207–14.

Woodford, J. (2001). *The Secret Life of Wombats*. Melbourne: Text Publishing.

Wordsworth, W. (1888 (1802)). 'My Heart Leaps Up When I Behold', in *The Complete Poetical Words of William Wordsworth*. Retrieved from: www.bartelby.com/145/wordchrono.html

—(1888 (1803–6)). 'Ode on Intimations of Immortality from Recollections of Early Childhood', in *The Complete Poetical Words of William Wordsworth*. Retrieved from: www.bartelby.com/145/wordchrono.html

—(2001 (1802)). 'Preface to Lyrical Ballads'. Retrieved from: www.english.upenn.edu/~jenglish/Courses/Spring2001/040/preface1802.html

Wyness, M. G. (2008). *Contesting Childhood*. London and New York: Falmer Press.

Yipirinya School Council (2012). Yipirinya School website. 'Teaching Two Ways'. Retrieved from: http://www.yipirinya.com.au/index.phtml.

Young, R. M. (1985). *Darwin's Metaphor: Nature's Place in Victorian Culture*. Cambridge: Cambridge University Press.

Young, T. (2008). 'Creating specific features to foster nature connections', in S. Elliott (ed.), *The Outdoor Playspace – Naturally – For Children Birth to Five Years*. Castle Hill, NSW: Pademelon Press, pp. 43–74.

Zonn, L. E. and Aitken, S. C. (1994). 'Of pelicans and men: symbolic landscapes, gender and Australia's *Storm Boy*', in S. C. Aitken and L. E. Zonn (eds), *Place, Power, Situation and Spectacle: A Geography of Film*. Lanham, MD: Rowman and Littlefield, pp. 137–59.

Zornado, J. L. (2001). *Inventing the Child: Culture, Ideology and the Story of Childhood*. New York: Garland Publishing.

Index